Becoming a Personal Trainer For Dummies®

Cheat Sheet

Tips for Tip-Top Telephoning

- **Introduce yourself by name and position.** "This is Pat Pectoral of Pat's Perfect Personal Training."

- **Ask for your prospect's first name, then use it when addressing her questions.** But don't overdo this, or you'll sound like a particularly insincere used-car salesman.

- **Ask how you can help her.** Then let her talk, and make sure you listen to the answer.

- **Ask questions if you're not clear on the caller's needs.** Your job is to find out what the caller is looking for and how you can give it to her. Don't be afraid to ask questions to clarify the prospect's needs.

- **Modify your rate of speech to match your caller's.** This is an old trick that helps the prospect feel comfortable with you.

- **Let her know it's okay to interrupt you if she doesn't understand what you're saying.** Talking with a trainer can be intimidating — especially for someone who isn't a big exerciser! Assure the prospect that she can ask you anything at any time.

- **Keep your answers short and definitive.** Getting too wordy can confuse your caller or make her lose interest in you.

- **No matter what your mood, be upbeat and maintain a positive attitude.** You want to exude health and confidence.

- **Smile during your conversation.** Your caller *can* hear it!

- **Make sure your voice reflects enthusiasm and cheer.**

- **Speak with confidence.** As the saying goes, "It's not what you say but how you say it!"

- **Know what you're talking about.** If you don't know an answer, admit it — don't make one up.

- **Make notes to refer back to during the conversation.** That way you can go back if you have a question about something the prospect said.

- **If you're able to schedule an initial consultation with the potential client, reiterate the date, time, and location of your next meeting before closing the conversation.** This will eliminate any potential confusion.

- **Always thank the prospective client for calling, and wish her a good day/afternoon/evening before saying goodbye.**

How to Ace Your Certification Exam

- **Get ready to study.** Make sure you have a quiet place where you can concentrate on the course materials, whether your kitchen or the local library. Turn off the TV, the radio (unless listening to classical music helps get your brain cells moving), and your Internet connection (unless you're using online course materials). Unplug the phone or turn on the answering machine. And make sure your study area is equipped with pencils, paper, and a good light source, such as a task lamp.

- **Find course materials.** Each certifying organization offers its own course materials to help you study for the exam. You may receive (or be able to purchase) textbooks, online study guides, sample tests, and access to live seminars and courses. Check out the certifying organizations' Web sites for information on the course materials that are available.

- **Role-play.** If the exam includes a practical portion, you'll need to get your hands on such equipment as skin-fold calipers and blood-pressure cuffs. Recruit some friends and use them to practice measuring flexibility, measuring body fat, performing submaximal cardio evaluations, and anything else you may have to perform on the test.

- **Use sticky notes.** Learning anatomy is an active process — you have to get up and get moving to understand how the body works. Stick labels on your muscles and joints to remember what they're called and how they move.

- **Draw up flash cards.** Make up flash cards with definitions and formulas. You can test yourself whenever you have a free minute — in line at the grocery store, in the dentist's waiting room, while stuck in traffic — or have a friend flash you (the cards, that is).

- **Get moving.** Get off your chair and perform movements to find out which muscles are involved. Which muscles do you use when you kick? How about when you're doing a bench press?

Becoming a Personal Trainer For Dummies®

Cheat Sheet

Keys to Personal Training Success

- **Be a professional.** Be sure to dress professionally (a polo shirt and clean sweat pants work well), always show up on time, and keep accurate files.

- **Don't be afraid to "fire" a client.** If the client has become increasingly noncompliant, refusing to stick to her plan; if you find yourself ending workouts early; or if the client has started to complain a lot (or a lot more than usual), the best course of action may be to let her go. Tell her that you feel that Trainer X can offer her more than you can.

- **Scope out the competition.** Your competitors are the personal trainers and personal training companies in your area that are already catering to the people you hope to train one day. The best way to "know your foe" is to "shop" them. Call as a prospective client, and ask what type of services they offer, how much they charge, whether their trainers are certified, when they're open, whether they travel to the client's home or office, and so on. Not only will you get the information you need to compete in the marketplace, you may pick up an idea or two for yourself.

- **Provide personal solutions.** Your clients don't all fit into one mold, and your programs and solutions for them shouldn't, either. Ask questions to find out about the client's unique situation and tailor your response to fit it.

- **Plan one step at a time.** Break down tasks into manageable steps. For example, if your client has never been on a treadmill, don't just put him on one and hit the On button. Tell him how to get on the treadmill, how to turn it on, how to step onto the tread, how to adjust the intensity, and how to turn it off.

- **Change up the program.** We humans get bored doing the same thing every day. Keep your client motivated by occasionally upping the intensity, changing the exercises, or switching the order of exercises.

- **Provide positive reinforcement.** Encourage and motivate your clients to keep them coming back. Tell your client how her performance compares to her past performance (if it's better, that is), compliment her, include positive notes about her performance in her workout log, and send her an occasional e-mail or greeting card to let her know you're proud of her.

- **Respect your clients' privacy.** Don't tell other clients, trainers, or anyone else about a client's home, personal life, or training program.

- **Follow up.** Following up with clients holds them accountable for following their exercise plan and gives them little motivational boosts to boot. It's simple — just check in once or twice (via phone or e-mail) when the client is between sessions.

- **Keep in touch with former clients.** Staying in touch with your former clients is a good business practice. If you have clients who have moved on, shoot them an occasional phone call, letter, or e-mail to touch base and make sure they're on track. You never know — they may decide to come back to you!

Copyright © 2004 Wiley Publishing, Inc.
All rights reserved.

Item 5684-3.

For more information about Wiley Publishing, call 1-800-762-2974.

For Dummies: Bestselling Book Series for Beginners

Becoming a Personal Trainer

FOR

DUMMIES®

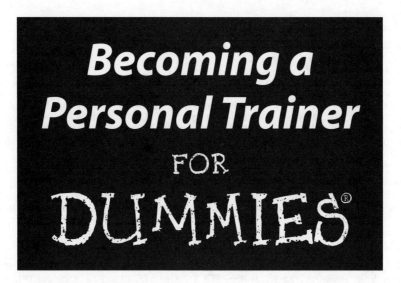

Becoming a Personal Trainer

FOR

DUMMIES®

by Melyssa St. Michael and
Linda Formichelli

WILEY

Wiley Publishing, Inc.

Becoming a Personal Trainer For Dummies®

Published by
Wiley Publishing, Inc.
111 River St.
Hoboken, NJ 07030-5774
www.wiley.com

For general information on our other products and services or to obtain technical support, please contact our Customer Care Department within the U.S. at 800-762-2974, outside the U.S. at 317-572-3993, or fax 317-572-4002.

Wiley also publishes its books in a variety of electronic formats. Some content that appears in print may not be available in electronic books.

Library of Congress Control Number: 2004111123

ISBN: 0-7645-5684-3

Manufactured in the United States of America

10 9 8 7 6 5 4 3 2 1

1B/RT/QZ/QU/IN

About the Authors

Melyssa St. Michael: Melyssa St. Michael is a certified personal trainer and certified nutrition consultant. She was named one of the top 40 entrepreneurs under age 40 by *Baltimore Magazine* in 2001. Setting out to "raise the bar" in the personal-training industry, Melyssa founded her first personal-training company in February 1995. She rapidly expanded her business into a thriving entity with over 2,000 clients, a 3,000-square-foot state-of-the-art personal-training/nutrition facility, and a staff of ten full-time trainers. Currently, Melyssa consults within the fitness industry and is a renowned fitness expert appearing on national news channels, including CNN, CBS, NBC, and ABC. She has been interviewed by such publications as the *Los Angeles Times, U.S. News & World Report, SHAPE, Muscle & Fitness,* and the *Sunday Times* (London).

Linda Formichelli: Linda Formichelli is a freelance health and fitness writer who lives in Massachusetts with her writer husband and two cats. She is the co-author of *The Renegade Writer: A Totally Unconventional Guide to Freelance Writing Success.* She's a karate enthusiast (okay, she's a karate freak) who enjoys sipping port and reading weighty tomes (okay, it's lemonade and Archie comics). Linda has an M.A. from U.C. Berkeley in a subject completely unrelated to writing.

Dedication

Melyssa dedicates this book to her best friend and soon-to-be-husband, Brian, and to her sister, Krys.

Linda dedicates this book to Eric.

Authors' Acknowledgments

Melyssa and Linda would both like to thank Jennifer Lawler, for her awesome photography skills; Project Editor Elizabeth Kuball, who did an excellent job guiding us through this book; Technical Editor Jason Teno, whose feedback was much appreciated; Aly Leone, Donny Rutledge, and Brian Flach, for being willing (super)models; Laurie St. Michael, for making our models look great at the photo shoot; our agent, Carol Susan Roth; and Tracy Boggier, Holly Gastineau-Grimes, and Joyce Pepple, the helpful Acquisitions team at Wiley.

From Melyssa: Foremost, to the people in my life who have supported me so selflessly. Thanks to Brian, who has proven to me that "you are where you are in your life at any given point and time for a reason, though you may not know it yet." Ranger, thank you for your enduring support and for being there for me in the way that only you can be. Thanks to my sister Krys, without whom I would not have made it past my first year of being in business. Krys, you were my backbone, my sounding board, and my voice of reason. I know it was difficult (and so was I!) at times, but please know this: I couldn't have done it without you. Mom, thank you for your love and complete belief that I could do it. Dad, thank you for your mentorship and teaching me FileMaker. Laurie, thanks for giving us your wonderful makeup artistry so that we all looked our best. Thanks to my co-author, Linda Formichelli, for her exceptional talent that has truly made this book what it is. And last but not least, thanks to my clients, mentors, and employees, who taught me more about business than they ever will know: Dan C., Doctors Dean and Lauri K., "Dr." David S., Edie B., Mark S. Thank you all for touching my life.

From Linda: I'd like to thank Eric, one great husband and also a great proofreader; my parents, for encouraging my writing habit; Jennifer Lawler, for her great advice and willing ear; Branchaud Dojo in North Smithfield, Rhode Island, for keeping me sane; and last but not least, Melyssa St. Michael, who's as good at writing as she is at personal training (and I mean *really* good!).

Publisher's Acknowledgments

We're proud of this book; please send us your comments through our Dummies online registration form located at www.dummies.com/register/.

Some of the people who helped bring this book to market include the following:

Acquisitions, Editorial, and Media Development

Project Editor: Elizabeth Kuball

Acquisitions Editor: Tracy Boggier

Assistant Editor: Holly Gastineau-Grimes

Technical Editor: Jason Teno

Media Development Coordinator: Sarah Cummings

Editorial Manager: Michelle Hacker

Editorial Assistants: Courtney Allen, Elizabeth Rea

Cover Photos: © Zoran Milich/Getty Images/Allsport Concepts

Cartoons: Rich Tennant, www.the5thwave.com

Composition

Project Coordinator: Maridee Ennis

Layout and Graphics: Jonelle Burns, Andrea N. Dahl, Joyce Haughey, Stephanie D. Jumper, Michael Kruzil, Barry Offringa, Lynsey Osborn, Jacque Roth, Mary Gillot Virgin

Proofreaders: David Faust, Carl William Pierce, TECHBOOKS Production Services

Indexer: TECHBOOKS Production Services

Publishing and Editorial for Consumer Dummies

 Diane Graves Steele, Vice President and Publisher, Consumer Dummies

 Joyce Pepple, Acquisitions Director, Consumer Dummies

 Kristin A. Cocks, Product Development Director, Consumer Dummies

 Michael Spring, Vice President and Publisher, Travel

 Brice Gosnell, Associate Publisher, Travel

 Kelly Regan, Editorial Director, Travel

Publishing for Technology Dummies

 Andy Cummings, Vice President and Publisher, Dummies Technology/General User

Composition Services

 Gerry Fahey, Vice President of Production Services

 Debbie Stailey, Director of Composition Services

Contents at a Glance

Table of Contents

Introduction

● ●

Maybe you're a fitness buff who would like to help people get healthy for a living. Or maybe you're already a professional personal trainer, and you want to boost your business or update your skills. Either way, *Becoming a Personal Trainer For Dummies* is for you.

You're in the right place at the right time. According to American Sports Data, Inc., more than 5 million people in the U.S. pay for the services of personal trainers every year, with the average personal training client attending 20 sessions per year. The size of the U.S. personal training market is approximately $4 billion — that's a lot of dough!

About This Book

Personal training requires more than the ability to bench-press your own bodyweight or run an hour on the treadmill without breaking a sweat. Personal training is a business, just like, say, a print shop, a doctor's office, or a grocery store. You need to have a solid grasp not only of exercise, but also of marketing, business structures, legal issues, accounting, customer service, certification, and more.

Don't flip out! We know that's a lot to think about, but we're here to help. In *Becoming a Personal Trainer For Dummies,* we give you the scoop on everything you need to know to start, run, and even expand your personal training business.

Becoming a Personal Trainer For Dummies tells you all the stuff you really want to know, such as:

- How do I know if personal training is for me?
- How do I become certified?
- How do I write a business plan?
- Should I go solo or work for someone else?
- How do I get clients in the door?

✔ Do I need an accountant, lawyer, and insurance agent?

✔ How do I perform an initial consultation and fitness assessment?

✔ How do I create exercise plans that will get my clients strong and healthy?

✔ How do I keep my clients motivated?

✔ What are some ways to expand my business?

Foolish Assumptions

They say that to assume makes an ass out of you and me, but were going to take that risk — because we need to assume certain things about you, our reader. We assume that you're interested in personal training. We also assume that you have some basic knowledge of anatomy and physiology, cardiovascular exercise, and weight training. You may already be certified, or you may be studying for your certification. Or you may even be a full-fledged professional personal trainer who wants to build your clientele or motivate your clients.

How to Use This Book

You can use this book in two ways:

✔ **If you want to know everything there is to know about becoming a personal trainer,** read this book from cover to cover. You'll get a thorough overview of what it takes to start and run a successful business, and you'll even find out about things you may not have thought of, such as how to write a marketing plan, how to name your business, and where to find a mentor who can guide you to success.

✔ **If you want to find out about a specific topic,** flip to that page and start reading. For example, if you plan to take your certification test, you can turn to Chapter 2 to get study tips. You can read any section in the book without reading what comes before or after — though we may refer you to other parts of the book for related information.

How This Book Is Organized

Becoming a Personal Trainer For Dummies is divided into five parts. The chapters within each part give you more detailed information on each topic within that part. Here's an overview:

Part 1: Shaping Up to Be a Personal Trainer

So, you want to be a personal trainer. What type of trainer do you want to be? What kinds of clients do you want to work with? And most important, how do you get started? If you don't know the answers to these common questions, this part is for you. We give an overview of the personal training business and tell you how you can get a piece of the action, including tips on developing your personal training identity, finding your niche, getting certified, interning and apprenticing, and weighing the pros and cons of going into business for yourself.

Part 11: Being a Successful Personal Trainer

Before you start training clients, you need to have all the business basics in place — like a business plan, a business name, a record-keeping system, a marketing plan, and a support system of professionals, such as a lawyer and an accountant. If you jump into training without these basics, you can land in trouble when, say, the taxes are due, you want a business loan, or you gain so many clients that you can't keep track of them (because you don't have a record-keeping system!). That's what this part is all about. We also tell you not only how to bring in clients, but how to keep them coming back with tips and tricks that will help them stay happy and motivated.

Part 111: Putting the Personal into Personal Training

Clients — they're the people who make your business a business. Without them, you'd be doing chest presses all by your lonesome. That's why in this part, we tell you all about how to understand, work with, and advance your clients. You'll find out how to perform an initial consultation and a fitness assessment, plus how to create individualized exercise programs and how to advance your clients to the next level.

Part 1V: Growing Your Personal Training Business

When you're ready to get big — and we're not talking about your muscles — this part is for you. To expand your business, you may want to hire employees — and in this part, we tell you how to hire, motivate, and alas, fire workers. You can also expand by offering additional services like massages, workshops, and nutritional services, or by selling products like exercise equipment — and in this part, we show you how.

Part V: The Part of Tens

You may notice that *Becoming a Personal Trainer For Dummies* is chock-full of valuable information. In this part, we put that information into easy-to-read lists for your convenience. We provide you with great ways to expand your services, highlight equipment that will help your clients reach their goals, and outline ways to be the best personal trainer you can be.

Icons Used in This Book

Icons are those little pictures you see in the margins of this book, and they're meant to grab your attention and steer you toward particular types of information. Here's what they mean:

The Tip icon points you to great strategies for running your personal training business.

We use this icon to give helpful reminders. This is information that you may already know but that's easy to forget.

This icon flags information about potential pitfalls to your business, from business snafus to common exercise mistakes to client-relations gaffes.

This icon flags information that's great to know but isn't mandatory for your success as a personal trainer. You can use this information to impress your buddies in the gym, but if you're short on time, you can skip this material without missing anything critical.

We use this icon to tell a story about one of Melyssa's adventures in personal training. You can discover a lot from these stories!

Part I
Shaping Up to Be a Personal Trainer

The 5th Wave   By Rich Tennant

"I appreciate you sharing your dreams and wishes for starting your own personal training business, but maybe I should explain more fully what we at Make-A-Wish Foundation are all about."

In this part . . .

So you've decided to become a personal trainer.
Congratulations! This part is for you.

First, we give you all the basics you need to get started.
We tell you what it takes to be a personal trainer — and
we don't mean muscles. Mental agility, listening skills, and
professionalism are all important traits. We also give an
overview of personal training, information on how to get
certified, and details on how to find out more by interning
or apprenticing.

Do you want to work with the general population?
Pregnant women? Seniors? Kids? In this part, we help you
decide what kind of personal trainer you want to be and
whom you want to work for. We also help you answer that
most important of questions: Do you want to work as an
employee or as an independent contractor?

Chapter 1

Personal Training 101: Do You Have What It Takes?

*W*hen it comes to choosing a career, unless you're a masochist, you probably want to do something that you enjoy. Well, here's news that may interest you: Personal trainers love their jobs. According to a survey of personal trainers by IDEA (a professional fitness organization), 88 percent of respondents reported that they were "satisfied" or "very satisfied" with their work, compared to the national average of 71 percent.

Numbers don't lie — personal training is indeed a fulfilling and rewarding profession. Watching your clients achieve health and wellness as a result of your guidance is an incredible experience.

To an outsider, personal training may look pretty easy — you just stick your client on a piece of equipment, throw some weight on the stack, and start yelling at him to "do one more!" until he drops, right? Not exactly. This chapter gives you the scoop on what it takes to become a personal trainer and how you can get started in this challenging and rewarding field.

Determining Whether You and Personal Training Are a Match Made in Heaven

If we asked you what a successful personal trainer looks like, what would you envision? A guy or gal in great shape, with California good looks, a bright white perma-smile, and an everlasting bronze tan? Now what if we asked you what an unsuccessful personal trainer looks like? Maybe you'd think of your local gym rat, perched on top of the piece of gym equipment you want to use, glorifying the benefits of the latest fad supplement.

Truth be told, you can't tell a "good" trainer from a "bad" trainer based on looks alone. No matter how much a person looks the part on the outside, what makes trainers good is what they have on the inside — solid skills, knowledge, experience, intuitiveness, dedication, professionalism, and understanding. Take all those attributes, roll them up with the ability to teach, and — voilà! — you have the stuff great trainers are made of.

The question is, do *you* have that stuff?

Defining the role of a personal trainer

By definition, a *personal trainer* is a fitness professional who uses the body's response to exercise to improve clients' overall physical health. Trainers do all the following:

- ✔ Perform in-depth evaluations of their clients' base fitness levels.
- ✔ Prescribe exercises appropriate for their clients' level of conditioning and specific fitness goals.
- ✔ Show clients how to properly implement the prescribed exercises.
- ✔ Monitor and record clients' progress, making adjustments as necessary to ensure clients reach their goals in a safe and healthy manner.

Think that's the whole shebang? Not quite. Much like your old Aunt Bertha, personal trainers wear many hats. When working with clients, personal trainers act as friend, teacher, motivator, disciplinarian, troubleshooter, therapist, equipment rep, and wellness consultant, all wrapped up in one. When working alone, personal trainers take on the roles of secretary, salesperson, student, accountant, business owner, and customer-service rep.

Knowing what skills you need

Being a personal trainer requires more than knowing exactly where your gluteus maximus is, or what the best exercise is to keep it from drooping. As a trainer, you need many skills to match the many roles you play for your clients. Here are some of the skills you need to hone before putting up your shingle.

You need to be accountable

You alone — not your clients, not your mother, not your annoying neighbor with the yappy dog — are responsible for yourself and your actions. If you're continually coming up with reasons (read "excuses") as to why you were late, why you didn't write out the new travel program, or why you had to cancel, clients and employers will lose trust in you. Being able to own up to the truth of your actions and working to prevent those snafus from happening in the future gains you trust and credibility in the eyes of your peers.

When you're a trainer, the only thing you have is your credibility and your reputation.

You need to be agile

No, we don't mean physically agile! (We *know* you can touch your toes!) In this case, we mean *mentally* agile — as in, the ability to come up with a completely different course of action on the fly if the original one isn't working out. Working with people's bodies requires insight and the ability to think outside the box. Each client's body is unique, and what works for one client may not work for another.

Melyssa had a client who had suffered a stroke and lost the ability to use her muscles — she was in a wheelchair, because her brain couldn't communicate with her muscles to tell them to walk, sit, or even lift things. She had hired Melyssa to show her how to "work out" with her disability. Melyssa was perplexed — how do you work out if you can't lift a weight? Then she realized that, even though the client couldn't lift the weight, she still had the ability to *resist* the weight (this is called a *negative* in trainer-speak). Bingo! They created a workout consisting of negatives in every sort of manner. Negative bicep curls, negative leg extensions — you name it, they did it. The client made great strength gains and, as a result, was eventually able to perform small lifting movements. Now, that's being agile!

You need to be a good teacher

Good teachers inspire and excite their students by involving them in the activity. They watch their students carefully, discover how they learn, and match their teaching methods to their students' learning methods.

As a personal trainer, you need to take the time to discover how each of your clients learns. By not overwhelming your clients with too much information at one time and allowing them to lead the learning process, you'll ensure that your clients retain what you teach them. When your clients realize that you've taught them something, their perceived value of you and your services increases. When you give your clients that precious gem of knowledge, they'll be back for more — guaranteeing that you'll have repeat business.

You need to be a good leader

Leaders inspire people to do their best by example. Trainers need to walk their talk and be a role model for their clients. The old "do as I say, not as I do" adage doesn't cut it in this biz. You won't be getting any repeat business if you tell your clients they need to watch their fat intake — while you're stuffing a candy wrapper in the trash can. Clients follow trainers who have demonstrated that they can be successful with their clients on a consistent basis. People naturally want to follow someone who is confident, charismatic, and successful. In this profession, that means creating a successful clientele, and working with each client as if she's the only one you have. You must provide positive reinforcement to your clients, even when they have setbacks, and celebrate each and every one of their victories, no matter how small.

You need to be a good listener

Sometimes, being a personal trainer is like being a therapist — the closer you get to your clients, the more they open up and divulge personal information about themselves. By listening more than talking, you'll find out a lot about who your clients really are — which not only helps you understand where they're coming from and why they're working with you, but also prepares you to help them as a trainer.

You need to be a good observer

In addition to being a good listener, you need to be a good observer. Sometimes, your clients will tell you something different from what they're *really* thinking or feeling. Figuring out how to read your clients' body language, tone of voice, and physical cueing will help to improve your communication with your clients as well as the programs you create for them.

You need to be knowledgeable

Today, trainers are often expected to know the answers to just about everything related to health and wellness. Does the ThighMaster really work? If I put black yam cream on my thighs, will I burn fat faster? Not only do you have to master the technical and practical aspects of training, but you also need to know what science is saying about the latest fitness fads. Being able to separate fact from fiction — and to explain the difference — gives you credibility points in the eyes of your clients.

You need to be likeable

Have you ever met someone who rubbed you the wrong way from the start? You can't quite put your finger on what it is about her that you don't like, but for some reason you two simply don't hit it off. No matter how hard you try, you can't prevent this from happening with at least some of your clients. For one reason or another, not every client is going to like you — and you aren't going to love every client. But you're a professional, and working with all types of people comes with the territory.

Being likeable means knowing how to mirror a client's tone, actions, and body language until you've developed enough of a rapport that he feels comfortable with you. If your client is the strong-but-silent type, recognize this, and don't blab away about the latest strongman competition on ESPN. By using the skills discussed earlier in this chapter, such as being a good listener and observer, you can match your tone and actions to those of your client, creating a smooth start to your relationship.

You need to be passionate

Having passion about what you do and the people you do it for is essential to being a good trainer. It means being in the moment with your client, with every ounce of your attention focused on him. It means giving her 100 percent (or more if you can spare it), day in and day out. It means being upbeat and positive, and showing your client how enthusiastic you are about helping him achieve success.

We bet you've been in a gym and witnessed a trainer sitting down on the floor or on a piece of equipment, staring off into space while his client struggles through an exercise. You've probably also seen a trainer who's whipping her client through what looks to be a pretty intense workout, all the while smiling and offering the client encouragement. Which trainer would *you* want to work with?

You need to be professional

Being professional sounds easy if you're waltzing around a plush office with an Armani suit and a leather briefcase. It's not so easy when you're a personal trainer on your tenth client of the day, completely exhausted, and running late because of a traffic accident. Your client yells (even though it wasn't your fault), and now you still have to work with her even though you're boiling mad. No matter how badly you want to walk out, you tell her that you hear her and understand how she feels, apologize for the inconvenience, and get on with the session. Now that's professionalism.

You need to be positive

Much like that nasty strain of the flu that goes around every year (but without the nausea), enthusiasm is contagious. If you maintain an upbeat outlook, you'll be able to keep yourself and those around you motivated. Having a positive outlook and manner helps retain clientele — after all, working out is hard enough for your client without having to deal with a depressed trainer on top of it. Your clients aren't paying you to lament about your woes of the day. They hired you to motivate them and positively support their efforts. Think about it — would *you* want to work out with a crying Christina or a sobbing Sam?

You need to be understanding

Being understanding means remembering why you became a personal trainer in the first place. You're here for your client, not the other way around. You don't need to lecture your client when she fails to comply; she *knows* she didn't do what she was supposed to.

When your clients don't follow your plan, it's not that they're dissing you, or that they don't believe in what you're telling them. More likely, what you suggested doesn't work for them for whatever reason. Your job is to understand what went wrong — why they didn't/wouldn't/couldn't do what you told them to in the first place. When you understand the reasons behind the snafu, you'll be able to adjust your plan so they can succeed at the task. Understanding is putting yourself in your clients' shoes — getting beyond yourself and being aware of your clients' needs.

Assessing your skills

No matter how much you know about adenosine triphosphate or how well you can demonstrate the clean and jerk (if you think that's a system for getting your significant other to pick up his dirty socks, you're in trouble), knowledge and technique are only a small portion of what makes a successful personal trainer. How you perform your job on a day-to-day basis and how consistent you are in your job are what makes you successful and your job enjoyable.

For all the aspects of personal training that you can control — like your attitude and your knowledge — there are twice as many intangible things that you can't — like your schedule, your work location, the type of people you work with, your management, and so on. These are the little things that you can't plan for and that make any job loveable or leaveable. The personal training industry has quite a few intangibles that have been known to break a trainer or two. So before you sign up for the job, take an honest look at yourself and decide whether you have what it takes.

Answer *true* or *false* to the following 15 statements to determine whether you've got the goods for personal training:

- ✔ I am at my best any time of the day.
- ✔ I get along with everyone I meet.
- ✔ I can do several things well at once. (Walking and chewing gum doesn't count.)
- ✔ I have a flexible schedule.

✔ I enjoy working with different types of people.

✔ I enjoy a fast-paced life.

✔ I perform well under stress.

✔ I am organized.

✔ I am good at planning.

✔ I am a self-starter.

✔ I am detail-oriented.

✔ I can communicate my thoughts clearly and concisely.

✔ I enjoy explaining "why."

✔ I enjoy being challenged.

✔ I enjoy helping others.

✔ I have a thirst for learning.

✔ I enjoy being mobile.

If you answered false to five or more of these statements, you may find the demands of being a personal trainer challenging. These statements represent typical, day-to-day occurrences for a trainer — and we'd hate to see you invest all your time, energy, and effort breaking into the field, just to find out that it's not what you thought it would be. As they say, forewarned is forearmed!

Hitting the Books

So you know how to perform a prefect squat? Well, we hate to be the ones to tell you, but knowing how to do a squat doesn't mean squat when it comes to succeeding as a personal trainer. Before you jump into the job, you'll need to practice, study, cram for exams, rehearse, train, and drill. (Okay, we'll back slowly away from the thesaurus now and keep our hands where you can see them.) You'll also need a sheet of paper from an accrediting agency proving that you did all the above.

These days, personal trainers are looked to as experts in the field of fitness — not just gym rats who can bench-press their own bodyweight and yell, "No pain, no gain!" Apply for the position of personal trainer at any gym, and the first thing they'll ask is, "Are you certified?" Certification is a badge of honor — it tells prospective employers or clients not only that you know what you're doing, but also that you take your job seriously. Being certified builds your credibility — and credibility is what attracts clients to you.

A gazillion fitness organizations (yes, we counted) offer certification, and they all claim to be the most popular, the most respected, the most gosh-darn wonderful. Boning up on the top organizations out there takes a little work up front, but in the long run, it'll save you time, energy, and money.

Finding the right certification for you is important — you don't want to pay for a test that's geared to athletic training when you're looking to work with seniors, or one that requires a four-year degree in kinesiology if you don't have one. In Chapter 2, we provide all the information about certification that you need.

We know that right now you're absolutely champing at the bit to get your hands on some "body" to work on! But personal training is definitely an art — and one that has to be practiced to get it right. Taking body-fat measurements, spotting an exercise, and estimating submaximal VO_2 are not skills that anyone is born with. Don't be shy about asking friends and family if you can practice on them. If you work with people you're comfortable with, you'll be able to learn from your mistakes more easily — after all, better to bollix up a body-fat reading with your friends than with paying clients.

Getting Started

Are you ready to get out there and train the heck out of those people who need your services so badly? Great! So what's stopping you? Time's a-wastin'! Go on, get to it!

"Wait just a second," you say. "How can I get started if I don't have anyone to start with?" All dressed up but no place to go? Don't quite know where to find those people who need your services so badly? Never fear. Keep reading, and that little obstacle will soon be but a fading memory.

Creating your plan of attack

All the training, reading, studying, and practicing you do to hone your personal training skills to perfection won't make a darn bit of difference if you don't have any clients to use them on.

Lay out your goal in advance; then work backward from there. For example, if you want to train clients at a gym, your plan of attack may look like this:

1. **Call a few area gyms and ask what certifications and experience they require.**

2. Contact the appropriate certification body, and sign up for the appropriate exam (see Chapter 2 for more details).

3. Study for and take the exam (see Chapter 2).

4. Fulfill any other job prerequisites (CPR training, for example).

5. Apply for the position you want (see Chapter 4 for the scoop on résumés and interviewing).

6. Intern or get the job (Chapter 3 tells you all about apprenticing).

7. Train clients! (See Part II for the scoop on training clients.)

When you lay out your plan step-by-step, staying on track and identifying any potential pitfalls before they occur is much easier. This habit is a good one to get into, because you'll be using this method frequently with clients, outlining step-by-step how they can reach their goals.

Personal trainer for hire: Getting work

Getting your first client is a momentous occasion. Melyssa remembers how she got hers — he approached her at the gym while she was working out and asked if she was a trainer. At the time, she had just been certified and hadn't yet been hired by anyone. She told him she was, and he asked if she could train him. Melyssa told him that she would love to, but she wasn't sure if the gym would let her. So she contacted the owner of the gym, explained her situation, and worked out a deal where she was able to train clients as long as they were gym members and she paid the gym a percentage of her training fee as an independent contractor. Thus, Melyssa's personal training business was born, and she was its sole employee.

Preparing for success

The power of the mind is an awesome thing. Stepping into a new career or taking on new responsibilities can be scary, and maybe you're a little doubtful that you'll be able to succeed. We've all been there before — we look over what's involved, shake our heads, and ask, "Can I do it?" If you feel that kind of doubt creeping up on you, shake it off and set your mind straight. Even though you may need to step back and reevaluate what you're doing once in a while, don't let the little voices in your head convince you that you won't be successful.

Having a positive mindset and the core belief that you *can* succeed and *will* succeed keeps you going on the tough days, energizing you to push on toward your goal. *Remember:* What the mind can conceive the body will achieve!

No matter how it happens for you, getting work is additive. All you need to start is one client — one single, solitary person who wants to get healthy through exercise. After you start training your client, people will see you working with her and approach you, or, if you're working with your client in a private setting, your client will start telling his friends about how wonderful you are (and you *are* wonderful!). Trust us — snagging new clients is all about word of mouth (more about that in Chapter 8). Nothing boosts your business faster than a psyched client pumping you up to his friends.

If your services aren't stellar or if your client is dissatisfied, word-of-mouth promotion can hurt you just as easily as it can help you.

Building your base

After you have a few clients on board, you'll be a bona fide personal trainer, managing multiple exercise programs for multiple clients. Thinking about your time constraints (How many people can you train in a day?), examining your career goals (Do you want to make lots of moolah? Work part-time? Hobnob with celebrity clients?), and choosing how you work with clients will help you lay the foundation for a viable personal training business. For instance, if you're going to make this a full-time deal, do you want to keep your client base small and concentrate on long-term clients? Or do you want to work with people short-term, so you can continually work with new clientele? There is no right or wrong way to do it — you're free to decide what you want. When you know what that is, you can gear your service offerings and build your client base accordingly.

Performing Your Art

As we've said, personal training requires more than knowing one muscle from another. Customer service, planning client programs, following up, and everything in between are the elements that will take your personal training from so-so to so great!

Making a great first impression

You know it, we know it, even your dog knows it — the first impression is a lasting one. That means your first client meeting is *the* most important meeting in your client relationship. You want to start out on the right foot, because you are — if you're lucky — going to be working very closely with this person for a long time. No matter what happened that day, even if your cat ate your goldfish and you got a speeding ticket, you need to slap on a smile and fake it 'til you make it.

The Midas touch

Clients may sign up with you because they appreciate your knowledge and enthusiasm, but it's the little touches — and the consistency with which you supply those touches — that keep them coming back.

After she started her own company, Melyssa insisted that every employee learn how to provide five-star service — hold the client's dumbbells for him while he's resting; get a towel and water for him *before* he needs it; manually stretch him between his sets. This differentiated Melyssa's company from the competition so well that when clients left her services to train elsewhere (which

all clients do at some point or another), they always ended up coming back. Why? Because of her attention to detail. The places they defected to didn't have towel service, didn't anticipate their need for water, or didn't stretch them between sets, making their workout experience excruciating instead of exquisite. By performing these little services for your clients, you change their perception from simply receiving a workout to experiencing a professional personal training session.

We talk more about motivating and connecting with your clients in Chapter 9.

If you're happy, you exude confidence and excitement, and your client will pick up on your positive outlook. If you're blue, getting your client excited about doing crunches and lat pull-downs will be difficult.

We delve deeper into the topic of making a good first impression in Chapter 10.

Evaluating your client

Before you start your client on a program, you need to evaluate her medical history, current physical status, goals, and lifestyle. Knowing as much about your client as possible is important — after all, her health is in your hands. If you prescribe an exercise program that doesn't account for your client's schedule, her physical status, or whatever, she may become discouraged. You can't expect a woman with three young kids to succeed with a two-hour-per-day routine, or a client who's mainly concerned with heart health to get excited about doing exercises to boost his butt.

Put on your investigator hat and ask your clients as many questions as you can think of. For example, you can query them about their:

- ✔ Exercise habits
- ✔ Medical history
- ✔ Lifestyle
- ✔ Health goals

A lot of trainers skip this step. We can't overemphasize the importance — from both a professional and liability standpoint — of evaluating your clients. For more information on client evaluations, see Chapter 10.

Programming your clients

If you liked science in school, you're going to love this — creating programs is like coming up with a new hypothesis for each client you work with. You come up with a theoretical program based on your assessment of the client, and then you get to test your theory and see if it holds up. You need to take into account your client's time availability, equipment availability, strengths, weaknesses, and goals to create a program that he'll not only find doable, but also enjoy. Here is where you, the trainer, get to shine as you take your client from what he is to what he wants to be via the exercises you prescribe. (And if you didn't like science, don't worry — we make it easy for you in Chapter 12.)

Performing a training session

If you ask any trainer what the easiest part of his job is, you'll most likely hear "training clients." Performing the training session is fun! After all, this is why you got into personal training in the first place — to work with clients hands-on, showing them the proper way to exercise, spotting them and encouraging them, providing positive support. And now that all the hard work — finding your client, assessing her needs, planning the program — is behind you, you can actually put your plan into motion and see how it works for her!

The only trick is, you'll need to create plans for your clients that break their goals into manageable steps, that keep them motivated, and that get results. More on this in Part III.

Staying in touch

Every good salesperson knows that the follow-up is crucial to making sales and keeping customers happy — and so should you.

Call your clients, whether they're active with you or not. Follow-up calls to active clients can help you determine the effectiveness of your previous training sessions, or provide an opportunity to answer questions about a new workout routine. Follow-up calls to inactive clients can bring them back to you for more services. However you decide to handle following up, remember that doing so is the key to maintaining healthy client relations. The personal training industry is based on relationships, and nurturing your client relationships is vital to the success of your business.

Meeting your clients, evaluating your clients, planning programs, conducting training sessions, and following up — these are the basics of performing your art, and we delve into these topics in more detail in Part II.

Our Little Trainer's All Grown Up!: Growing Your Business

Eventually, you may want to kick your personal training business up a notch. Growing your personal training business means different things to different people. It could mean accepting a management position at a gym, or leaving a gym to start your own studio. However and whenever the bug bites, you need to plan, plan, and plan some more in order to be successful.

Preparing for growth

Getting ready to grow is exciting and invigorating. The prospect of tackling new business and career challenges excites a lot of trainers. But before you jump into anything, do your homework to make sure your vision is viable. Your future is at stake here, and a mistake at this point in the game can be costly.

List the pros and cons of making your change. Talk with people who have been in your shoes to see how they handled the decision. Make sure you have everything you need — financial support, skills, knowledge, and the right tools — should you decide to make the change. Involve those close to you so they can be prepared to give you the emotional support you need.

For more information on determining your career path, check out Chapter 4.

Adding profit centers

If you're looking to increase your income — and who isn't? — you don't necessarily have to increase your working hours. Trainers have plenty of ways to add dollars to their bottom line without spending more time. Selling fitness-related products that clients can use on their own, such as heart-rate monitors or body balls, is a great way to make extra cash while helping your clients. And creating specialty training sessions allows you to diversify and possibly garner more dollars for those sessions.

We give you the 411 on adding profit centers in Chapter 16.

Duplicating yourself

Another way to grow is to take on trainers who can handle additional clients. Because no one will be an exact duplicate of you (and if someone is, be afraid, be very afraid), before hiring, you need to create a list of attributes and qualities you feel the candidate should possess. Check with your lawyer and accountant to understand your state's laws regarding employment. Create a job description for the position so your new hires will have a clear understanding of what is expected from them.

You can find more information on hiring a staff in Chapter 17.

Creating consistency within your business

A successful business provides its customers with consistent quality and service. (And we probably don't need to say this, but the quality and service must be consistently *good*.) Have you ever heard people complain about the hot new restaurant in town? Some nights everything is fabulous, and other nights it takes forever to get seated, the service is horrible, and the food is colder than Vermont in January. That restaurant won't be open long.

If you can't give dependable service, your clientele won't be around long either. You want to strive to create a great experience for your clients each time they work with you. That means you must provide the same training to all your staff members; document your rules and policies; make sure everyone on board understands your company's vision, mission, and objectives; and most important, make sure that that you are the embodiment of what you preach — that you lead by example.

Chapter 2

Getting Certified

. . . .

In This Chapter

▶ Finding your niche

▶ Understanding the acronyms

▶ Choosing the right certification for you

▶ Studying for the certification exam

. . . .

*M*any people who are athletes or who love working out dream of becoming a personal trainer. The fact that you've picked up this book proves you know that there's more to personal training than just enjoying your daily workouts. Success is in the details. What kind of a trainer do you want to be? Who is it that you want to train — kids, seniors, elite athletes? Do you want to train your clients in groups or one-on-one? And, most important, why do you want to train them?

When you have an idea of what kind of personal training you want to do, you need to decide which letters you want after your name — that is, what kind of certification you should get. No two certifications are alike, and clients and employers take some more seriously than others.

In this chapter, we help you decide what kind of clients you'd like to work with, determine whether to train individuals or groups, find the best certification, study for (and pass) the test, and keep your credentials up to date.

Think of the information in this chapter as the foundation for your career as a personal trainer — if you skimp where these decisions are concerned, your house is likely to fall down around you. But if you give these decisions the attention they require, your foundation will last you for many years to come.

It's a goal!

A goal is more than a point in hockey — it's something that will help you decide who to work with, where to work (at a health club, say, or a corporate facility), and whether to work for yourself or for someone else. Do you dream of living large? Then you probably want to focus on segments of the population that don't mind shelling out for a training session, and avoid group classes where you can't charge as much per person. If your goal is to help kids become healthy adults, then becoming certified to work with children is the right path. And if the thought of being your own boss makes your heart go shang-a-lang, then you'll take a different path from someone whose goal is to work at a posh health club.

Take a minute to write down your goals — the reasons you want to become a personal trainer — and keep them in mind as you read the rest of this chapter. They'll help you decide which certification is best for you and what type of personal trainer you want to be.

Finding Your Niche

The type of certification you seek is directly tied to the kinds of clients you hope to work with. In this section, we help you find your niche, the place where you can best put your skills and talents to use.

Looking at the possibilities

When personal trainers talk about their businesses, they often use the term *client population,* which is just a fancy name for the type of people that a personal trainer works with. Each client population has its own needs, advantages, and disadvantages. In the following sections, we cover the most common types of client populations. As you read these descriptions, make a mental note of the groups that most appeal to you.

Healthy adults

This population is the one you'll probably encounter the most — healthy adults who want to lose a few pounds or strengthen sagging muscles. These clients don't have any major aches or pains and, for the most part, have a clean bill of health. Generally, your primary personal training certification covers everything you'll encounter in training this population.

Healthy adults are a great group to get your feet wet with. After you're comfortable working with these clients, you can study to be certified with more specialized groups, like the ones in the following sections.

Seniors

Older people not only require different training parameters than the general population, they also require a completely different set of skills from you as a trainer. Working with seniors involves a strong knowledge of the aging process and how it affects the body.

In more instances than not, older people have chronic medical issues that can be made worse if you're not careful. With seniors having less range of motion and strength, and often lacking the endurance to sustain activity for very long, you can easily injure them without realizing it. *Remember:* This shouldn't prohibit you from working with seniors — it just means that, before you start working with them, you need to have the right training.

The American Senior Fitness Association (www.seniorfitness.net) offers comprehensive certifications for trainers who look to specialize in this area.

Kids and teens

With childhood obesity at epidemic levels, working with children as a personal trainer isn't such a crazy idea. However, you can't load a kid down with heavy weights like you would a power-lifter.

Unlike adults, children have *growth plates,* areas of soft growing tissue near the end of each long bone. Placing excessive stress on these plates can cause them to fracture, especially in the hip, knee, and ankle areas. As a result, "kid-friendly" guidelines have been established, and training the young now requires secondary certification.

The American Council on Exercise (ACE) is one of the top certifying bodies that offers specialized certification in training wee ones. For more information, visit www.acefitness.org.

Pregnant women

Don't be surprised if you see a mom-to-be stretching at the gym with her legs wrapped around her shoulders. Pregnant women produce *relaxin,* a very effective pregnancy hormone that helps "relax" ligaments in the pelvis to allow the hips to spread for childbirth.

Relaxin is a little *too* effective, though — it makes all the other joints in the body super-flexible as well! The bad news is that because of this handy-dandy, mommy's-little-helper hormone, pregnant women can accidentally overstretch, pulling muscles and tendons. Expectant mothers also can't sit or stand in certain positions because doing so places stress on the uterus, possibly leading to pregnancy complications.

Specializing in pre- and postnatal clientele requires mom-savvy knowledge and skills gained from a specialty certification. ACE (www.acefitness.org) offers certification in this area.

Athletes

If your client wants to cream her opponent in tennis, she'll need exercises that improve her lateral power. If he wants to perform a spinning side kick at the karate dojo, he'll need exercises that work on his *explosivity* (the ability to perform quick, powerful movements). Personal trainers who work with athletes have to create and implement sport-specific programs designed to improve performance and decrease the risk of injury.

You don't need to be an expert in the sport yourself to train athletes, but you do need to have an excellent grasp of which muscles do what during sport-specific movements. The base certification offered by the National Strength and Conditioning Association (NSCA) is an excellent primer in training to enhance athletic performance. For more information, visit www.nsca-lift.org.

Deciding which client group you're best suited for

Even if you want to specialize in a client population like athletes or kids, you should probably start out working with healthy adults. Not only will you build a bigger client base to help get your business off the ground, but many certifying bodies also require you to earn a primary certification in personal training before they allow you to test for specialized certification. For example, to be certified as a Sports Fitness Specialist (SFS) through the National Academy of Sports Medicine (NASM), you must first be certified through the academy as a personal trainer.

After you have your personal trainer certification and are pulling in enough dough from a broad client base, you can choose to work with the client population that makes you feel motivated and that pushes you toward your goals.

Still not sure which client population is right for you? Here's a quick quiz that will help:

1. Which of these adjectives defines you best?

    a. Patient

    b. Careful

    c. Gung-ho

    d. Enthusiastic

    e. Slow and sure

2. If you weren't a personal trainer, you would be a:

    a. Teacher

    b. Doctor

    c. Drill sergeant

    d. Customer-service manager

    e. Eldercare nurse

3. Your favorite exercise style is:

    a. Hula hoop!

    b. Pilates

    c. Cross-training

    d. Treadmill

    e. Stretching

If you answered mostly As, think about training kids; mostly Bs, try pregnant women; mostly Cs, train athletes; mostly Ds, go for healthy adults; and mostly Es, seniors may be your client population.

Becoming Certified (Not Certifiable!)

Watch out! It's the attack of the acronyms! ACE, ACSM, NASM — the choices in certifications are enough to make any aspiring personal trainer's head spin. In this section, we outline the various certifications available and help you decide which certification is best for you.

Knowing your ABCs: The personal training alphabet

In the following sections, we cover the six certifying bodies that are the most well known in the industry.

American Council on Exercise

The American Council on Exercise (ACE) Personal Trainer Certification is one of the most popular in the industry. To pass the ACE Personal Trainer Certification exam, you have to demonstrate your knowledge of basic exercise science, nutrition, fitness assessment, exercise programming, and instructional and spotting techniques.

You can contact the ACE at 4851 Paramount Drive, San Diego, CA 92123; phone: 800-825-3636 (toll-free) or 858-279-8227; e-mail: certify@acefitness.org; Web site: www.acefitness.org.

American College of Sports Medicine

The American College of Sports Medicine (ACSM) credentialing exam is the most rigorous in the industry, so you can be sure that it weeds out those who don't know a sphygmomanometer from a goniometer. In your studies, you'll find out how to help healthy individuals as well as individuals with controlled disease.

You can contact the ACSM at P.O. Box 1440, Indianapolis, IN 46206-1440; phone: 317-637-9200; e-mail: publicinfo@acsm.org; Web site: www.acsm.org.

National Strength and Conditioning Association

The National Strength and Conditioning Association (NSCA) is the first certifying body ever accredited by the National Commission for Certifying Agencies (NCCA). Their certifying exam is no cakewalk, either; it assesses your knowledge in the areas of exercise sciences (such as anatomy, exercise physiology, and biomechanics) and nutrition, and tests your knowledge of program design, exercise techniques, testing and evaluation, and organization and administration.

You can contact the NSCA at 3333 Landmark Circle, Lincoln, NE 68504; phone: 888-746-2378 (toll-free) or 402-476-6669; e-mail: commission@nsca-cc.org; Web site: www.nsca-lift.org.

Three's a crowd: Choosing classical or group certification

Personal trainers can choose to work with individuals (referred to as *classical training*) or groups (referred to as *group training*). Many certifying organizations offer certifications in both of these options. If playing to a crowd gets your motor running, group training may be for you. However, be aware that the risk of injury is higher because you can't give each client your undivided attention. Although you can earn more money per hour by training several people at once, you can't charge as much as you would for an individual session, because the *perceived value* (what clients think your services are worth) is lower.

National Academy of Sports Medicine

The National Academy of Sports Medicine (NASM) certification is focused on developing a fitness professional who's well rounded and well versed in correct biomechanics and exercise implementation. Most of their certification programs are completed online.

You can contact the NASM at 26632 Agoura Road, Calabasas, CA 91302; phone: 800-460-6276 (toll-free) or 818-878-9203; Web site: www.nasm.org.

International Sports Sciences Association

Since 1988, the International Sports Sciences Association (ISSA) has provided certification and continuing education for over 50,000 fitness professionals. The organization gives you the option to study at home and also offers a live weekend seminar.

You can contact the ISSA at 400 East Gutierrez Street, Santa Barbara, CA 93101; phone: 800-892-4772 (toll-free) or 805-884-8111; e-mail: webmaster@issa online.com; Web site: www.issaonline.com.

Aerobics and Fitness Association of America

Founded in 1983, the Aerobics and Fitness Association of America (AFAA) has certified more than 150,000 fitness professionals in areas ranging from personal training to kickboxing. The AFAA produces a variety of educational materials, including *American Fitness Magazine,* textbooks, reference manuals, and videos. Each year, the AFAA produces over 2,500 educational workshops.

You can contact the AFAA at 15250 Ventura Boulevard, Suite 200, Sherman Oaks, CA 91403-3297; phone: 800-446-2322, ext. 215 (toll-free); e-mail: contactafaa@afaa.com; Web site: www.afaa.com.

Making your choice

Now comes the hard part: choosing which certification you want to pursue. The tips in the following sections will help you make the decision that's right for *you.*

Ask for advice from personal trainers you respect

If you're looking for a good restaurant, chances are you'll ask your friends what they think of the food and atmosphere at La Maison du Snob before you drop a bundle there. Do the same with a certifying body.

Start by talking to personal trainers in your area. Ask them about their certification experiences. Don't be shy — personal trainers love to talk about their jobs!

Contact the certifying organization you're interested in and request the names and numbers of a few personal trainers who have gone through their certification process. Then contact those people and ask whether they were happy with the program. How was the exam? Were the study materials helpful? Do the organization's reps act professionally? What are the advantages and disadvantages of this certification? Would they recommend the program to others?

Find out which certification is required at the places where you'd like to work

Dropping hundreds of dollars and spending lots of time getting a certification only to find out that the certification you received doesn't help you get a job would be more than annoying.

If you hope to work in a health club or other business (as opposed to working for yourself), contact potential employers in your area and ask which certifications they require for employment.

Find out what additional requirements the organizations have

You'd think that after you paid the fee, crammed your head full of facts, and passed the exam, you'd be all set. But some certifying bodies require that you be certified in CPR and/or Advanced First Aid, have a college degree, or even have work experience in addition to passing their exam before you can be fully credentialed by their organization.

Check out the organizations' Web sites for specific information, and make sure you'll be able to meet their additional requirements before you get started.

Preparing for the Test

No matter which certification you decide to pursue, you'll most likely have to pass an exam to prove you have what it takes to be a personal trainer. Organizations that require in-person (as opposed to Internet-based) testing offer exams on different dates in different testing centers around the country. Check out the organizations' Web sites for information on test dates and locations.

If a certifying organization doesn't require you to take an exam, run — don't walk — in the other direction. The purpose of the exam is to weed out those people who give personal trainers a bad name. Your certification won't mean anything — to you or anyone else — if you don't have to pass an exam in order to get it.

Understanding the exams

The following sections fill you in on the exams required by each of the top certifying organizations.

American Council on Exercise

The ACE test has 150 multiple-choice questions, and you have three hours to complete the exam. The three types of questions you have to answer are "knowledge" questions (for example, "Which muscle extends the elbow joint?"), "application" questions (such as, "Sarah's measurements are X. What is her body fat percentage?"), and "analysis" questions (such as, "The per-serving nutritional data for a bag of chips is X. What is the total amount and percentage of calories that come from fat in the entire bag?").

American College of Sports Medicine

The ACSM written examination contains approximately 115 multiple-choice questions. Questions are in the areas of anatomy and biomechanics, exercise physiology, human development and aging, pathophysiology and risk factors, human behavior and psychology, health appraisal and fitness testing, safety and injury prevention, exercise programming, nutrition and weight management, and program administration/management.

The practical examination is composed of 3 separate test stations, each 20 minutes in length. You'll need to demonstrate your abilities in the areas of assessing body composition/flexibility, demonstrating strength and conditioning exercises, and assessing cardiovascular fitness with a Monark Cycle Ergometer.

National Strength and Conditioning Association

To earn certification as an NSCA-CPT (Certified Personal Trainer), you have to pass a three-hour written examination that includes 140 multiple-choice questions focusing on client consultation/assessment, program planning, exercise techniques, safety/emergency procedures, and legal issues. Thirty-five questions correspond to a videotape, which assesses knowledge in the areas of exercise techniques, functional anatomy, and fitness testing protocols.

National Academy of Sports Medicine

This online exam has two parts: multiple-choice questions and a case study. The multiple-choice portion consists of 100 questions and lasts 90 minutes. For the case-study section, you must develop a training program based on information the NASM provides about a real-life client. You have 24 hours to complete the case study. You can prepare via a two-day workshop, an interactive CD-ROM, traditional text and videos, or an online course. The course covers flexibility training, exercise physiology, strength training, program design, and more.

International Sports Sciences Association

ISSA offers three ways to take its exam: online, during their two-day seminar, and at home as an independent study. The exam consists of 50 multiple-choice questions, 50 true/false questions, case-study calculations, and a practical video section, where you watch clips of exercises and answer questions about them. If you choose home study, the exam isn't timed, but you're required to fill out a workbook and complete ten learning experiences in lieu of the video portion of the exam. One example of a learning experience is to go to a gym, list all their exercise equipment, and describe how each piece of equipment works the body.

Aerobics and Fitness Association of America

The AFAA offers an intensive three-day workshop and certification exam that covers fitness testing procedures, obesity, nutrition and weight control, behavior-modification techniques, special populations, and special medical considerations. The AFAA Personal Trainer/Fitness Counselor Certification course consists of a practical and written exam. The written exam lasts 75 minutes and consists of 100 multiple-choice questions.

Making the grade

Unless you were born with a knowledge of exercise programming, fitness assessments, and weight management, you'll need to study for the certifying examination. Cramming the night before a test may have worked in high school, but this technique probably won't cut it for the personal training exam. Starting a few months before the exam, set aside an hour or two every day to study.

Getting ready to study

If you went to high school or college in the days of Boy Toy belt buckles and neon leg warmers (or even earlier), you may be out of practice when it comes to studying. Don't worry — we'll refresh your memory.

Make sure you have a quiet place — whether that's your kitchen or the local library — where you can concentrate on the course materials. Turn off the TV, the radio (unless listening to classical music helps get your brain cells moving), and your Internet connection (unless you're using online course materials). Unplug the phone or turn on the answering machine. And make sure your study area is equipped with pencils, paper, and enough light.

If you have roommates or family members living with you, be sure they respect your need for quiet time. If your house resembles Grand Central Station, consider going to the library or even a local coffee shop to do your studying — a place where you can concentrate without distraction is what you need.

Finding course materials

Each certifying organization offers its own course materials to help you study for the exam. When you sign up to take the test, you may receive (or be able to purchase) textbooks, online study guides, sample tests, and access to live seminars and courses. Check out the certifying organizations' Web sites for information on the course materials that are available.

Take a look at sample tests

Many of the certifying bodies have sample tests on their Web sites or in their program literature. Check them out and ask yourself the following questions:

- ✔ **Do I understand the language?** For example, do you know what a quadratus lumborum is, if that's mentioned on the test?

- ✔ **Am I capable of performing everything that is required in the test?** For example, can you demonstrate the proper spotting technique for a flat dumbbell bench press, if that's a requirement on the test?

- ✔ **Can I recite the Karvohnen Formula while hopping up and down on one foot?** Okay, we're kidding about that one.

- ✔ **Is the exam difficult enough to weed out those who would be better off staying out of the gym?**

After you've examined the contents of the test and what's involved, try taking the sample test. The answers are usually provided so you can see how well you do. Taking the sample test is a good way to see exactly what you do — and don't — know.

TIP

Not your mama's studying tips

When Melyssa was studying for her certification exam, she didn't just bury her nose in a book. Bor-ing! She used all sorts of unconventional studying techniques to help her understand the material. Here are some of the tricks she used to ace her exam:

- ✔ **Use yourself.** Studying anatomy is an active process — you have to get up and moving to understand how the body works. Melyssa and a friend stuck labels on their muscles and joints to memorize the muscle names and how they move. Also, get off your chair and perform movements to find out which muscles are involved. Which muscles do you use when you kick? How about when you're doing a bench press?

- ✔ **Be lazy.** Just like during a workout, take short rest breaks. Psychological studies have shown that a five-minute rest break every half hour can increase information retention (in English, that means you'll remember more of what you study).

- ✔ **Use flash cards.** Melyssa drew up flash cards with definitions and formulas. You can test yourself whenever you have a free minute — in line at the grocery store, in the waiting room at the dentist's office, while stuck in traffic. Or have a friend flash you (the cards, that is).

Equipping yourself

If the exam includes a practical portion, you'll need to get your hands on such equipment as skinfold calipers, blood-pressure cuffs, stethoscopes, and tape measures. You can order this equipment from an online medical source such as QuickMedical (Web site: www.quickmedical.com; phone: 888-345-4858).

Recruit some friends (offer them free lunch if you have to) and use them to practice measuring flexibility, measuring body fat, performing submaximal cardio evaluations, and anything else you may have to perform on the test.

Maintaining Your Certification

Most certifying organizations will require you to keep your credentials up to date by earning Continuing Education Credits (CECs). For example, to renew and maintain your ACE personal training certification, you must earn 1.5 CECs every 2 years through ACE-approved courses or professional activities. You can generally earn CECs through correspondence courses, online courses, practical and comprehensive training, and live classes. Some certifying organizations also require you to keep your CPR or Advanced First Aid training current — this is a good idea even if it isn't required to maintain your certification. Check out the Web site of your certifying organization for detailed information about how to maintain your certification.

You may think that taking more courses after you earn your certification is a waste of time, but Melyssa knows from experience that scientific knowledge is always changing and improving — and that keeping your skills updated can save your clients' lives! Melyssa learned in one continuing education course that if a client's nose turns purple during exercise, it can indicate a heart condition. Soon after, one of Melyssa's clients came up for air after doing some toe-touches, and his nose was bright purple. Melyssa suggested he see his doctor immediately, and sure enough, his doctor admitted him to the hospital, where he underwent a quadruple bypass. Thanks to her continuing education course, Melyssa's client is alive and well. So don't ever stop learning, and remember this mantra borrowed from one of Melyssa's mentors: When you're green you grow, and when you're ripe you rot.

Chapter 3

Practicing Your Art

In This Chapter

▶ Interning and apprenticing

▶ Finding a good place to start

▶ Working with friends and family

▶ Practicing what you preach

The only way to become a stellar personal trainer is to get out there and train. But if you're not employed yet and you don't have any clients, exactly how do you go about doing that? It's the old catch-22 — you can't get clients until you have experience, but you can't get experience without clients.

Except that you *can*. In this chapter, we give you the scoop on interning, apprenticing, and practicing on your friends (and how to do it so that they *remain* your friends).

Getting the Scoop from Those in the Know

A great way to get real-world experience before you try hanging your personal-trainer shingle is to become an intern or an apprentice. Internships and apprenticeships allow you to discover the technical aspects of the job by working with people who have been there and done it — and who can show you how to do it, too.

Interning

When you think of interns, you probably imagine someone running around serving coffee to spoiled executives as a low-paid gofer yearning to climb the corporate ladder. But as an intern in the personal training industry, you won't be serving any coffee, kowtowing to any execs, or climbing any ladders.

Instead, a personal training internship is a temporary work experience in which you receive training and gain experience in your field. If you have no practical experience under your belt, interning will:

- ✔ Give you in-the-field experience that you can't get in a classroom or a book
- ✔ Give you the opportunity to explore and understand the industry before committing to it full-time
- ✔ Let you create relationships with potential employers
- ✔ Help you earn credit toward your certification or degree
- ✔ Help you acquire the skills necessary to perform your job well
- ✔ Teach you valuable new skills with which to build your résumé
- ✔ Establish vital career networks and mentors
- ✔ Enable you to collect references for future employment

Many internships provide compensation through minimum wage, stipends, or hourly wages comparable to full-time pay. Others don't pay but do provide perks and invaluable experience. Internships vary in duration.

The best place to start is with your local gym. Ask the gym owner or manager if you can shadow one of his trainers or maybe start working the front desk to learn the business. Also, don't hesitate to call other personal training companies to see if they would be open to taking you on as an intern. It's a great way for a personal training company to train you in the way they want things to be done — and it works for you too, because you get to learn the ropes!

Apprenticing

Apprenticing provides education and on-the-job training. Typically, you work in a structured apprentice program for a company under the watchful eye of one of their veteran staffers. Unlike internships, apprenticeships are *always* paid positions. The benefits of apprenticing include the following:

- ✔ Paid on-the-job training, under the guidance of a skilled employee
- ✔ Additional instruction, classroom theory, and hands-on training
- ✔ Progressive, increasing wages as your skill level increases

If you're just starting out as a personal trainer, you can earn entry-level income as an apprentice and gain the skills you need to become a higher-ranking trainer. Plus, you'll typically get a raise in pay after you've successfully completed the apprenticeship program. The bonus here is that, when you go through an apprenticeship, your employer is able to train you in the way *they* want you to work, so your chances of being taken on as a full-time trainer at that facility are greater than they are if you were just an intern there.

If you're interested in apprenticing but aren't sure where to start, try your local college. Colleges with Exercise Physiology programs typically have a list of companies that offer apprentice programs to their students, because their students have to complete an apprenticeship for their degree requirements. Even though you may not be a student, they can give you a few names and contact numbers of companies you can apply to as an apprentice. If you don't have any colleges or universities in your area, don't hesitate to approach a company yourself and ask if you can work with them as an apprentice — it never hurts to ask!

Tailing other trainers

If you can't find an internship or apprenticeship in your area, you may consider trying to find a job at a small personal training facility where you can work more closely with a skilled trainer.

Before Melyssa owned her own personal training facility, she worked for a bodybuilding couple who owned a small gym. She learned all about training and servicing clients from them before breaking out on her own. But even then, Melyssa asked another fitness guru in the area if she could assist him one or two days a week at his gym so she could see how he operated. He allowed her to help out, and she learned things there that she wasn't able to learn at her previous job, because they were two completely different types of gyms.

When Melyssa started her business, this behavior was one she found herself duplicating often. If she didn't completely understand some aspect of personal training, she sought out an expert to shadow until she understood the real-life application. This strategy helped Melyssa develop a network of advisors who had a lot more experience, knowledge, and education than she did. She found herself going back to these people time and time again with her questions and concerns.

Training to train

If you haven't done it yet, you may want to think about coughing up a few pennies to work with a personal trainer yourself. Although you want to be training other people — not be trained yourself — spending time with someone who's been doing it for a while and is successful at it can be worth way more than the money you shell out for the session. Trust us, if you tell your trainer that you're interested in being a personal trainer, too, and you'd like to work with him for a couple of sessions to get a feel for it, he'll be delighted. For the most part, trainers are very supportive of one another — a good personal trainer will want to see you succeed. A bonus to working with another trainer is that, when you do get certified and start training clients, you have a colleague whom you can call when you need help troubleshooting or you just need a quick answer to a question.

To this day, Melyssa still works out with other trainers. The trainers she works with are very experienced and very successful, and in some cases Melyssa even travels out of state to work with them. She does this because other trainers always know something she doesn't, and to stay in top form, she needs to keep learning. Melyssa gleans invaluable tips and techniques from the other trainers — things that she wouldn't have learned if she had stayed at her own facility and worked out all on her lonesome. Now she can pass on to her clients the new techniques she's discovered.

Taking advantage of other learning opportunities

If you belong to a gym, work out with a friend who's slightly less advanced than you are. While you're working out with her, practice your training and spotting techniques. We guarantee that your partner won't mind — after all, she's going to get stronger as a result of your practice!

If you can't find anyone to work out with, try role-playing. (And no, we don't mean meeting your significant other at the local watering hole wearing a wig and dark glasses.) While you're working out, run through a mental dialogue of what you would say to yourself if you were the client. Practice explaining what the exercises do and which muscle groups are involved in the exercise. Just be sure to do this in your head, not out loud — unless you want to gain a rep as "the crazy guy on the treadmill." Practicing your dialogue prevents you from being tongue-tied when you're working with a live, flesh-and-blood client. The last thing you want when you're on the job is to draw a blank and forget the names of the body parts you're training!

One great way to expand your mind and elevate your glass ceiling is to visit the leaders of your profession — and what better way to do that than to visit a conference? Try attending conferences put on by different certifying bodies or groups such as IDEA (www.ideafit.com) or the National Strength and Conditioning Association (www.nsca.com — click on Meetings). Also check out the seminars by Northeast Seminars (www.neseminars.com), an outfit that gathers some of the top people in the fitness and rehab industries to discuss functional training and rehabilitation.

Study or practice one of your training skills every day. Read up on medical literature, listen to a lecture at the hospital on preventing back injuries, practice stretching a friend. However, whatever, and whenever you decide to practice, when the time comes that you actually need that skill or tidbit of knowledge, you'll be glad you did!

Interning resources

If you'd like to read more about interning, check out these popular books on the subject:

✔ *Internships For Dummies,* by Craig P. Donovan and Jim Garnett (published by Wiley). This book tells you how to decide which industry is for you, score the internship of your dreams, and succeed in the business world.

✔ *The Internship, Practicum, and Field Placement Handbook: A Guide for the Helping Professions,* 3rd Edition, by Brian N. Baird (published by Prentice Hall). This book starts with information on how to find an internship, and then delves into the real-world issues of being involved in the helping professions.

✔ *Internships 2004,* 24th Edition (published by Petersons Guides). Petersons is the publisher that prints all those directories for college students. This book has nearly 50,000 paid and unpaid opportunities plus information on how to apply for internships and how to get the most out of an internship.

✔ *The Internship Bible,* 2004 Edition (published by Princeton Review). This annually updated guide gives the scoop on more than 100,000 internships.

Or try these Web sites:

✔ **FitnessManagement** (www.fitness management.com): Click on Job Fair, and you can post an ad yourself saying that you're looking for an internship, as well as browse job openings.

✔ **FitnessJobs.com** (www.fitnessjobs. com): Here you can post your own ad looking for internships.

When you write an ad seeking an internship, be sure to include your contact information, the region you're looking to work in (so you don't get calls from people in Peoria when you live in Seattle), and a description of your experience or education.

Using Test Subjects (Or, Getting Your Family and Friends to Jump When You Say Jump)

Who knows you better or loves you more than your friends and family? (If you said "the pizza delivery guy," you're in trouble.) You can bounce your business ideas off of them and practice your techniques on them when they're not looking, er, we mean when they're *willing*.

Because your friends and family members have no problem with telling you that your teaching skills stink or that you don't know your gluteus maximus from your elbow, they can be trying to work with. Develop a thick skin and remember that their suggestions get you used to dealing with straight-talking clients!

There's more to training than, well, training. You need to pinpoint all the other areas where you may need improvement. Ask the people you've been practicing with to give you feedback on things like:

- ✔ **Your professional demeanor.** Do you seem like a professional, or like their goofy sibling/spouse/friend?

- ✔ **Your ability to explain the exercises.** Do they understand what the exercises are for and how to do them correctly?

- ✔ **Your ability to demonstrate the exercises.** Do your demonstrations help them understand the proper form?

- ✔ **Your spotting technique.** Do they feel like they're in good hands, or are they afraid that they're going to wind up getting dumbbells dropped on their heads?

- ✔ **The overall quality of the session.** Was your session something they'd shell out money for, or do they feel they'd get more value buying an exercise video?

- ✔ **Your overall knowledge and ability to communicate what you know.** Do you seem like someone in the know or someone who needs to go to the back of the class?

Make a list of the skills you need to brush up on, and build time into your schedule to devote to strengthening those skills. With practice and good feedback from your clients, you'll have this personal training thing down in no time!

Training Yourself

Have you ever noticed how people naturally gravitate toward the buff trainer in the gym? That's because the trainer with the washboard abs *looks* like he knows what he's doing, even though that may be the farthest thing from the truth. People want to look fit, lean, and buff — if you know someone who wants to look flabby and out of shape, we'd like to meet that person — so they figure, "Well, if that person knows how to make *himself* look like that, then he'll know how to make *me* look like that, too."

Now, the reality is that this is bunkum. What you look like doesn't really have any correlation to your skill as a personal trainer. You need to be able to prescribe different exercises for different people, based on their unique needs. Looking the part does help; your health and fitness can be the greatest advertisements you'll find. But more important than talking the talk, you have to be able to walk the walk.

Practicing what you preach

Can you perform a modified push-up? How about a full push-up? Guy or gal, you need to have the physical strength to demonstrate any type of exercise to any type of client you take on. That means you need to learn and practice every exercise that you plan on being able to teach.

Reading up on it

Check out your library's fitness section for exercise and advanced weight-lifting books. Your certifying body will have publications along those lines as well. After sifting through them, pick out the new exercises you're going to master, and write them out in your workout log. Be sure to keep the new exercises in your log until you develop mind-muscle connection and can really nail the form and feel the isolation of the movement. Incorporate a few more new exercises and do the same with them until you've built an enviable exercise repertoire.

Getting moving

Despite popular opinion, personal training entails more than pumping iron. Start getting to know the cardio equipment in your gym. Knowing how to set the programs is helpful if you're looking to change up a client's workout with a little interval training. Trust us, this recommendation comes from personal experience — throwing a client on a piece of cardio equipment that's unfamiliar to you and then not being able to get the darn thing to go on while you're trying to do a body blitz workout won't exactly impress your client (at least not in the way you *want* her to be impressed).

Dear diary . . . : Keeping a workout log

It may sound corny, but you're going to be keeping a workout log for your clients, so you may as well get used to it now by keeping one for yourself. While you're in your experimental phase and you're discovering new exercises and training styles, keeping a workout log can be extremely helpful. You can record the elements that got you the results you were looking for, and then you can duplicate them for your clients. Make notes about how you felt and how you recovered, and plan your next workouts based on that.

Being a not-so-mad scientist: Experimenting on yourself

Every person's body is unique, and what works for one person may not work for another. When you train clients, think of yourself as a scientist. You have to step outside of your normal thought process and ask "What if?" (What if I increased the pace? What if I slowed down this movement? What if I had the client work on this machine first?)

On top of knowing every exercise there is to know, you need to be well versed in every style of training — you need to know how different tempos feel, how increased weights and/or reps affect the sensation of your workout, how changing your recovery time affects your performance. These are all things you need to experiment with personally so that one day you'll be able to say to your client, "What if we try this instead?" — and you'll have a good idea of what the results will be.

Developing your professional skills

According to some guy named Webster, a *professional* is somebody who shows a high degree of skill or competence. Becoming a professional doesn't occur overnight. Professionalism is a combination of your technical skills, practical skills, people skills, and that little indefinable something called *finesse*. It's the ability to perform your job as a trainer in a proficient and skilled manner. To do that — and to do it well — takes time and practice.

Your speaking style and manner are extremely important when working with clientele, both paying and nonpaying; they indicate to your clients how well versed you are in your technique, how comfortable you are in your role as a trainer, and how disciplined you are as a professional.

One of Melyssa's favorite topics with her trainers was professionalism. They got together for a staff meeting every two weeks or so, and one of the first things they talked about was client issues and how to handle them professionally. During one meeting, they decided to make a list of what a professional trainer looks like. Here's what they came up with.

A professional trainer:

- ✔ Is responsible and reliable
- ✔ Has exercise programs written out for clients ahead of time
- ✔ Stays knowledgeable and current
- ✔ Is focused on the client 100 percent of the time
- ✔ Admits to not knowing the answer to a client question

✔ Is early or on time for training sessions and meetings

✔ Doesn't let clients distract him with too much talk

✔ Performs all requirements of the job

✔ Completes duties fully and in a timely manner

✔ Offers to help out other staff members

✔ Doesn't gossip about others, with clients *or* staff

✔ Is respectful of the people he works with

✔ Takes responsibility for his own actions

✔ Maintains appropriate boundaries with clients

✔ Doesn't blame others for problems or shortcomings

✔ Takes up any problems or issues with the appropriate person

✔ Takes clients and staff out for ice cream on a regular basis (Okay, we made that one up.)

A cautionary tale

Here's a story from a trainer we know (we'll call her Angie) that underscores the importance of being professional.

Shortly after Angie expanded her service offerings to include massage therapy, her masseuse called in sick 30 minutes before she was to meet one of Angie's first — and best — clients. Not wanting to cancel and disappoint her client, Angie thought, "I'll go myself!" With that, she grabbed the portable massage table and massage cream and loaded up her car.

The client met Angie at the front door. She looked behind Angie. "Where's your masseuse?" she asked. "Well, she's sick, so I'm going to give you your massage," Angie answered. The client looked surprised. "Have you ever given a massage before?" "No," Angie replied. "Have you ever *gotten* a massage?" the client asked, her eyes even wider. "Well, no," Angie replied.

Looking doubtful, the client led the way to her bedroom, where Angie proceeded to set up the table without sheets (the client brought out her own towels and placed them on the table so she could cover herself).

To make a long story short, the client knew that Angie didn't know what she was doing, and even though Angie thought the session went fine, it wasn't until three years later, when she got her first massage, that she realized the errors she had made with her client. Boy, was her face red! Angie realized that she had compromised her relationship and her professionalism by trying to do something she wasn't qualified to do.

Make sure when you're meeting with a client — whether for the first time or the 50th — you're prepared and know what to do. You can't just wing it when it comes to being a personal trainer or offering services to your clients.

Melyssa's trainers could have come up with 20 more ways to be professional. But these were the most predominant in the organization — the ones that they dealt with most often.

No matter who you are practicing with or working on, you must take yourself seriously. If you don't, no one else will. If you're practicing with friends and family, stay in character. As easy as it is to joke around and gab about the latest reality show, keep in mind that you need to develop two skills: how to keep your client moving through a session, and how to keep yourself focused and on track while you direct your client. The whole purpose of practicing with friends and family is to find your *training rhythm* (the manner in which you'll be most comfortable working with clients).

Chapter 4

Planning Your Start

. . . .

In This Chapter

▶ Exploring your personal training options

▶ Deciding if business ownership is for you

▶ Choosing whether to work for someone else

▶ Discovering the types of facilities where you can work

▶ Applying for a personal training job

. . . .

*Y*ou're certified, your skills are buffed and polished to perfection, and you're raring to go. Go where? Some personal trainers work as employees at health clubs and other facilities, while others work for themselves.

Being your own boss may sound like a dream come true. But if you're not prepared, it can be a nightmare. In this chapter, we help you decide whether to work for yourself or for someone else, figure out what kind of facility you'd like to work at, get hired by the employer of your dreams, and figure out where to train your clients if you're a lone ranger.

Assessing Your Lifestyle Needs

If you're like most people, you just want to dive right in and get working. But if you take some time up front to really think about what you want from your life and your career, you'll reap the rewards in the years to come. So, grab a pen and paper, and write down your answers to the following questions:

✔ Are you a night person or a morning person?

✔ How many hours per week would you like to work?

✔ How much money would you like to earn as a personal trainer?

✔ How often would you like to go on vacation, and for how long?

✔ Is family life important to you?

✔ What are your hobbies? What hobbies would you like to have?

These questions don't have right or wrong answers. They're just supposed to get you to think about your priorities.

Refer back to your answers as you read about the realities of starting your own business and working for someone else. You'll find that, for example, if you like to take two months of vacation time every year, you can do that as an independent personal trainer. But if your family life is important to you, starting your own business may not leave you any time to spend with your kin.

Being Your Own Boss

Who doesn't dream of telling his boss to "take this job and shove it," and forging his own way as a freelancer or business owner? No more getting up at 6 a.m., no more fighting traffic, no more surly bosses, no more tiny paychecks.

Hold on a second . . . before you decide that you want to go it alone, you need to be aware of the pros and cons. Running your own business isn't a surefire way to wealth or free time — if it were, everyone would be doing it.

Keep reading to find out the truth about going it alone. Being a successful business owner takes a certain kind of personality, and sometimes the disadvantages can outweigh the advantages.

Figuring out if you have what it takes

You need more than an independent spirit to make it on your own. To find out if you have what it takes, answer the questions in the following sections. If you answer "no" to any of them, think long and hard about how you can change the answer to "yes" — or whether you should rethink the whole freelance thing.

Getting other people on board

Before you make your final decision about whether to strike out on your own, put together an informal advisory board of friends and family members, health professionals, small business owners, and personal trainers you may know (you probably called a few when you were deciding which certification to pursue — but if you didn't, now is as good a time as any to make some connections). These people can give you honest feedback on your strengths and weaknesses, true tales about working for yourself or for someone else, and advice on where to start and how to get started.

Are you a self-starter?

When you work for yourself, you don't have a boss to cluck his tongue (or dock your pay) when you punch in late. The only thing that makes you get out of bed on time, focus on your work, balance your books, and create new client programs is — wait for it — you. Be truthful: Are you motivated enough to do your own marketing, programming, accounting, and everything else you need to do to keep a business running (at least until you start making enough money to hire other people to do some of it for you)?

Do you get along well with different personalities?

As an independent professional, you'll be dealing with insurance agents, journalists (who can give you good PR), doctors (who can give you referrals), accountants (when you can afford one), landlords or health-club owners (you need *somewhere* to work!), and — don't forget — clients. You need to be able to communicate and get along with a wide variety of people.

Are you good at making decisions?

If the idea of choosing between PB&J and chicken noodle soup for lunch sends you into a tailspin, you're in trouble. You'll need to make decisions galore, from what to name your business and what color your logo should be, to whether you should take on a new client. And sometimes you'll need to make snap decisions, such as when a client has a complaint or a reporter from the health section of the paper is on the phone asking you to give him ten rules for making healthy New Year's resolutions. (Don't think this will happen to you? Check out the information about appearing in the press in Chapter 8.)

Do you have money in the bank?

Unless you find some magic formula for getting clients to pound down your door, your business will probably start out slowly as you gain a reputation and get referrals. This isn't bad — it's just par for the course. But in the meantime, you need money to live on.

Most experts suggest that you have at least six months' worth of living expenses socked away before making the leap.

Are you good at organizing?

When you work for an employer, somebody else writes up your schedule, supplies client forms, creates training programs for your clients, and so on. When you work for yourself, you need to be able to create, use, file, and find all sorts of documents. You'll probably have a Rolodex, a Palm Pilot, or the equivalent, as well as contact-organizer software — and you'll use them to keep track of clients, doctors, and other contacts. You'll also need to keep track of how much money you're making, who owes you money, and how much you owe. All of this requires you to be more organized than Martha Stewart's fruit preserving calendar.

Are you a leader?

If your business takes off, you may want to hire other trainers to boost your income and to be able to serve more customers. Now *you'll* be the boss whom everyone wants to tell to "take this job and shove it." Can you give orders without creating a mutiny? Can you inspire people to give 100 percent?

In addition to potentially leading a staff, you'll need to be a leader to your clients. They look to you for instruction and advice, and you need to be able to lead them to better health.

Do you have management skills?

If you own a company with employees, you may find yourself doing more managing than training. Can you deal with constantly keeping an eye on your employees — and cutting down on your training hours to do so? Can you discipline an underperforming employee?

Do you have your the support of your family and friends?

When you start your own business, at first you have to work overtime to lay the foundation and get the business off the ground. Your family and friends need to understand that your schedule will be different; that you'll need privacy during certain hours while you work on marketing, creating client programs, and other tasks; and that you may not be able to handle all the household chores on your own. If your family and friends aren't already on board with your new business venture, you'll need to get them there — fast.

Understanding the pros and cons of going it alone

Think you have what it takes? If you read the questions in the last section and answered yes to all of them, read on about the pros and cons of owning your own business to find out whether you really want to make the leap into the freelance lifestyle.

Pro: Unlimited income potential

When you work for yourself, you set the rates and you work as much as you want to. If you can charge $100 per session (who knows, maybe you'll have some celebrities on your client list!) and can cram in eight sessions per day, that's nobody's business but your own. If you work for a health club, you'll usually be paid an hourly wage for working the floor, plus a commission for bringing in new clients and a set fee for doing personal training sessions. Your employer dictates how much you get paid and how many sessions you can conduct.

Pro: You choose your clients

If someone rubs you the wrong way, you don't have to accept her as a client. If you work for an employer, you have to grit your teeth and deal with — and even be nice to — rude or annoying clients.

Pro: You choose your hours

No 9 to 5 for you! If you want to be there to walk your kid home from the bus stop, that's your choice — as long as you can schedule your clients around it. And if you want to take off to Tahiti for a week, you can do it (as long as you don't mind not getting paid for that week).

Pro: Your income lines your own pockets

Your hard work and long hours directly benefit you, as opposed to increasing profits for some CEO in an ivory tower. Many successful freelancers are people who had a "bad attitude" at work because they resented busting their buns to profit someone else.

Pro: Going it alone is exciting

Nothing makes your heart go pitter-patter like signing on a new client, scoring a public-relations coup, or finding a new way to help a client beat back pain through exercise. Every day is a new learning experience as you figure out how to best serve your clients while boosting your bottom line.

Pro: You can work where you like

Instead of getting paid to "walk the floor," you can walk wherever you like! Design T-shirts with a snazzy logo and your business name and go to the beach — you're advertising, not slacking. Work at different gyms that allow independent trainers. Travel to out-of-town fitness-industry conferences. The *world* is your floor to walk!

Pro: You get to keep (almost) every penny you earn

When you work for someone else, in many cases the business owner pockets up to 40 percent of what you earn. When you work for yourself, you get to keep everything you earn (minus taxes, of course). No middlemen need to be paid.

Pro: You get to deduct your expenses

As a business owner, you can deduct expenses related to your business from your taxes, such as gas to get to work, clothing, office supplies, computer equipment, and more. Consult your accountant for more information.

Con: No company health-insurance plan

Most working people take health insurance for granted — but not those who work for themselves. Trying to get a health-insurance plan when you're a free-lancer can be as painful as repeatedly jabbing yourself in the eye with a pen.

Linda, who is an independent professional, went without insurance for four years and finally decided to sign up through the Chamber of Commerce — to the tune of $550 per month for herself and her husband. Some industry associations offer health insurance to members, but it usually isn't cheap.

Con: No company-sponsored retirement plan

Traditional retirement plans such as 401(k) plans, where employers often match your retirement contributions, are for employees. If you want to put aside money for retirement, you'll have to set up an Individual Retirement Account (IRA), Keogh, or Simplified Employee Pension (SEP), and remember to contribute to it regularly. No automatic deductions for you!

Con: Higher taxes

When you're an employee, your employer pays half of your Social Security tax. As a freelancer, you have to cough up the entire 15 percent on your own.

Con: Feast or famine lifestyle

If you work for yourself, you can kiss your biweekly check goodbye. In the freelance world, when you don't work, you don't get paid. You don't get paid to walk the floor, you don't get paid when you're sick, you don't get paid when you take a break.

When you have a lot of clients — such as in January, when people are trying to stick to their New Year's resolutions — you work like a dog but get paid like a prince. When times are lean, so is your paycheck. You need to be able to put aside money when you're flush to tide you over when clients are scarce.

Con: No paid vacation or sick days

Can't work because you're laid low with the flu? Too bad, you don't get paid. Want to go on vacation for a week or two? Hope you don't mind taking a pay cut, because you don't get those two weeks per year of paid vacation time like your 9-to-5 brethren. (Of course, you can vacation as long as you like — as long as you can afford it — a definite advantage.)

Con: No equipment and supplies

When you work for someone else, all the equipment and all those pencils and paper clips are provided by the Business Supply Fairy. When you work for yourself, all those supplies — not to mention the computer, printer, fax machine, sticky notes, business cards, Internet access, ink cartridges, paper, and long-distance service — come from your *own* magic wand. And unless you rent space in a gym or a personal training center, you may even have to supply your own exercise equipment. These goodies are tax deductible, but that's small consolation when they used to be free.

Con: No locker room chitchat

Forget Friday morning gabfests in the locker room about who got kicked off *Survivor.* Even if you hate working for an employer, working for yourself often gets very lonely — so lonely that you can suddenly find yourself down at the local juice bar making small talk with anybody who gets within five feet of your smoothie. Sure, you have your clients — but you can't complain to *them* about how awful your clients have been lately or how you're afraid to raise your fees.

Trading spaces: Finding a place to train your clients

After you've asked yourself the tough questions and been honest with yourself about the answers, and after you've considered all the pros and cons of going it alone, if you still want to do it, you're off to the right start.

Now's the time to get down and dirty. Although you don't have to apply for a job when you pursue the freelance path, you do have to deal with some other details, such as where you'll work. When you don't work for a gym, where are you supposed to train your clients? You can't very well outfit a van with exercise equipment and become a wandering personal trainer, can you? (Actually, that's not a bad idea. Someone steal it, quick!)

In the following sections, we cover your options for places to train clients when you work for yourself.

Gyms

Some gyms will let you train clients there — for a price. They may ask for a percentage of your fee, a set amount per client, or a set amount per month. The bonus is that you'll have all the equipment you need, and your clients will have use of the locker rooms, showers, and so on. Contact local gyms through the Yellow Pages to find out whether they rent space to personal trainers.

Your clients' homes

Some of your clients will be blessed with full gyms — in fact, 30 percent of Melyssa's clients had complete gyms in their homes. Instead of having to take their chauffeured limos to the gym, these people may pay you to train them in their own homes. But even if your client isn't loaded, and she has nothing but a rug on the floor, you can often get by with just a set of dumbbells and a body ball.

When you work in a client's home, behaving like the professional you are is even more important than usual. You may get the urge to slack off because you're not in a professional environment, and this is a definite no-no.

If you're driving from house to house giving training sessions, you probably won't be able to book as many sessions in a day, because you'll be spending a lot of time whizzing down the highway or waiting in traffic.

Local businesses

Sometimes you can rent space from compatible businesses. Melyssa started her personal training business in a room she rented from a physical therapist. The room was 400 square feet and completely empty, and Melyssa stocked it with equipment and ended up employing two other trainers and an administrative assistant in that space.

The advantage to renting space from a business is that it won't break your bank and you don't have to worry about a lease. The drawback is that you'll be at the mercy of your landlord's schedule and rules.

Personal training facilities

Some bigger cities have personal training facilities where you can rent space — just like a hairdresser rents a station from the salon he works at. Check the Yellow Pages under "Personal Training" to see if a facility like this is located near you.

Working the 9 to 5

If you'd like to get hired at a gym or other facility, this section is for you. We give you the scoop on places that are looking for trainers like you, the pros and cons of working for someone else, and how to get your foot in the door at the facility of your dreams.

Knowing whether you're the perfect employee

Answer the questions in the following sections. If you answer "no" to any of them, ask yourself how you can change your answer to "yes" — and if you can't, you may want to consider going solo. (Turn to the beginning of this chapter to find out if being a lone ranger — er, we mean trainer — is for you.)

Can you take direction?

As an employee, you'll need to take directions from your boss, whether that's the business owner or a manager. This doesn't mean, of course, that you have to blindly follow instructions, but too much questioning can land you in the soup.

Do you play well with others?

See those other people working at the gym you hope to work for? If you get hired there, you'll be interacting with them for the majority of your waking hours. Do you get along with all types of people? Can you handle working with someone who thinks or works differently from you?

Are you punctual?

Of course, being punctual is important for both freelancers and employees — but as an employee, excessive lateness or tardiness can land you on the unemployment line. Do you have the willpower to get up when your alarm goes off and be at your workplace, bright-eyed and bushy-tailed, at the appointed hour?

Can you stick to someone else's schedule?

Your employer will make up a schedule for you, and chances are she doesn't care that you like to watch your favorite reality TV show on Monday nights. If she says you work Monday nights, guess what? You work Monday nights. If you need a certain day off, you need to let your boss know well ahead of time so she can work it into the schedule.

Can you do it someone else's way?

Your employer may have a different outlook on exercise programming, client relations, employee relations, or business operations than you do. A good employer will give you leeway to do your job your own way, but you'll probably have to make some changes to your preferred way of doing things to fit in your place of employment.

Identifying the pros and cons of being an employee

If you answered "yes" to all the questions in the preceding section and you're thinking about going to work for someone else, read on to find out about the pros and cons of your decision. Just like any other situation, working for someone else has its advantages and disadvantages.

Pro: Your company pays for your health insurance

Freelancers have to shell out megabucks in some areas to get insured — but not you! If you work full-time for your employer, chances are you'll be offered health insurance as part of your benefits package.

Pro: You get a company-sponsored retirement plan

You can have a certain percentage of your paycheck automatically deposited into your retirement account so your savings will grow — and it will be painless, because you probably won't even notice that the money is gone. If you're lucky, your employer will match your retirement contributions up to a certain amount — that's free money (something you should definitely take advantage of, if you can).

Pro: You get a regular paycheck

Every week (or every two weeks), like clockwork, your employer will put a check in your hands — unlike freelancers, who get paid when the have clients, and get zilch when they don't.

Pro: Your employer provides everything you need

Need a particular form? Your employer has a whole drawer full of them. Not sure what to wear? How about that snazzy polo shirt your employer gave you? Want to start your client on a new exercise? Have him hop on that brand new treadmill, courtesy of — you guessed it — your employer. As an employee, you don't have to drop money on supplies, equipment, or other work-related goodies.

Pro: You can make new friends

As an employee, you'll always have someone else to talk to, whether it's to trade ideas for client programming or chat about the latest news. You'll never get lonely with other employees around.

Pro: You get paid vacation and sick days

Unlike your freelance brethren, if you get sick and have to stay home, you still get paid (as long as you still have sick days left). Your employer will most likely also give you paid vacation time, so you can relax for a couple of weeks without worrying about how the bills are going to get paid.

Con: Your income potential is limited

You can make only as much as your employer pays you (except when you get a raise). Unlike freelancers, you can't make more moolah by raising your prices, adding more clients, adding more services, or working more hours.

Con: You don't choose who you work with

Don't like that new client? Too bad. You have to work with — and even be
nice to — all clients, no matter how annoying they may be. You also don't
choose your workmates, and may get stuck with a stinker of a co-worker.

Con: You work set hours

Working set hours can make it hard for you do the things you like. For example,
if you're scheduled to work the 9-to-5 shift, you'll have to find some way to do
your errands — like dropping off dry cleaning, going to the bank, and going to
the post office — after hours or during your lunch break. If you're scheduled
for Tuesday night and that's the night your son has a baseball game, you're
out of luck unless you remember to ask your employer for the day off weeks
ahead of time.

Con: Your employer takes a cut of what you make

If your employer charges clients $50 for an hour-long session, why do you
make only $20 per hour? Because your employer has to take a cut of what
you earn from each client to pay for *overhead* — things like heat, light, rent,
and other operating expenses. Employers also pay additional taxes on their
employees, as well as matching employees' Social Security withholdings.

Picking from the job jar

Don't think that because you're a personal trainer your working options are
limited to gyms. Plenty of businesses that deal with health are willing to hire
a sharp specimen like you. In the following sections, we give you a guided
tour of some of your options.

TIP

Going from employee to employer

If you really want to start your own personal
training business, but you answered no to our
questions earlier in this chapter, don't worry!
Working for an employer will help you get your
skill set up to snuff — especially if you work at
a facility where you're able to get involved with
all parts of running the business.

Melyssa was working for a large health-club
chain when the owner tried to pressure her into
signing a noncompete deal and coughing up
$1,000 per month to work exclusively for him — a
tactic that's known as *reverse hiring*. This jerk-
iness on the part of the club owner motivated
Melyssa to quit and start her own personal training business. Working at the gym gave Melyssa
plenty of skills — such as how to hustle for work
and how to treat clients — that helped her build
a successful business.

Hospital-based wellness centers

Hospital-based wellness centers are the latest health trend. They operate like any other gym, except that your client base will consist of a lot of doctors, nurses, and patients (though members of the community are also welcome to join). The good news is that being surrounded by medical professionals will be a great learning experience for you. The bad news is that working with doctors and nurses can be intimidating — after all, they'll know for sure if you're pronouncing *gastrocnemius* correctly!

A lot of doctors and nurses don't know nearly as much as you think when it comes to physical fitness. Many of them also live such busy lives that they suffer from poor nutrition. They need *you* to show them how to adopt a healthy lifestyle!

University gyms

Many large universities have gyms for their students and faculty. You'll be working with plenty of brainy people, and the benefits package is usually impressive.

Where the jobs are

Surf to these job sites to find personal training jobs in your area:

✔ **GymJOB.com** (www.gymjob.com): Gym JOB.com is a free benefit for ACE-certified fitness professionals, or you can pay for access ($9.95 for one week, $24.95 for one month, $59.95 for three months). You'll have access to job postings in over 20 categories.

✔ **Monster.com** (www.monster.com): This popular job-search site lets you search key-words or browse job categories. For personal training jobs, select the categories "Personal Care and Services" and "Healthcare — Other."

✔ **The International Health, Racquet & Sports-club Association** (www.ihrsa.org): Start by clicking on "Running Your Business" and

then click on "Career Center." Job seekers can choose to browse through all available job listings or search for jobs by using specific criteria. The ads are mostly for directors and managers, but why not contact the businesses and offer your services?

✔ **FitnessManagement.com** (www.fitness management.com): The job selection is skimpy, but you can post your job-wanted ad free for 30 days.

✔ **Exercisejobs.com** (www.exercisejobs. com): This site has a good selection of fitness-specialist/personal-trainer jobs. You can also post your résumé (preferably in a way that stands out from the dozens of pages of other trainers' résumés). The site includes career resources, such as interview tips and a résumé guide.

Chain health clubs

You know these places — they're the ones with the TV and magazine ads depicting hot young men and women wearing Lycra bodysuits and thongs. In this large gym environment, you have plenty of opportunity for advancement. However, much of your salary is based on sales, so you'll feel the pressure to sell, sell, sell — whether you're pushing nutritional supplements or personal training sessions.

If your goal is to help people, you may feel uncomfortable handing them a slick sales pitch in order to boost your income.

Independent or small health clubs

Because the staff is small, you'll wear many hats in an independent or small health club — such as working the front desk, answering phones, scheduling clients, cleaning, taking part in marketing campaigns, and, oh yeah, conducting personal training sessions.

If you hope to own your own personal training business someday, this may be the best workplace for you, because you'll get to see all aspects of running a business.

Private personal training studios

Private personal training studios do nothing but personal training. Clients don't go there to work out on their own, to drink smoothies, or to get facials. You may also be sent out to train clients in their home gyms or in small corporate facilities.

YMCA/YWCA

The YMCA, immortalized by the Village People, caters to families (as does the YWCA). This employer will give you a good, solid base of experience. If you want to work with a diverse group of people, then the Y's for you. The Y is the poor man's country club, and it typically offers everything from badminton to basket-weaving. If you're looking to get a feel for what the gym industry is like, a great place to start is the Y, where you can test your skills in different areas of fitness services.

Senior centers

If you want to work at a senior center, you'll need to be aware of the changes the body goes through as it ages and you may need advanced certification as well. State-run senior centers may not pay as much as other fitness facilities. The good news is that even if your local senior center doesn't offer a fitness program, they may be open to new ideas, so you can propose a program or a class to them.

Management fitness companies

These companies are like staffing agencies for fitness professionals. Management fitness companies outsource personal trainers to corporate fitness centers and other businesses that need staff but that don't want to take on staffing themselves. These employers have very stringent requirements; you'll probably be required to know CPR, turn in a résumé, and even take a test.

Alternative healthcare centers

Alternative healthcare centers are into natural care and an Eastern philosophy of medicine, so they offer treatments like acupuncture, massage therapy, naturopathy, and chiropractic services. Clients may be trying to avoid surgery or medication, and they may have ailments they're trying to resolve. Personal training fits in with this environment perfectly, because clients are looking for natural ways to improve their health — and what's more natural than exercise? Only those with open minds need apply.

Physical-therapy businesses

Some physical therapists hire personal trainers to work with patients after they get past the acute stage of an injury, to regain strength and mobility. You'll be teaching exercises under the supervision of the therapist to help patients lose weight (because excess weight can affect the joints) and prevent re-injury. Because you'll be working for a licensed or registered therapist, you're in for a great learning experience.

Health resorts

These are the exclusive playgrounds of those with a lot of cash to drop. They usually boast a full-blown gym in addition to spa services, healthy meals, and activities. Most health resorts require trainers to show proof of certification plus a résumé, and they'll likely expect you to be certified in CPR as well. Because these are vacation spots, you won't have long-term clients, and you'll have to pack a lot of information into a short amount of time.

Day spas

Day spas are like toned-down health resorts. Clients usually visit for a few hours or a day to get massages, facials, and other treatments. The difference between working at a day spa and working at a health resort is that you'll see clients on a more continuous basis.

Sussing out potential workplaces

Before you go to all the trouble of convincing an employer to hire you, make sure that *you* want to work for *them*. Nothing's worse than knocking yourself out to get hired and then finding out that you're working for Satan himself.

Head to the facility and take a look around. You can even ask for a day pass or a week pass so you can work out at the facility yourself. Do you like the equipment? Do the employees seem happy, bored, suicidal? What kinds of clients do they cater to — women, men, bodybuilders, young adults, seniors?

Corner a personal trainer and ask her some questions. If she's busy or doesn't want to talk while on the job, ask if you can have her e-mail address or phone number and contact her later — or give her your contact information and ask if she'll call or e-mail you. Don't be shy — personal trainers love to talk about their jobs! Here are some questions you want to be sure to ask:

- How is the facility's management to work with?
- What's the pay like? Do you get a commission for bringing on new clients?
- Is there a lot of pressure to bring in new clients or push products like nutritional supplements?
- What are the hours like?
- Do you like the equipment?
- Does the employer take good care of the equipment?
- What are the clients like?
- What kind of certification do you need to work there?
- Do you find it difficult to get clients?
- What are the pros and cons of working for this employer?

Getting hired

Finding out where you'd like to work is the easy part. The hard part is convincing the owner or manager that you're the best darn personal trainer this side of the Mississippi and that she should hire you right away (preferably for a lot of money).

Your best bet is to visit the facility of your choice in person, hand your résumé to the person behind the counter, and ask to make an appointment, with the manager or owner (if it's a small facility). But don't make a move before sharpening the tools in the following sections.

Polishing your résumé

Your résumé is you — on paper. Is the résumé sloppy? This tells an employer that you may do a sloppy job. Is it riddled with typos? This shows a lack of attention to detail. Is it well organized? You'll probably be just as organized when dealing with client programs.

A résumé is also a sales tool. You're presenting information about yourself in such a way as to convince someone to hire you.

Here are some tips that will take your résumé from "ho-hum" to "hire her!":

- ✔ **Start with your most impressive credentials.** If you studied physiology or exercise science in college but have no job experience, start your résumé with a section that describes your education. If you have no formal training but you've worked in the fitness industry, put your job-experience section first.

  Résumés can be chronological or functional in format. A *chronological résumé* lists your jobs and education from most recent to least recent. A *functional résumé* focuses on skills rather than job titles. A functional résumé is best if you want to highlight skills and strengths that your most recent jobs or education don't necessarily reflect. If you don't have much experience in the fitness industry, a functional résumé may be the way to go.

- ✔ **Use active verbs and phrases to give your résumé punch and help the employer understand how you can benefit the facility.** Rather than weak verbs (as in "Was a trainer for Club X" or "Was responsible for training at Club X"), use strong, active verbs that stress accomplishments (as in "Trained clients at Club X"). Here are some active verbs you can use:

  - Trained (clients, employees)
  - Implemented (programs)
  - Reduced (costs, accidents)
  - Increased (profits, sales, safety)
  - Improved (clients' fitness levels, customer service)
  - Managed (employees, programs)
  - Helped/assisted (clients, management)

- ✔ **Fake it 'til you make it.** Never worked as a personal trainer before? Stress the responsibilities you held at previous jobs that will help you in your new position. For example, if you worked in retail, you know how to treat customers and handle complaints. If you worked in sales, you have the skills you'll need to bring in new clients. Just make sure that your résumé is truthful — you don't want to fake it *too* much.

- ✔ **Check it over.** Much like Santa, you should check your résumé twice — not to find out if you've been naughty or nice, but to make sure your résumé is free of typos and misspellings. Don't rely on spell check, which can't tell the difference between *you're* and *your.* If you have time, put your résumé in a drawer for a few days so you can look at it with fresh eyes before turning it in. Even better, have a friend look it over for you. Or, if you have a little extra time and money, consult a freelance editor who can take your résumé up a notch.

Writing the perfect résumé is a huge topic — huge enough to have hundreds of books devoted to it! We suggest *Resumes For Dummies,* 4th Edition, by Joyce Lain Kennedy (published by Wiley).

Knowing what to wear

Even though you're applying to be a personal trainer, you shouldn't wear your sweats when dropping off your résumé or during the interview. Don a suit, even if it makes you feel overdressed — your professionalism will shine through.

Brushing up on your interview skills

You don't want to lose your cool when you're being grilled by a potential employer. Follow these tips to become an ace interviewee:

✔ **Research the employer thoroughly.** This strategy will help you ask intelligent questions and show your enthusiasm for the job.

✔ **Ask a friend to pretend he's an interviewer and ask you questions.** Typical questions you may have to answer are:

- Why do you want to become a personal trainer?

- What are your strengths and weaknesses?

- What would you do if a client hurt herself while doing a lat pull-down (or a chest press, or whatever)?

- What certifications do you have?

- Why did you leave your last job?

- Why should we hire you?

✔ **If you have the equipment, videotape yourself answering interview questions.** Check for mumbling, slouching, fidgeting, wandering eyes, and saying things like "um" and "y'know."

For many more tips, check out *Job Interviews For Dummies,* 2nd Edition, by Joyce Lain Kennedy (published by Wiley).

Part II
Being a Successful Personal Trainer

"C'mon, give me 10 more! 10 more copies! Okay,
now 5 more! 5 more copies! That's it! That's it!"

In this part . . .

*P*ersonal training is about more than pumping iron and doing cardio. You're a business, which means that you need to think like a businessperson. In this part, we tell you all about how to create a business plan, project your income and expenses, develop your fee structure, and develop a marketing plan — just like a Fortune 500 company!

Next, we help you hire other professionals, such as an accountant and a lawyer (yes, you do need them). We also tell you how to create a business name and logo and how to determine your business structure (that's those modifiers that come after your business name like *Inc.* and *LLC*).

Keeping with the business theme, the following chapters describe how to develop sound business practices that will keep your business running smoothly, how to bring clients in the door, and how to keep those clients happy and motivated so they keep coming back.

Chapter 5

Creating Your Business Plan

· ·

· ·

Most trainers, eager to strike out on their own, jump feet-first into business ownership. They have a vague idea of what they need to do — go out, get clients, train them, collect money — but no real plan.

Success doesn't happen by accident; you plan for it. In this chapter, we tell you how to develop a business plan, fee structure, and marketing plan, plus how to project income and expenses so you don't find yourself in a financial hole.

Developing a Road Map for Success

Before you rent a space, before you start advertising for clients, before you decide how much you're going to charge, you need a plan — a business plan, that is. A *business plan* is a detailed blueprint of how you're going to reach success. You can — and should — refer to it occasionally to make sure you're on the right track. (You also need a business plan if you ever decide to apply for a business loan.)

Here are some of the questions you answer in your business plan:

✔ **What are your personal goals?** Do you want to make more money, have a flexible schedule, work with the rich and famous?

✔ **Where do you want your business to be six months, a year, five years from now?** Do you want to stay solo or grow your business to become the first national personal training franchise?

- ✔ **Whom do you want to train?** If you're not sure about the answer to this question, turn to Chapter 2, which offers information on the different types of clients you can work with.

- ✔ **Where do you want to train your clients?** Do you want to travel to their homes or gyms, meet them at their offices, or have them come to you?

- ✔ **What services or products will you provide your clients?** Will you offer specialty services like sport-specific training? Will you sell nutritional supplements or fitness equipment?

- ✔ **How are you going to let clients know that you're available?** Read more about marketing yourself in Chapter 8.

- ✔ **Why will clients hire you?** What makes you and your services different from Big George's Deep Discount Personal Training?

For a sample business plan, check out www.wiley.com/go/personaltrainer.

For more information on writing business plans, visit the Web site of the Small Business Administration (SBA) at www.sba.gov. In particular, check out the "Starting Your Business: Business Planning" page at www.sba.gov/starting_business/planning/basic.html.

Sounds like a plan to me: Writing your business plan

After you've thought about what services and products you want your company to provide (your goods), who you want to provide those services to (your clients), and where you're going to provide them (your location), your next step is to create a business plan.

The business plan contains seven parts:

- ✔ **Executive summary:** The executive summary is an overview of your entire plan, highlighting all key strategic points. You typically write this last but list it first.

- ✔ **Company description:** The company description is, well, a description of your company — your vision and mission statements, a company overview, and an overview of your legal structure (the letters that come after your business name, such as *Inc.* or *LLC*). We give more information on legal structures in Chapter 6.

- ✔ **Products and services:** This section describes in detail the types of products and services your business will offer, any research and development that you may have done to support them, how much they'll cost, and how you plan to deliver them to your clients.

- **Marketing:** In this section, you define the market you'll be operating in (the health and fitness industry), the type of client you expect to service (your target market), your competition (Big George's Deep Discount Personal Training), and your strategy for attracting clients (putting flyers on the windshields of Big George's clients' cars when he's not looking).

- **Operations:** This section describes your business's physical location, any equipment you need, the kinds of employees you need, your inventory requirements, and any other applicable operating details, such as a description of your *workflow* (how your business will perform its day-to-day activities). For more information on workflow, turn to Chapter 7.

- **Management:** Here you outline your key employees (even if you're the only one), external professional profiles (that's your accountant and lawyer, as well as another other professionals you've hired to help you with your business), the members of your advisory board (if you don't have one yet, include this section for the future), and your human-resource needs (how many staff members you'll need to run your business and service your clients).

- **Financials:** This section contains financial projections that will show whether your concept is viable or whether you need to head back to the drawing board. The projected financial statements — the income statement, the cash-flow projection, and the balance sheet — are estimates based on research of your start-up costs and projected sales.

You can find a sample business plan on the Web site for this book. For even more information on this huge topic, check out *Business Plans Kit For Dummies* by Steven Peterson, PhD, and Peter E. Jaret (published by Wiley).

Developing your mission statement

An important part of your employee manual is your mission statement. Your mission statement captures the essence of your business and makes sure you and your employees are on the same page and moving toward the same goals. It also signals what your business is about to your clients and vendors. Include it in your business plan, your marketing materials, and your employee manual (after all, if your employees don't know your mission, that's not a good sign).

Your mission statement tells people:

- Who you are
- What you do
- How you do it
- Who you do it for

Where to find your competition

Don't know where to go to find the competition? Start asking around. Get friendly with your local gym manager — gym managers typically have the scoop on the training scene, such as who's hot, who's not, and where to go to find people in the know. Also try your local fitness-equipment store — personal trainers often leave business cards on their counters, and the managers there can fill you in on who's a poseur and who's the real deal. And don't forget the Internet and the Yellow Pages.

For example, your mission statement might be:

> The mission of Wanda's Personal Training Emporium is to promote longevity and quality of life for health-conscious individuals through scientifically proven methods of exercise, nutrition, and positive lifestyle modification.

This mission statement contains all four elements:

- **Who you are:** Wanda's Personal Training Emporium
- **What you do:** Promote longevity and quality of life
- **How you do it:** Through scientifically proven methods of exercise, nutrition, and positive lifestyle modification
- **Who you do it for:** Health-conscious individuals

You can start formulating your mission statement by answering these questions:

- Who are my clients? What is my client population, and what do they want?
- Who are my competitors, and what makes my business different?
- What can my business do for my clients?
- How do we do this for the clients?
- Why am I in business? What do I want for myself, my clients, my family?

Now compose a brief paragraph incorporating who you are, what you do, how you do it, and who you do it for.

Before you start framing your mission statement and hanging it all over the walls, put it to the test:

✔ Ask your clients if they would want to do business with a company that has your mission statement.

✔ Ask your employees if they understand the mission statement and if they would support it.

✔ Ask your vendors (like equipment suppliers and supplement vendors) if it helps them understand your business.

Incorporate all the feedback you get from your clients, employees, and vendors into the mission statement, and then repeat the testing process until you have a mission that sparkles with perfection.

Your mission statement clearly articulates what your business is all about. Post it on the wall, include it in your marketing materials, and put it on your Web site.

Make sure that your employees help support your business's mission. Put the mission statement in their employee handbook, and use weekly staff meetings as an opportunity to discuss the mission and how the employees can live up to it.

Researching your market

When you were a kid, didn't you dream about being a spy? C'mon, we know you did. Well, here's your chance. Here's where you go undercover to get the dirt on your potential clients and your competition.

Gathering demographic data

If you don't know the demographics of your chosen location, you need to do research to determine whether the area you want to do business in can support your personal training prowess. You need to know your area's population, a breakdown of the ages and genders of the inhabitants, and the average income of the area. If you're planning to open a personal training business that caters to seniors, you probably don't want to open it across the street from a college campus.

A great — and free — way to get information on your chosen location is to check out the Census Bureau Web site (http://factfinder.census.gov), which lets you look up the demographic makeup of towns, states, or zip codes. Click "Fact Sheet," then enter information about the location you're considering. You can narrow it to a particular zip code or look at a town or city as a whole.

Don't forget your own eyes and ears. If you're interested in opening a business in a particular part of town, drive around and see what kinds of businesses are already located in the area. Spend some time there and get a feel for the atmosphere.

Scoping out the competition

Another important aspect in determining your venture viability is having a strong awareness of your competitors. Your competitors are the personal trainers and personal training companies in your area that are already catering to the people you hope to train one day. The ones you want to scope out are the successful businesses, not the poseurs who think that *lat pull-down* is short for *lateral pull-down*.

The best way to know your foe is to "shop" them. Call as a prospective client and ask for information about their services. You'll want to know things like:

- ✔ What type of services do they offer?
- ✔ How much does it cost?
- ✔ Are their trainers certified? If so, how?
- ✔ How many trainers do they have?
- ✔ How long have they been in business?
- ✔ Are they insured and bonded as a business?
- ✔ When are they open?
- ✔ Do they travel to clients' homes or offices?

Not only will you get the information you need to compete in your marketplace, but you may also pick up an idea or two for yourself.

Pinpoint all your competitors within a five-mile radius of your proposed business location. (An industry survey by the International Health, Racquet & Sportsclub Association [IHRSA] reported that consumers generally travel to fitness facilities that are within five miles of their homes or workplaces.) Make a chart listing the competitors you want to call and the specific items you want to know. This chart will make it easier to compare and contrast.

Selecting a location

Now that you know everything about everyone — including where your target market lives, where your competitors are located, and what Big George had for breakfast this morning — selecting a location should be a snap.

If you're still having a hard time deciding, photocopy a map of the area you live in. Outline the zip-code boundaries, then label the map with the demographic information you turned up for each zip code — the average household income, the number of households, the predominant gender and class — and take a step back. Does anything jump out at you? Do you notice certain areas with similar profiles that are close together? If you see similarities in certain areas, and those similarities match your objectives, that is most likely where you want to be!

Deciding How Much to Charge

You know about how much a computer, a car, or a house should cost. But how do you put a price on something as intangible as your personal training services? One of the ways your prospective client determines the value of your services is through your fee structure. Whether you realize it or not, what you charge says a lot about you. If your prices are too low, your prospect will think that you're not too confident with your skills as a trainer or that you're not really a pro. If your prices are stratospherically high, your prospect will think that you're a little *too* confident. Setting your fee structure at the right level is imperative — both for you and for your client.

Make a list of how much your competitors are charging. Add together all the prices, and divide that number by the number of companies you surveyed. Round up to the nearest dollar, and — voila! — you have an average price per session. You should be fine as long as your prices are close to that average — you don't want to be too far under or too far over. Just like Goldilocks, you want your price to be "just right."

If you don't have many competitors in your area to help you set your price point, first do a dance of joy. Then log on to the IHRSA Web site at www. ihrsa.org for industry statistics — such as average session price by state or club type — to point you in the right direction.

Too often, newbie trainers are so hungry for clients that they'll do just about anything for the business — from offering multiple free sessions to charging bargain-basement rates. Whenever Melyssa asks trainers why they set their fees so low, the answer is always the same: "I could never charge $40 a session! No one would pay me that!" The truth is, most trainers simply aren't prepared to *ask* for fair and adequate compensation — they don't believe that they're worth it.

Be confident that you're offering a valuable service. After all, what can be more important than keeping people healthy? Recognizing and standing by your worth tells your client that you know what you're doing and you know what it's worth. Charging fair prices even helps your clients — the confidence that you exude gives your clients the confidence to let you help them.

When Melyssa was starting out, she created a menu of prices for her services. She was so proud of the way her menu looked that she ran over to her physical therapist's office to ask his opinion. Another personal trainer was in the waiting room, and he glanced down at the paper in Melyssa's lap, turned to her, and asked, "Are you a trainer?" Melyssa nodded and smiled, not knowing that he was a trainer, too. He snickered, pointed to the menu in Melyssa's lap, and said, "You'll never get that much money for training, you know. No one will pay that much." Though her mind was screaming, "But I did my research!", Melyssa calmly replied that she was going to try out the fee structure and see how it worked. Five years later, Melyssa had a 3,000-square-foot private training facility with six full-time trainers. She ran an ad in the paper looking for new trainers — and guess who showed up looking for a job? The moral of the story: Charge what you're worth, and don't listen to the whining of trainers who charge bargain-basement prices.

To Market, to Market: Getting the Word Out about Your Services

Owning a personal training business is not like *Field of Dreams* — if you build it, they may *not* come. You can go ahead and open your business, but you won't have any clients if they don't know you're there. Marketing is all about letting people know — repeatedly — that you're there. That's where your marketing plan comes in.

You versus the competition: Knowing what sets you apart from the crowd

Before you can write a marketing plan, you need to know what makes you different from your competition. After all, to convince clients to sign up with *you,* you need to differentiate yourself from the rest. After all, why should clients go to you when they can go to Big George's Deep Discount Personal Training? What do you offer that sets you apart? By understanding and establishing the unique points of your service, you form the foundation on which you'll base your marketing strategy.

Refer to your competitor survey chart. Consider each competitor's selling points. Do they have a good location? Are all their trainers certified? Are they bottom-of-the-barrel cheap? Make a comparative list of their selling points versus your selling points.

Developing a marketing plan

A marketing plan outlines the specific actions you need to take in order to get your name in front of potential clients. In your marketing plan, make sure you detail:

- ✔ **Your services and what makes them unique:** Refer to the preceding section, "You versus the competition: Knowing what sets you apart from the crowd."

- ✔ **Your pricing strategy:** Refer to the "Deciding How Much to Charge" section, earlier in this chapter.

- ✔ **Your sales and distribution plan:** How are you going to get your services and products to clients — online, by mail, in person? Will you accept credit cards or checks? Will you offer refunds?

- ✔ **Your advertising and promotion plan:** See Chapter 8 for more-detailed information on advertising.

Doing the Math: Projecting Your Income and Expenses

The last section of your business plan is the most important: your financial plan. The financial plan tells you whether you can do what you hope to do — that is, whether your business will make money.

Getting help estimating expenses

If you're having a hard time estimating expenses, turn to the International Health, Racquet & Sportsclub Association (IHRSA) for help. IHRSA performs extensive surveys every year of the entire health-club industry. They publish industry-specific periodicals and custom reports geared toward very specific sectors of the population. You need to be a member to access some of their information, but you can purchase their reports and books through their online store. Call them at 800-228-4772 or visit www.ihrsa.org for more information.

Estimating expenses

Here's where you get a grip on what you're going to have to shell out to be in business for yourself. Divide your expenses into two groups: *start-up expenses* (typically, one-time costs) and *operating expenses* (which occur on a regular basis).

Start-up costs

Think of your business as a car: Before you can get anywhere, you have to fill up the tank. Start-up costs are all the things you have to pay for to get your business started. Start-up costs include the following:

- ✔ Business registration fees
- ✔ Business licensing and permits
- ✔ Rent deposits
- ✔ Equipment
- ✔ Promotional materials
- ✔ Uniforms
- ✔ Utility setup fees (phone, electricity)

This list is just a small sample of possible start-up costs. You'll find that, as you write down your own start-up costs, the list will seem to grow faster than the national debt.

Operating expenses

A full tank will get you moving, but as with your car, your business requires regular infusions of cash to stay in gear. Your operating expenses may include the following:

- ✔ Payroll (your salary and/or staff salaries)
- ✔ Rent
- ✔ Loan payments
- ✔ Phone and utility bills
- ✔ Advertising
- ✔ Continuing education
- ✔ Supplies

Again, this is just a sample list to put you on the right track. After you've completed your list of operating expenses, add up all the expenses to know how much dough you need to come up with each month.

Projecting income

Now that you have a clear idea of how much you need to pay the bills, you have to figure out how many clients you need in order to earn that money! Bear in mind when you're projecting your session load for the week that you need to leave room for:

- **Travel time:** If you travel to your clients' homes or workplaces, you need to factor in that driving time.

- **Cancellations:** People inevitably cancel, and you have to figure that it'll happen — you're better off planning for at least some of your clients to cancel. That way, if they all keep their appointments, you'll be ahead of the game.

- **Administrative time:** Your clients don't pay you for the time you spend balancing your books or doing filing, but you have to do it anyway.

- **Personal time:** If you don't want to burn out within six months, we recommend you build this into your schedule now.

Okay, here comes the fun part. Break out your calculator and use this formula to determine how many sessions you need to conduct per week to meet your monthly income goal:

1. **Add your total monthly expenses (see the "Operating expenses" section, earlier in this chapter) to the amount you want to make as a profit.**

   Be realistic! This profit has to pay for your mortgage, food, entertainment, and all other nonbusiness expenses.

2. **Divide the number you came up with in Step 1 by your session price (refer to "Deciding How Much to Charge," earlier in this chapter).**

   The resulting number is how many paid sessions you need to conduct per month in order to pay your bills.

3. **Multiply the number you came up with in Step 2 by 12 (the number of months in a year).**

4. **Divide the number you came up with in Step 3 by 52 (the number of weeks in a year).**

   This figure is how many paid sessions per week you'll need to conduct in order to make your desired monthly income.

   If you plan to take vacation time, you need to account for this in your calculations. For example, if you plan to take two weeks of vacation time, divide by 50 rather than 52.

Now that you know how much you need to make, project your entire financial scenario — by month for the first year, then by year for the following years.

Chapter 6

Setting Up Shop

- -

- -

*Y*ou have a client. Now you're a full-fledged personal training business, right?

Not quite. As you probably know, personal training involves more than just the training. You need to get all your ducks in a row in terms of handling taxes, registering your business, and deciding on a business structure. And you have to work with more people than just clients to get your business off the ground. Professionals such as lawyers, accountants, doctors, and other trainers will serve as your advisory board, mentors, and networking group. In this chapter, we show you how to connect with the people who will help you reach the pinnacle of personal training success.

Shakespeare said a rose by any other name still smells as sweet. But will a personal training business called Lazy Louie's Personal Train-o-rama still bring in the clients? Probably not. In this chapter, we also help you come up with a winning business name (and come up with a logo to match).

A Little Help from Your Friends: Forming Your Support System

You'd think that an independent professional like yourself would be — how should we put this? — independent. Far from it. No matter how much of a take-charge person you are, to get your business up and running (and jogging, and lifting weights, and jumping rope), you'll need to rely on lawyers, accountants, bankers, insurance agents, doctors, friends and family, and other trainers. Sure, you can aspire to be the next Oprah Winfrey, an uber-entrepreneur who has her hands in a thousand pies — but even she had a million assistants doing her bidding behind the cameras.

Drafting your professional team

At first, you may feel that hiring a team of professionals is out of your league — after all, you're not Donald Trump. But at the very least, you need to rely on a lawyer and an accountant to take your business from the field of dreams and make it a reality. And because all businesses change with time — whether they're hiring new employees, moving across town, or opening branches — you need the advice of some pros to keep yourself on the up-and-up.

In the following sections, we tell you about the people you need and how to find them. We also tell you which kinds of questions you should ask before you put someone to work for you. *Remember:* You need to interview these professionals just like you would a potential employee. Finally, we let you know whether going it alone, without a team of professionals, is an option.

Knowing which players you need

Before you start drafting your team, you need to know which players you need (that is, which professionals have the kind of expertise that can help you out). In the following sections, we tell you about the four biggies: lawyers, accountants, insurance agents, and bankers.

Hiring a legal eagle

What do you need a lawyer for? You're not planning to sue anybody, are you? Despite the impression you may get from TV shows like *Law & Order,* lawyers do a lot more than represent you when clients mysteriously disappear after hitting on your spouse or missing a payment. A lawyer can

- Help you make sure your business is registered and IDed properly.
- Defend you if someone decides to bring legal action against you.
- Give you legal advice related to the operation of your business (such as when you hire and fire employees).
- Create and interpret contracts and leases — even the small type!
- Choose the right business structure (such as a limited liability corporation, partnership, sole proprietorship, or corporation — more on this in the "These entities mean business" section, later in this chapter).

The very first thing Melyssa did when she started her business was hire a lawyer, who helped her choose the proper business structure that would allow for growth. Melyssa wanted to make sure that everything she did was by the book. Doing this helped Melyssa avoid potential business pitfalls, and she recommends that all personal trainers do the same.

Don't know where to start your search for a lawyer? Try these tips:

- ✔ **Contact the American Bar Association.** The ABA Web site has a Lawyer Locator page, where you can search by location and area of expertise. Do a search for business or incorporation attorneys. You can reach the ABA at 321 North Clark Street, Chicago, IL 60610; phone: 800-285-2221 or 312-988-5522; Web site: `www.abanet.org`.

- ✔ **If you already have a banker, accountant, or insurance agent — professionals that we recommend hiring — ask them for recommendations.**

- ✔ **Go to Find Law (`www.findlaw.com/business.html`), which has an attorney listing plus a helpful Small Business Center.**

- ✔ **Be old-fashioned: Check ye olde Yellow Pages.** In Melyssa's experience, the professionals with the big ads are serious about putting themselves out there and about what they're doing.

- ✔ **Consult the Martindale-Hubbell Law Directory (`www.lawyers.com`), which specializes in finding lawyers for small businesses.**

- ✔ **Ask your clients for suggestions.** Who knows? One of them may actually be a lawyer who would be willing to trade advice for training, although his billing hour probably equals a handful of yours!

When in doubt, ask local salons for recommendations. Salons are similar to personal training businesses in that they're often small and they provide regular service to their clients.

Getting accounted for

They're often called bean counters — though you shouldn't call them this to their faces if you want them to help you — but accountants do a lot more than count legumes. In fact, they can make the difference between a personal trainer who thrives and one who gets tossed into the pokey for tax fraud. An accountant can

- ✔ **Work with your lawyer to help you decide what type of business structure to have.**

- ✔ **Design and set up your accounting system so that year-end financial reporting will be easier.**

- ✔ **Keep Uncle Sam off your back by making sure you pay the correct types of taxes in the right amounts.**

✔ **Make sure that you send out W2 and 1099 forms to the right people at the right times.** If you hire independent contractors, the accountant will make sure that they actually fit the criteria for independent contractors (who get 1099s) and are not considered employees (who get W2s) by the government.

✔ **Let you know whether that smoothie or pair of wind shorts is a legitimate business expense.**

✔ **Show you how to separate your personal and business expenses, from home offices to work mileage to postage.**

✔ **Advise you through the process if, God forbid, the IRS ever audits you.**

✔ **Help you decide whether you're better off leasing or buying that exercise equipment or office machine.**

✔ **Compile your financial records for the past period.**

✔ **Advise you regarding tax shelters or direct you to professionals who specialize in investing and protecting your hard-earned income.**

✔ **Help you understand your financial statements.**

Even if you have an accountant making sure your finances and taxes are on the up-and-up, you should be able to understand your business's finances so that you'll always know how your business is doing. Check out *Accounting For Dummies,* 2nd Edition, by John A. Tracy, and the latest edition of *Taxes For Dummies* by Eric Tyson and David J. Silverman (both published by Wiley) for more help.

Start your search for an accountant by following these tips:

✔ **Check with the National Association of Small Business Accountants (NASBA).** The NASBA Web site lets you search for an accountant in your area. You can contact the NASBA at 205 West Randolph Street, Chicago, IL 60606; phone: 866-296-0001; e-mail: nasbaccts@northshore.net; Web site: www.smallbizaccountants.com.

✔ **Let your fingers do the walking through the Yellow Pages.**

✔ **Ask your friends, family, and clients who their accountants are.**

✔ **Ask local small businesses, such as salons, for their recommendations.**

Insuring yourself

No matter how careful, thoughtful, and just plain wonderful you are, a claim of personal injury, bodily injury, or sexual harassment can wipe out your bank account — even if it's not true. That's why you need to find an insurance agent. An insurance agent can help you determine how much coverage you need if you set up your own place of business. (If you work for a gym, the owners will tell you how much coverage you need, but an independent agent can still help find the right insurance for you.)

Here are the different types of insurance you may need:

✔ **Liability insurance:** Most personal trainers can purchase this insurance, which is relatively inexpensive, through their certification body. Liability insurance covers you if your client gets injured while you're training her.

✔ **Professional liability insurance:** Although liability insurance covers you for most claims made against you, *professional* liability insurance is more specific. It covers you if you specifically perform against general accepted standards of practice — such as asking the client to juggle three dumbbells in between each rep.

✔ **Personal liability insurance:** This insurance covers you if you defame or humiliate a client. It protects you if a client says something like, "Johnny told everyone I weigh 500 pounds!"

It goes without saying, of course, that just because you're insured doesn't mean you have a free pass to do things that are irresponsible (just like car insurance doesn't mean you smash your car into everyone in sight). Ideally, you'll never even file an insurance claim — but you still need the insurance in case an accident happens.

Most small-business owners seek out independent agents in their area; agents are independent businesspeople who deal with different types of insurance from different companies. Your insurance agent will be able to find the best liability insurance as well as health insurance and other policies.

Personal trainers can also find fitness-instructor insurance through credentialing organizations and insurance agencies that specialize in the fitness industry.

Check out these resources for finding an independent insurance agent:

✔ **Consult the Independent Insurance Agents & Brokers of America (IIABA).** The IIABA Web site lets you search for agents by name, location, or area code. Contact the IIABA at 127 South Peyton Street, Alexandria, VA 22314; phone: 800-221-7917; e-mail: info@iiaba.org; Web site: www.iiaba.org.

✔ **Check your local Yellow Pages.**

✔ **Ask other local businesses whom they use.**

The following organizations offer insurance policies specifically for personal trainers (some of the organizations require you to be certified through them in order to get insurance through them):

- ✔ **United States Personal Trainers Organization:** www.uspto.npginc.com/pl

- ✔ **TrainerInsurance.com:** www.trainerinsurance.com

- ✔ **IDEA Health & Fitness Association:** www.ideafit.com/membership/pro_insurance.htm

- ✔ **American Fitness Professionals & Associates:** http://afpa.npginc.com/pl

- ✔ **National Endurance & Sports Trainers Association:** www.nesta certified.com/insurance.html

- ✔ **Fitness and Wellness Insurance Agency:** www.fitnwel.com/personal_trainers.html

- ✔ **International Sports Sciences Association:** http://issa.npginc.com/pl

Banking on it

Most small businesses (like you!) have banks, but no bankers. But a banker — the person who handles your account at the bank — can help you get credit, avoid fees, and enhance your business opportunities through the banker's extensive personal contacts.

Personal trainers rarely bother with bankers at all — and when they do, they don't understand how to cultivate an alliance with them. Follow these tips to build a good relationship with your banker — after all, good rapport is like money in the bank!

- ✔ **Invite your banker to tour your facilities.** Just don't do this right before asking for a loan, because you don't want to look like you're pleading for sympathy or special favors.

- ✔ **Let your banker know when something important occurs — for example, when you've landed new clients, reached a profit goal, or faced a new competitor.**

- ✔ **Don't ask for favors at the beginning of your relationship.** First create goodwill by giving the bank your business and even trying to bring in other accounts.

- ✔ **If something bad happens in your business — for example, if you lose several clients — try to determine the cause and develop a plan of action *before* contacting your banker.**

The best way to find a banker who will help keep the money flowing is to ask other personal trainers and small-business owners in your area which banks they use, and then research the banks to figure out which one fits your needs. If you want to bank online, does the bank offer this service? How long does getting a loan approved usually take? How much red tape will you have to go through to, say, replace a missing ATM card? Then interview bankers at the banks of your choice and pick the one with whom you feel the most comfortable.

Separating the good from the bad

Have you ever walked into a hair salon without checking it out first — because you just *had* to do something about your hair right then and there — and walked out with a do that made you look like a mulleted refugee from the '70s?

If you hire a lawyer, an accountant, or any other professional without checking her out first, you can end up with a lot worse than a bad-hair day. We're talking about taxes and lawsuits here.

Ask to meet with the professional for a consultation (many will do this free of charge) and make sure she:

- ✔ **Has experience working with small businesses like yours.**

- ✔ **Asks more questions than Barbara Walters.** The person should interview *you* in addition to being interviewed *by* you. She may ask you where you want to be in five years, what your goals are, how you expect to reach those goals, what your major concerns are, and what you expect from a lawyer/accountant/banker/insurance agent. Be prepared to answer these questions so your interview is productive.

- ✔ **Has time for you.** A lawyer or accountant who constantly interrupts your meeting to answer her phone and deal with crises probably won't have the time to give you the attention you need.

- ✔ **Explains her fee structure so that you understand it.**

- ✔ **Defines industry terms you need to know, such as *LLC* and *1099*, in plain English.**

Going it alone: Should you or shouldn't you?

Maybe you took a tax-preparation class, or maybe you were a lawyer before you realized that you'd rather pump iron than push papers. Can you save money by handling the accounting or legal tasks yourself?

It depends. Every hour you're sweating over tax filings or contracts is an hour that you're not making money or building your business. Sure, you may save money by filing that form yourself, but you're simultaneously *losing* money because you could have been training a client in that hour. The question is: How much will you save by doing these tasks yourself, and how much will you lose by not being able to spend the time training clients?

When you're training a client, you're building goodwill and giving the client something to tell all his friends about (and referrals are the lifeblood of the personal training business — see Chapter 8 for more information on referrals). While you're hassling over a form, you're building nothing but a headache. You can also be spending that time working on meeting your business goals by networking, marketing, and dreaming up new ways to bring on more clients.

If you're strapped for cash when you first start out, doing as much as you can yourself may make sense. But as soon as you're able, we suggest hiring professionals to do their thing so that you have time to do *your* thing — that is, train clients and build your business.

Someone to look up to: Mentors

A mentor is someone who will tell you, "Jane, I prefer this logo to that one" or, "Bob, I think you need to drop that client to save your sanity." A *mentor* is someone you trust, who has an interest in you and your business. A mentor can be:

- A friend
- A professional, such as a doctor
- Your spouse, son or daughter, parent, or sibling
- The owner of a local business
- Another personal trainer

You don't need to create a formal mentor-mentee relationship; in other words, no one needs to sign on the dotted line. But as you develop your network, you'll find people whose opinions you trust, and you'll naturally gravitate toward these people when you have a question or a problem.

Keep these people's contact information in your Rolodex or Palm Pilot, and try to touch base with them often.

Networking with your peers

Your peers are the people who are doing what you're doing: personal training. "Peers? You mean competitors," you gripe. "Why should I network with them?"

Being active in the fitness community and networking with other trainers will keep you up to date on industry happenings, help you generate new ideas for running your business, and give you sympathetic ears to bend when your spouse is sick of hearing about that client from hell. In addition, personal trainers often refer potential clients to other trainers when they have too many clients to handle or when a client is looking for specialized services they don't normally provide.

Networking with your peers can give you more than a convenient sounding board — it can also boost your business. Melyssa bought a personal training business from a peer who decided to relocate. The trainer found Melyssa through a friend of a friend and offered to let her buy his business.

To get in on the networking loop, you can:

- ✔ **Attend industry conventions.**

- ✔ **Talk to other trainers in your area.** You can find them in the Yellow Pages, on the Internet (use a search engine, such as Google), and through some of the credentialing organizations we list in Chapter 2.

- ✔ **Participate in online discussion groups for personal trainers.**

Forming your advisory board

First we tell you to hire professionals, and now we're telling you to form an advisory board. Clearly, we have personal trainers mistaken with Microsoft or IBM. But wait! An advisory board isn't just for multinational conglomerates bent on global domination, and it doesn't have to consist of dozens of pinstripe-suited old men sitting around a mahogany table complaining about women who wear pants.

An *advisory board* is simply a group of people you go to for advice on running your business, and it can be as formal or as informal as you like. With their expertise, these people can help you get funding, make smart business decisions, and avoid costly mistakes.

Melyssa's advisory board helped her obtain financing to expand her business. One of them personally loaned Melyssa money. When she needed more funding, that same member turned her over to his banker and helped her get approved for a loan when she didn't have any credit. Among many other decisions, Melyssa's advisory board also helped her decide to write her own business-management software rather than buy a generic system off the shelf.

An advisory board can consist of:

- ✔ Your lawyer
- ✔ Your accountant
- ✔ Your mentors
- ✔ Professionals in related fields (such as physical therapists or orthopedic surgeons)
- ✔ Public relations (PR) people
- ✔ Other small-business owners

To form your advisory board, simply ask these people if they'd like to serve on your board. Be clear as to what this means — do you expect to contact them only when you have a problem or a question, or do you expect more hands-on advising?

You're already paying your accountant and lawyer; if you feel bad asking other people to advise you for free, you can offer them personal training sessions in exchange for their counsel. In addition, if they agree to meet you in person, you can treat them to a cup of coffee or a nice restaurant meal — the calories from which you can help them burn off later!

If you feel the need and you can corral several busy people at once, you can gather your advisory board together every once in a while to take the pulse of your personal training business. To hold a successful meeting of your advisory board, follow these tips:

- ✔ **Create an agenda, outlining the major points you want to cover.** Make sure your advisory board has copies of your agenda before the meeting.
- ✔ **At the beginning of the meeting, give an overview of the points you want to cover, then go over them one at a time.**
- ✔ **Allot a certain amount of time for each issue.** If the issue isn't solved in that amount of time, come back to it later.
- ✔ **Have someone take notes, or use a tape recorder to record the session.** You want to be able to refer to the comments that are made, because you can't possibly remember everything. (And you want to be free to discuss and ask questions — not worried about whether you'll be able to recall everything that's said.)

Structuring Your Business

Y'know those letters businesses have after their names, like *Inc.* or *LLC?* They aren't there just because they sound cool. They indicate the legal structure of the business. The legal structure has an impact on how much you pay in taxes, the amount of paperwork you have to do, the personal liability you face, and your ability to raise money for your business.

These entities mean business

Liability, taxation, and record-keeping are what you need to keep in mind when choosing your type of business entity. The following sections offer a brief look at the differences between the most common forms of business entities.

A lawyer can help you decide on and set up your business structure.

Sole proprietorship

A *sole proprietorship* is the most common form of business organization. In this type of business, you're the proprietor and you have complete managerial control of the business. The drawback to sole proprietorship, however, is that you're personally liable for all financial obligations of the business. If someone sues your business, they can come after you personally to ante up the dough from your own personal bank account.

Partnership

A *partnership* is a business relationship between two or more people who share the profits and losses of the business. The partners report any losses or profits on their individual income-tax returns. The benefit of this business structure is that it's easy to set up and operate. Unfortunately, as in a sole proprietorship, the partners remain personally liable for all financial obligations of the business.

Corporation

A *corporation* is taxed (just like an individual is) and can be held legally liable for its actions. The corporation can make a profit or take on a loss. The key difference between a corporation and a sole proprietorship is that, if someone sues your business, your personal assets remain safe at home underneath the mattress. In other words, your personal finances are separate from your business finances. The drawback is that running a corporation requires extensive record-keeping.

Limited liability corporation

Want to have it both ways? The *limited liability corporation* (LLC) is the one to pick. It's taxed like a partnership but has limited liability like corporations (meaning your personal finances are separate from your business finances).

Getting Registered and IDed (Even if You're Over 21)

When you start a business, you need to get the proper licenses, permits, and ID numbers so that all those government officials can look busy when the boss walks by.

The permits, licenses, and IDs required of you depend on where you live, but we offer some general guidelines in the following sections.

We're giving you only a sampling of the licenses, permits, and ID numbers you may need to do business in your city or state. A lawyer will be able to help you navigate the maze of requirements in your particular location.

Employer Identification Number

The Employer Identification Number (EIN), also known as a federal tax identi-fication number, is used to identify a business entity. You'll use the EIN in place of your Social Security number on tax forms. You can apply for an EIN on the IRS Web site (www.irs.gov), or you can download Form SS-4 from the Web site to apply by mail or phone.

Business license

No matter where you decide to set up shop, you'll likely need a business license to operate legally. If your business is located within an incorporated city's limits, you should get a license from the city; if you're outside the city limits, you'll probably get your license from the county.

For more information, contact the county or city office in your area. The Small Business Administration (SBA) Web site offers a list of links to individual states' business-license forms; go to www.sba.gov/hotlist/license.html for more information.

Certificate of occupancy

If you plan to occupy a new or used building with your new business, you may have to apply for a Certificate of Occupancy from a city or county zoning department. For more information, contact the county or city office in your area.

You can also try going to your state's Web site (find a list of state sites at `www.sba.gov/world/states.html`). Locate their search feature, and type in **certificate of occupancy** or **county information**.

Fictitious business name

Businesses that use a name other than the owner's must register the fictitious name with the county. This rule doesn't apply to corporations doing business under their corporate name or to those practicing any profession under a partnership name. For more information, contact your state or local government (see the SBA's list at `www.sba.gov/world/states.html`).

A Rose Is More than a Rose: Naming Your Business

Can you imagine people referring their friends to "that personal trainer, um, what's his name, the guy down the street"? Probably not. That's why you need a catchy, memorable name for your business.

Your business name should convey your expertise, value, and uniqueness. You want something that will tell potential clients that you're a personal trainer, and a darn good one (so "Fat Fanny's Personal Training" is out). Don't stress — in the following sections, we show you how it's done.

Playing the name game

The first step to finding a business name that will have clients beating down your doors is to decide what you want your name to communicate. In Chapter 2, we help you decide what your client population will be, how you'll position yourself (an affordable alternative? trainer to the stars?), and whether you'll concentrate on individuals or group classes. Your name needs to convey this information in as few words as possible while avoiding potential misunderstanding by prospective clients. (For example, if you chose the name "We Pump You Up," people may not know if you're a personal training company, a balloon manufacturer, or a tire retailer.)

Many experts say that your business name should be made up of real words or combinations of words rather than made-up monikers. Sure, Xerox and Skechers work for those companies, but those companies also have million-dollar marketing budgets to help their names stick in consumers' minds. If your marketing budget consists of spare change and pocket lint, you're better off going for actual words that people will recognize.

Avoid narrowly constrained names that limit you to certain locations or services. For example, say you name your business "San Antonio Personal Training." What if you move to Walla Walla, Washington? And if you choose the name "Perfect Bodies for Pregnant Women," you won't be able to expand into another client population.

Ask yourself the following questions to decide on a moniker for your business:

- ✔ What is my target market? (See Chapter 8 for more information.)
- ✔ What problems do I solve for my target market? Do I help them lose weight, get healthy, increase their confidence?
- ✔ What words or phrases appeal to my target market? Perhaps words like *health, fit,* or *strong?*
- ✔ What are the best benefits my business brings to customers?
- ✔ What kind of name would differentiate me, in a positive way, from my competitors?

When you have a few contenders, run them by friends, family, and potential clients to get their reactions. Be sure to say the names aloud. Can you imagine answering the phone with this business name? If it doesn't roll off the tongue, 86 it.

If you're having trouble deciding on a name, you may want to hire a professional naming company. These companies can be pricey, but they do help you come up with a name that has mucho impact. They can also help you envision how the name will look on signs, stationery, and so on, as well as helping you with trademarking and registering your name. You can find a listing of naming companies on Yahoo! at `http://dir.yahoo.com/business_and_economy/business_to_business/marketing_and_advertising/naming/`.

Marking your territory: The trademark

Any word or image (or combination of words and images) used to distinguish your business or services from other businesses or services can be a trademark. You don't have to officially trademark the name, but doing so ensures that the guy down the street can't start using it next week.

Making sure your name isn't already taken

Earlier in this chapter, we advocate hiring a lawyer to handle all your legal matters. But in the case of searching out names, you can easily do this yourself.

Search the trademark filings on the U.S. Patent and Trademark Office (USPTO) Web site (www.uspto.gov) to ensure your name isn't already trademarked. Their Trademark Electronic Search System (TESS) contains more than 3 million pending, registered, and dead federal trademarks. They also have other helpful resources, such as instructions on how to submit your trademarks and information about how much it will cost to send in an application.

In addition, check the Internet by using several search engines (such as Google, Yahoo!, or All the Web) to make sure no one else has already staked a claim on your preferred name.

Filing a trademark application

You can file your application directly over the Internet with the Trademark Electronic Application System (TEAS) available at www.uspto.gov/teas/index.html.

If you prefer to send in your application the old-fashioned way, you can mail or hand-deliver a paper application to the USPTO. To request a printed form, call the USPTO's automated telephone line at 800-786-9199 (toll-free) or 703-308-9000. Send your application to Commissioner for Trademarks, 2900 Crystal Drive, Arlington, VA 22202-3514.

You don't have to have a lawyer submit your application, but if you do it yourself, you're responsible for complying with all requirements of the trademark statute and rules. If you use a lawyer, the USPTO will correspond only with the lawyer, not with you directly.

As they say, nothing in life is free, and that includes trademark applications. As of this writing, submitting an application costs $335. For up-to-date fee information, call 800-786-9199.

Image Is Everything: Creating Your Look

When you see a pair of shoes with a swoosh on the side, you know they're Nikes without reading the label. That's the power of a logo — a graphical depiction of your company. Your logo will help people recognize and remember your business. A logo gives you an image of substance and stability. It also shows you're serious about what you do.

But choosing a logo design involves more than pasting some clip art onto your letterhead. Your design needs to convey important information about your business. Your potential clients should look at your logo and know what you do. For example, an accountant may want a conservative design, but a personal trainer needs a more vibrant logo to project vitality and strength, with sweeping shapes and bright colors.

For Melyssa's first personal training business, she wanted a logo that projected health and change. For the color of the type, she chose purple, which is vibrant yet calming, and for the design part of the logo she chose a gold symbol that incorporated an arc and a triangle. The arc depicted action, while a triangle is the chemical symbol for change. (See, you knew those chemistry classes you were forced to take in high school would come in handy.)

Creating a logo that works

Here are the main criteria of a good logo:

- **Readability:** A busy design may make it hard for people to understand your logo or read the name of your business.

- **Memorability:** You want your logo to create interest, not yawns. When potential clients see your logo, they should think of your business.

- **Uniqueness:** If your logo looks like the logo of the personal trainer down the street, it won't distinguish your services from your competitors'.

- **Appropriateness to your business:** Weights, healthy bodies, training shoes? Good. Flowers, puppies, cookies? Bad.

- **Professionalism and stability:** You want to look like a professional business, and not some fly-by-night with a clip-art logo, so cutesy cartoons are out.

- **The ability to convey the message in any size and any medium:** You should test your logo to make sure it looks good on faxes, letterhead, photocopies, and the Internet.

- **A design that's not too trendy:** A trendy logo will quickly go out of date and make you and your business look out-of-date as well.

The psychology of color

To help you choose a color for your logo, letter-head, uniforms, and office or gym, check out this list of popular colors and the emotions they convey:

- **Red** symbolizes fire, heat, passion, excite-ment, power, and aggression. It can elevate blood pressure and respiratory rate. Red is an attention-grabber that makes people look.

- **Blue** is one of the most popular colors. It's peaceful and tranquil, and it relaxes the nervous system. On the other hand, it represents solitude and depression (that's why, when you're down in the dumps, you may say that you're "feeling blue").

- **Green** is a neutral, relaxing color. It can communicate the ideas of life, renewal, hope,

vigor, nature — or money. Green is the easiest color on the eye.

- **Black** is the color of authority and power — just think of a high-level exec wearing a black suit. Watch out, though, because in large doses it can represent somberness and mourning.

- **Yellow** denotes brightness, playfulness, creativity, and warmth. Yellow is the most visible of all the colors — which is why traffic signs are this color.

- **Purple,** the color of royalty, conveys luxury, wealth, and sophistication as well as passion and romance.

- **Brown,** the color of earth and wood, is solid, reliable, neutral, and comfortable. It also symbolizes credibility, strength, and maturity.

You don't have to answer *all* the questions about your business in your logo design.

Unless you have graphic-design experience, a logo must be done professionally if you want it to look, well, professional. But don't fret — try contacting art and design schools for students who would be willing to design a logo on the cheap. You can also do rough concept drawings yourself and hire a designer to do the finished product, or barter your services for designing (see Chapter 8).

Giving your logo some color

In addition to the graphic design of the logo — the image you choose — you'll need to decide on colors. Even though your logo should look good in black and white (in case you need to fax or photocopy your letterhead, for example), color will be an important part of your overall logo design. Color conveys emotions, so the colors you choose for your logo, your office or gym (if you have one), and your uniform (especially if you employ other trainers) are important aspects of your image. Check out the nearby sidebar, "The psychology of color," to get a feel for what different colors communicate.

Okay, so you decide on a three-color logo incorporating a duck-billed platypus lifting weights. You go all out and spend several thousand dollars getting some big-shot designer to draw it up for you. And the first time you fax a client or copy your logo on a black-and-white copier, that beautiful, expensive logo ends up looking like a big blob.

That's why you need to make extra sure that the logo you go with works in black and white, as well as in all different sizes. The solution: Keep it simple. The most common mistake made by anyone designing a logo is creating a symbol that is much too complicated and difficult to read — especially in smaller sizes.

You can trademark your logo if you like; this will ensure that other businesses can't snatch your awesome design. You trademark your logo in the same way that you trademark your business name (see the "Filing a trademark application" section, earlier in this chapter).

Chapter 7

Developing Sound Business Practices

In This Chapter

▶ Using legal forms

▶ Determining how to conduct your business

▶ Creating policies for working with your clients

▶ Maintaining records for your business

▶ Paying taxes

*Y*ou probably want to become a personal trainer because you love physical action and you'd rather do push-ups than push papers. But alas, every personal trainer must push a little paper in his time, from legal forms to activity logs.

In this chapter, we tell you how to keep your business organized and running smoothly. Here, you discover everything you need to know about setting policies, maintaining documentation, tracking your cash, and more.

Crossing Your T's and Dotting Your I's: Legal Forms for Your Business

Personal training is an injury-prone profession, and we're a litigious society. Add these together and what do you get? Clients who sue if they get a hangnail when they're using the elliptical trainers. Okay, maybe that's a bit of an exaggeration. But when people get hurt, they tend to sue, so you need to do everything you can to make sure you don't wind up on *The People's Court*.

Three kinds of forms will help you keep yourself out of hot (and by hot, we mean legal) water — accident-report forms, waiver forms, and disclaimer and informed-consent forms.

Accident-report form

The accident-report form is the one you'll need to fill out if a client gets injured while you're working with her.

The accident report form should include the following information:

- **Identification information:** Record the date and time, the name of the person in charge, the activity that was going on, the names and contact information for all witnesses, and the name of your insurance company. (See Chapter 6 for more information on getting liability insurance — a must.)

- **Location of accident:** Take note of the area where the injury took place plus the location of any witnesses and other participants.

- **Action of the injured party:** Describe in detail what was going on and specifically what action caused the injury.

- **Sequence of events:** Describe when, in the course of the workout, the injury happened (for example, during the warm-up).

- **Preventive measures that could have been taken by the injured party:** Detail what the client could have done to prevent the injury.

- **Procedures followed in giving aid:** Write down what first-aid measures were taken and by whom, including who called for help and when the help arrived.

- **Disposition or follow-up:** Follow up with the doctor or hospital and record how long the medical professional said the client must refrain from exercise after the injury.

- **Person completing the accident report:** Record the name of the person completing the report, along with the person's position and whether that person witnessed the accident.

Attorney (n): Your new best friend

In Chapter 6, we stress the importance of having a good attorney on your professional team. An attorney can help you create forms that reduce your liability and can represent you if you get sued. If you haven't found an attorney yet, follow the advice in Chapter 6 on how to find the one who's right for your business.

You should keep completed accident forms for seven years, although this number varies by state. Contact your lawyer for advice.

Waiver form

Before you go skydiving or take a dance class (or do just about anything these days), you have to sign a form that says you promise not to sue if you plummet to your death while skydiving or lose an arm while tap-dancing. That's a *waiver form* (shown in Figure 7-1), and you need one for your personal training business. Although not foolproof, a waiver form can go a long way toward keeping you out of court.

Waiver and Release of Liability

I, _____, intending to be legally bound, and recognizing the danger involved in physical exercise, do agree as follows:

In consideration for the services rendered by _____ in the establishment of a personal physical-fitness program for my benefit, I agree to waive any rights, claims, or damages for injuries that may occur as a result of my participation in said fitness/nutrition program.

I agree to disclose any physical limitations, disabilities, ailments, or impairments that may affect my ability to participate in said fitness program.

I understand that _____ is a personal-training company and not a medical doctor, and that they will, in fact, be relying on my representations and disclosures regarding my health and physical condition.

Figure 7-1: I also do not hold the aforementioned institutions liable for any personal
The waiver injuries, bodily injuries, or property damage while going to and from the
form aforementioned property.
protects you
if a client is
injured.

Signed: _____

Date: _____

Consult your attorney for help developing a waiver you can have clients sign.

Disclaimer and informed-consent form

The disclaimer and informed-consent form (see Figure 7-2) states that the client understands that there is a risk involved to personal training, and that he's disclosed all the pertinent medical, physiological, and lifestyle information that you need to create a program for him. It also gives you permission to work with the client based on the information the client has given.

Informed Consent

I, the undersigned, hereby expressly and affirmatively state that I wish to participate in the personal training program of _____.

I realize that my participation in these activities involves potential risk of injury, including but not limited to bodily injury, heart attack, stroke, or even death. I also recognize there are other risks associated with exercise and personal training and that it is not possible to list every one.

I know and understand the risks of exercise. Understanding that injuries are a possibility, I hereby assume all risks of injury that could occur by reason of my participation in this personal-fitness program.

Figure 7-2:
The dis-
claimer and
informed-
consent
form
ensures that
the client
gives you
correct
information.

Signed: _____

Date:_____

Witnessed: _____

If you have the client write out any past injuries and sign the disclaimer and informed consent form, you're somewhat protected if the client tries to sue you for causing an injury she already had. Not only that, but having this information allows you to design a program around the client's previous injuries and illnesses.

Going with the Flow: Determining in What Order to Conduct Your Business

When a prospective client comes to you and eventually (you hope) becomes a paying client, things happen in a certain order. A stranger doesn't just walk in off the street and hop on the treadmill. And a client you've seen for five years doesn't walk in one day and expect you to do an initial assessment. This order in which things happen is referred to as *client flow* — it's literally just the way your clients *flow,* or progress, through your business operations. Step 1, for example, may be when a prospective client expresses interest and you fill out a client lead sheet. Step 2 may be an initial consultation, and so on through the life cycle of a client.

In order for everything to run smoothly and efficiently, you need to plan what to do and when to do it. For example, what if someone expresses interest but then doesn't end up buying a package? Will you call in two weeks or send a card in a month — or both? When will you do a fitness reevaluation? When will you make stay-in-touch calls to former clients?

Much of this information comes from your business plan (see Chapter 5), which tells you who your client population is, how you plan to target them, and what you'll do when you have them.

Charts: They're not just for computer geeks

You may want to create a client flow chart to keep track of your client flow. Melyssa uses a chart that's six pages long and documents everything from administrative actions and client care to the trainers' duties when it comes to the client.

Your chart may have data like what you see in Table 7-1. *Remember:* This table is just to give you an idea of what kind of information a chart may contain — it doesn't contain all the steps or possible scenarios.

Table 7-1	What You May Include on a Client Flow Chart		
Situation	*Administrative*	*Client Care*	*Trainer*
Prospect buys a package and pays up front.	1. Take the client's picture. 2. Schedule a fitness assessment. 3. Collect the payment.	1. Assign the client a client ID. 2. Set up a service contract. 3. Have the client sign the waiver, cancellation policy, and service contract. 4. Give the client a tour of your facility. 5. Give the client a copy of the waiver, contract, and What to Expect sheet.	N/A
The client shows up for her initial fitness assessment.	1. Greets the client and alerts the trainer assigned to her that the client is here. 2. After the assessment, schedules the next session. 3. Rings up sales.	N/A	1. Has the fitness assessment, blood-pressure cuff, heart-rate monitor, and towel ready. 2. Greets the client. 3. Performs the assessment. 4. Enters a follow-up call two days out in planner.
Two days after the first session.	N/A	N/A	1. Calls to follow up with the client. Asks the client how she is feeling; whether the client is experiencing any unusual muscle soreness; asks whether the client has any chest pain, palpitations, or nausea; and asks if the client has any questions. 2. Confirms the next appointment. 3. Makes notes in planner.

Notice how detailed the chart is. This extra detail is there to ensure that every client gets the same exact treatment and that you (or your employees) don't skip any steps.

Be sure that you don't skip steps in your order of operations. If you skip the fitness assessment because the client is eager to begin, and then the client gets injured, you're in big trouble. Or if you send a thank-you note or special offer to one client and not another — and that second client finds out — you can create bad feelings.

Every step you take, every move you make . . .: Keeping track of everything you and your client do

Keeping notes on everything you do with a client — from the beginning of the client flow to the end — can keep you out of court. For example, if a client claims you stiffed him on sessions, you can whip out your client file that shows he had all the sessions he was entitled to. Or if a client is unhappy with your services, he may cancel the credit-card charge, and then you'll need to send the credit-card company a record of everything you've done with the client. If you have no documentation, the credit-card company may take the money from you.

Make a record of every time you have contact with a client. For example, you may write something like, "September 2, 2004: Talked with Eric about his interest in our services," "September 16, 2004: Made appointment for initial consultation," and "September 17, 2004: Followed up by phone. Eric will be calling within a week to sign up for a package."

You don't have to write the Great American Novel (besides, this isn't fiction!). You just have to write enough so that you know what you and your client have done and when.

Putting Policies in Place

Don't you hate it when you ask for a little flexibility somewhere — for example, to get onion rings rather than fries with the Super Gulp Meal at your local fast-food joint — and you're told, "We can't do that — it's against the policy"? Well, the time is ripe for revenge — now you get to set policies of your own.

Of course, the purpose of policies isn't to wield power over clients or to make them jump through hoops. It's to make sure that everyone is treated the same way and that you have a set way of dealing with every process in your business, from payments to refunds.

Your policies are in place for a reason, but you're also in the business of serving your customers. You don't want to become a dictator, shouting, "It's against our policies!" every chance you get. Instead, you want to try your best to adopt policies that make sense, and then explain them to your clients so that they understand that you aren't just setting rules for the sake of setting rules.

Setting a payment policy

Asking for money makes many people feel uncomfortable. People who go into personal training generally want to help people. When they ask for money, they feel greedy, miserly, like Ebenezer Scrooge on Christmas Eve. But money is, if not the main point of being in business, a big part of it. Without money, you wouldn't be able to run your business and you wouldn't be able to help your clients.

You have two basic options when it comes to accepting payment from your client:

- ✔ You can charge up front.
- ✔ You can charge for each session on an individual basis.

Although getting some or all your money from a client up front is a good idea, some states prevent you from collecting over a certain dollar amount without being *bonded.* (Being bonded means you pay an insurance company or bonding agent an annual fee to cover costs if you don't finish the job — bonding is a kind of insurance.)

In the 1980s, some gyms collected for lifetime memberships and then folded, leaving their lifetime members in the lurch. The government created this law to protect consumers from such snafus. Personal training falls under the recreation/gym category, which means that this law applies to you. Contact your lawyer to find out how the law affects your business (read more about finding and hiring a lawyer in Chapter 6).

Charging for a month's worth of sessions at a time has many benefits. Clients don't feel trapped as they may with a long-term package, and you get a steady monthly income. Because you're charging a smaller amount than you would for a large package, clients are more likely to pay cash — meaning you don't get dinged a transaction fee by the credit-card company. Finally, because you're collecting less money at a time, you may not need to be bonded.

Another option is to collect for one session at a time. Of course, if you do this, you have no guarantee that the client will sign up for another session.

If you're allowed to charge for sessions up front and choose to do so, budgeting your money is especially important. Some months you'll get $50,000 because many clients are signing up for packages and paying up front, and other months you'll take in nothing because the clients are still working on the sessions they already paid for. In the business world, this is called *feast or famine.* Make sure you save enough from your feast to get through the famine!

Try collecting a small amount of money by check up front and then collecting for services every six sessions. That way you get some money right away but still keep the cash flowing throughout the client's package. Also, this method eliminates the hassle of refunding a whole truckload of money if the client buys and pays for a huge package up front and then decides to cancel after a few sessions.

See Chapter 5 for information on how to set your fees.

Show me the money: Collecting fees

Now that you know how you plan to charge your clients, you have to have a way to actually collect the money. Unfortunately, getting paid in rolls of pennies won't cut it for your business. You can use any one or more of the following methods.

Checks

Checks are probably the easiest and most popular way to accept payments. You get the money fairly quickly, and you're not charged a fee as you are with credit cards and electronic funds transfers (more on these in the sections that follow). You also don't need to have a special setup to accept checks — just take them and deposit them in your business account.

Sometimes, whether on purpose or by accident, people bounce checks. When this happens, as unfair as it seems, your bank will charge *you* a small fee. Setting up a policy of charging clients to cover this fee if they bounce a check is perfectly within your rights. Just be sure that the client gets a copy of your check-bouncing policy in writing — do this the moment he signs on with you, *before* he bounces a check.

Credit cards

Many people prefer the convenience of credit cards. Although using credit cards is easy for your clients, it can be complicated for you.

Before you can accept credit-card payments, you must submit an application to a financial institution, which can cost between $75 and $200. Providing credit-processing services to merchants is risky for financial institutions. Credit-card users can return items or dispute charges, which means the bank loses money.

And if the merchant goes out of business, the financial institution is responsible for the charged amounts. That's why, before approving your application, the financial institution asks such questions as:

- ✔ Will you electronically authorize all credit cards?
- ✔ How long have you been in business?
- ✔ What prior experience do you have in managing a business?
- ✔ What type of refund or return policy does your business have?
- ✔ What is your anticipated *credit-card volume* (that is, how many credit-card payments do you expect to accept each month)?

If you're approved, you'll need to buy, rent, or lease credit-card processing equipment from the financial institution, which can range from $900 to $2,000 in total.

Accepting credit cards and debit cards isn't free. The financial institution will charge you approximately 20¢ to 35¢ per credit-card transaction and 40¢ to 60¢ per debit-card transaction. You may also be charged for your monthly statement and for chargeback fees.

EFT

Electronic funds transfer (EFT) lets you debit session fees directly from your clients' bank accounts. Your client will need to fill out a form that includes her bank name and address, routing number, bank account number, and signature to approve funds transfers. The bank will likely charge you a small processing fee for each transfer (much like with a credit card), as well as setup and monthly fees. Contact your bank for more information on how to set up EFT capabilities for your business.

Many people have a problem with letting businesses have access to their bank accounts. Talk with your mentor (see Chapter 6 for more about mentors) and other trainers to get their opinions on and experiences with using EFT.

Cash

You can always accept cash, but beware the allure — walking down the street with $500 in your pocket and not spending it is tough! Also, having a lot of cash hanging around your place of work is an invitation to thieves.

Billing your clients

Now that you know how you'll accept payment from your clients, you have to decide how you'll bill them.

House accounts

Y'know how you go to a bar, order a drink, and say, "Put it on my tab"? You can also allow clients to put what they owe on a tab, or a *house account.* The clients come in as often as they like for a certain period of time — for example, a month — and then pay the balance at the end.

If you set up a house account for your clients, you may want to:

✔ **Set a spending limit.** For example, you could decide to not allow the client to spend over $500 dollars with you without paying off her account first (if it's before the month's end).

✔ **Have your client sign a running account tab every time she makes a purchase on her account.** That way, she can't come back and say, "I never bought that!"

✔ **Write out your house-account rules and have your client sign the document, indicating she's read them.** Give her a copy and place a copy in her file.

Accounts on file

Some clients will allow you to keep their credit-card number on file and charge them for sessions they use. Each credit-card company will tell you what they need to have to validate the receipt. Generally, you write "signature on file" on the receipt and mail the client a copy of the receipt.

You're responsible for protecting the client's credit-card number from prying eyes.

Invoices

You may want to send your clients invoices that they can pay within a certain period of time, such as two weeks or a month. Make sure your invoices include the following information:

✔ **The name of your business:** If you prefer, you can write the invoice on your letterhead.

✔ **The client's name**

✔ **The date**

✔ **An invoice number:** This will help you keep track of your invoices.

✔ **The services rendered:** What kind of sessions? How many? On what dates?

✔ **The amount due:** You may want to break this down for the client — for example, "Ten sessions @ $50/session = $500."

✔ **The due date:** Expecting payment in two to four weeks is fair.

Determining a cancellation policy

Sometimes clients get sick, or they have work emergencies, or they're too lazy to return to a vertical orientation after lying down on the couch. In other words, sometimes clients call to cancel a session. You need a plan for what will happen when a client misses a session.

When a client cancels on short notice, that session time is gone, and you get paid nothing for it. If the client gives you enough notice, however, you may be able to schedule a last-minute session with another client and recoup your losses. That's why deciding how much heads-up time you need when a client wants to cancel is important. Will you let a client cancel an hour before her session without charging her? Or will you require 6 hours' notice, or 24 hours' notice?

Melyssa gave clients one free cancellation. After that, if they cancelled less than six hours before the session, she charged them the full fee. If a client missed more than 60 percent of his sessions, Melyssa would refund his money for unused sessions and suggest another personal training company that may be more flexible.

Whatever you decide, put your cancellation policy in writing and have the client sign it when she signs up for sessions.

Maintaining Records

If the very thought of paperwork makes your hair stand on end, you're not alone — keeping records and maintaining files is probably not on any personal trainer's top-ten list. But don't worry — in the following sections, we make record-keeping as easy and painless as possible.

Understanding why records rock

You may become a fan of record-keeping when you discover that keeping good records can save you hundreds of dollars. For example, say you forgot to record a $20 business expense, which would have taken you a mere five minutes to record had you remembered it. This oversight raises your business's net income by $20, for which you will now be taxed. As a result, your federal, state, and Social Security taxes go up — even if we're very conservative in our estimate, the taxes may go up by $5. If you had recorded the deduction, you would have saved $5 in taxes in five minutes — which comes out to a whopping $60 per hour!

If that's not enough to convince you, we have more. Accurate, well-maintained records:

✔ Provide a record of your business's financial performance so you always have a handle on the health of your business.

✔ Give you income-tax data, which will make your life easier come April 15.

✔ Give you ammo for when you're applying for a loan or a merchant account.

Keeping the books

Part of maintaining records is keeping the books, which will help you:

✔ Keep track of your income and expenses

✔ Have the data you need on hand to file tax returns

Whenever you're feeling overwhelmed by the daunting details of keeping your books, keep those two simple goals in mind.

You can keep your financial records in any way you want, as long as they work for you — but we'll explain the common methods that will make your life easier.

"I'm no number cruncher!" you cry. "I'm a personal trainer!" Well, have no fear — keeping books consists of just three easy steps:

1. **Keep receipts and records of every payment and expense.**

2. **Summarize these records on a regular basis.**

3. **Use these summaries to create financial reports, which will help you determine the financial health of your business.**

Keeping receipts

Unfortunately, Uncle Sam won't just go by your word when you claim that you spent $3,000 on a piece of equipment — or even $5 buying a smoothie for a potential client. Whenever you make or spend money, you need to have the transaction backed up with receipts or other records that show the amount, the date, and other relevant information.

Legally, you can keep all your receipts under a rock in your yard if you want, but choosing a system that fits your needs makes more sense. If you handle only a few clients, you can get by with a low-key system; if you have lots of sales and expenses, you'll need something stronger.

Make sure you have a place to keep all your records and to handle bookkeeping duties — an inexpensive filing cabinet or file box works well. You also need a desk or table, a comfortable chair, and good lighting for when you need to do some number crunching.

How long do you have to hold onto these pieces of paper? According to the IRS, you need to keep your records as long as they may be needed for the administration of any provision of the Internal Revenue Code. In plain English, most financial advisors recommend keeping all tax-related materials for seven years. After seven years have passed since your first year filing taxes as a business, you can throw a bonfire in the yard and burn your tax records for your first year of business if you want — unless you file a fraudulent return or don't file a return at all, in which case the IRS can come after you at any time.

Summarizing your records

You'll need to keep a summary of your income, expenditures, and anything else you need to track, all entered according to category and date. This wonderful document is what accountants call a *ledger*. This summary will help you determine, at a glance, how your business is doing — how much money you're making versus how much you're paying out.

Using a piece of ledger paper (you can get ledger pads at an office-supply store), transfer the amounts from your receipts and records into the ledger. You can keep one journal for receipts and one for *disbursements* (expenditures). Recording receipts and disbursements in the journals is called *posting*. You can do this as often as you like, but make sure it's often enough that you won't feel overwhelmed with a mountain of receipts to enter. If you have just a few transactions every month, you can post weekly or monthly.

If keeping records on dead trees is too old school for you, try using an accounting software package. A finance software package like Quicken will work well. Check out *Quicken 2004 For Dummies* by Stephen L. Nelson (published by Wiley) for more information on this popular software.

Creating financial reports

Financial reports bring together everything you've recorded in your ledger. Sure, you can see how much cash came in from your ledger, but you can't get the big picture about how your business is doing without measuring your income against total expenses. This is where the financial report comes in. The report will also tell you whether money from clients is coming in quickly enough to allow you to cover your bills.

If you're using software such as Quicken, you can have it generate reports for you with the click of a button. Pie charts, bar graphs — you name it, the chart is there.

Check out *Entrepreneurship For Dummies* by Kathleen Allen (published by Wiley), which has information on creating financial reports. Also take a look at *Financial Statements: A Step-By-Step Guide to Understanding and Creating Financial Reports* by Thomas R. Ittelson (published by Career Press) or *Managing by the Numbers: A Commonsense Guide to Understanding and Using Your Company's Financials: An Essential Resource for Growing Businesses* by Chuck Kremer (published by Perseus Books Group) for more information on financial reports.

Developing an accounting method

Choice is good. The red or the blue? Small, large, or super-size? Today or tomorrow?

Well, we're happy to tell you that you also get a choice in accounting systems: cash or accrual. These methods are different sets of rules for the timing of income and expenses. Usually, you report income and expenses in the year in which they're paid. So if you buy a piece of equipment in January 2005, you can't include it as a deduction on your 2004 taxes, even if you haven't filed your taxes yet. But what if you bought the equipment in 2004 but paid for it in 2005? The year in which you'll take this deduction depends on which accounting method you choose.

Cash

Using the cash system, you record an item of income or expense when it's paid. So when you receive money from your clients, you report it in that tax year. (Even if you invoice them for it in 2004, if they pay you the money in 2005, you report it in 2005.) And if you buy that piece of equipment in 2004, but you don't pay your credit-card bill until 2005, you can't deduct it on your taxes until 2005. Most businesses that sell services (such as yours) use this method of accounting.

Even though it's called the *cash* method of accounting, it actually covers any kind of payment, such as credit card, check, or even barter.

In some cases, you must report income as soon as it becomes available, even if you don't have it in hand. For example, if someone gives you a check in December 2004 and you don't deposit it until January 2005, you still must report the income for 2004. You're also not allowed to take a deduction for the current year for items paid for but not yet received.

Check with your accountant to make sure you're always on the right side of the tax law. (See Chapter 6 for more information on finding and hiring an accountant.)

There's no accounting for personal trainers: Handling your money like a pro

People who become personal trainers and people who become accountants are typically two very different kinds of people. You may not be excited by numbers — unless they're the number of calories your client has burned or the number of pounds he's lost — but you can still manage your money wisely. Here are some suggestions:

✔ **Open a separate checking account for your business.** Don't make the mistake of using your personal checking account for business purposes.

✔ **Pay all your bills by check, and note on the check what you purchased.** This tactic will help you keep track of expenditures.

✔ **Deposit checks and cash often.** Keeping checks and cash hanging around your place of business is an invitation for theft.

✔ **Record all your sales by using invoices, duplicate receipts, or some other method.**

This approach will help you keep track of who has paid and who is a deadbeat — er, we mean, who has not paid.

✔ **Keep a petty cash fund.** A small amount of cash lets you make payments without having to write out checks for small amounts. Whenever you make a payment from the petty cash fund, you should make out a petty cash slip and attach it to your receipt as proof of payment.

✔ **Keep records neat and tidy, the way your mom wanted you to keep your room.** You probably couldn't find your favorite baseball glove or Barbie doll when your room was a mess — and messy records will keep you from finding the data you need for tax purposes. (Your parents were the only people you had to contend with as a kid, but now you have Uncle Sam breathing down your neck. How's that for motivation?)

Accrual

Many C corporations, businesses with inventories of products, and manufacturers use the accrual method of accounting. It may not be the best for your service business, but we want you to know what it is just in case.

With the accrual method, you count the money as received as soon as it's earned, even if it isn't actually in hand. (That means if you've had a session with your client and invoiced her for it in 2004, but she doesn't pay you for it until 2005, you still report it on your 2004 taxes.) You record expenses when the obligation arises, even if you haven't actually paid it yet. This means if you buy a piece of equipment on your credit card in 2004 and don't pay for it until 2005, you still need to report the expense on your 2004 taxes.

If you decide to use the accrual method, you'll definitely need to consult your accountant to get set up and stay on the right track. (See Chapter 6 for the scoop on hiring an accountant.)

The Tax Man Cometh

Think paying taxes once a year is bad? Well, we hate to scare you, but as an independent contractor or business owner, you need to pay taxes four times per year. That's right, we said four. But don't worry — in this section, we tell you how to breeze through these quarterly tax payments without breaking a sweat.

If you're curious about why you need to pay taxes more often when you're an independent contract or a small-business owner, here's the lowdown: Essentially, when you're an employee of someone else, your employer withholds enough to cover your federal and state income taxes. (That's why your paychecks are always less than you think they'll be!) When you're working for yourself and your client writes you a check, no one is withholding anything for tax purposes. As an employee of a company, your tax dollars are going to the federal and state governments all throughout the year — every time you get a paycheck. So to even out the playing field a bit, when you work for yourself, you have to pay taxes four times a year. (Lucky for you, you don't have to pay taxes every time someone writes you a check!) Also, when you work for an employer, the employer is required to pay half your Social Security tax; the other half is deducted from your paycheck and turned over to the government. When you work for yourself, you have to pay the whole Social Security tax yourself. And you thought being your own boss was going to be all fun and games. . . .

Before we get started on the tax talk, we want you to know about something the IRS will give you for free: IRS Publication 3207, Small Business Resource Guide, is a great resource for every small-business owner or any taxpayer about to start a business. This interactive CD contains all the business tax forms, instructions, and publications you need to successfully manage a business. The CD provides other helpful information, such as how to prepare a business plan, how to find financing for your business, and more. The CD uses file formats and browsers that can run on virtually any computer. The Small Business Resource Guide is available in early April of every year. You can get a free copy by calling 800-829-3676 or by visiting the IRS Web site at www.irs.gov/smallbiz.

Computing your estimated tax

To avoid an underpayment penalty, your estimated tax must be at least the lesser of the following:

✔ **Ninety percent of the tax liability shown on the return for the current year:** This means that you predict how much you're going to earn (minus deductions), and you pay 90 percent of that estimated amount over four quarterly payments.

✔ **One hundred percent of the tax liability shown on the return for the prior year:** This means that you pay the same amount of taxes that you paid last year over four quarterly payments.

For example, say you paid $10,000 in taxes in 2004. For 2005, you can either predict what you're going to make and how much you'll owe in taxes and be sure to pay at least 90 percent of that amount in four quarterly installments, or you can pay $2,500 per quarter, which will add up to $10,000 — which is 100 percent of your liability from 2004.

In general, unless you expect your income to fluctuate dramatically one way or the other, your best bet is to pay 100 percent of what you paid last year. It's the surest way to avoid an underpayment penalty, even if your income skyrockets.

Knowing when to pay

Most businesses use the calendar-year accounting period, meaning that their business year ends on December 31 every year. You may also use a fiscal-year accounting period, which is a 12-month period ending on the last day of any month *other than* December.

Unless you have a reason to do so (for example, your accountant recommended it), using the calendar-year accounting period makes the most sense.

If you use the calendar-year accounting period, you need to pay your quarterly payments on:

✔ April 15

✔ June 15

✔ September 15

✔ January 15 of the following year

The idea is that your April 15 payment will cover what you earned January through March, your June 15 payment will cover what you earned in April and May, and so on. Don't ask why the payments aren't evenly spaced (in April, July, October, and January) — it's just a quirk of the IRS.

If you also earn a salary or wage in addition to your self-employment income — for example, if you have a "day job" in addition to your personal training clients — you can get around the whole quarterly tax deal by asking your employer to withhold more tax from your earnings. To do this, you need to file Form W-4 with your employer.

Filling out the forms

You'll use federal Form 1040-ES to determine the amount of your estimated taxes. You can get this form from the IRS (go to www.irs.gov/formspubs/index.html). After you file the form, it'll automatically be sent to you in following years. Your state will have a similar form — check with your state's income-tax authorities for more information.

Contacting Uncle Sam

Want to contact someone at the IRS to ask tax questions, get the status of your refund, or just shoot the breeze (okay, maybe not)? Here's how:

To order forms, instructions, and publications: Call 800-829-3676 to order current-year forms, instructions, and publications and prior-year forms and instructions. You should receive your order within ten days.

To ask tax questions: Call the IRS with your tax questions at 800-829-4933.

To solve problems: You can get face-to-face help solving tax problems every business day in IRS Taxpayer Assistance Centers. An employee can explain IRS letters, request adjustments to your account, or help you set up a payment plan. Call your local Taxpayer Assistance Center for an appointment. To find the number of the center in

your area, go to www.irs.gov or look in the blue pages of the phone book under "United States Government, Internal Revenue Service."

To listen to TeleTax topics: Call 800-829-4477 to listen to prerecorded messages covering various tax topics.

To get refund information: If you'd like to check the status of your federal income-tax refund, call 800-829-4477 for automated refund information and follow the recorded instructions, or call 800-829-1954 to speak to a representative. Be sure to wait at least six weeks from the date you filed your return (three weeks if you filed electronically) and have your federal income-tax return available because you'll need to know your filing status and the exact whole-dollar amount of your refund.

Saving for taxes

To get a head start on paying your taxes and avoid last-minute panic, why not do what an employer does and deduct taxes from every check? Using last year's figures, determine what percentage of your income goes to taxes. Then deduct that percentage from every check and deposit it in a special savings account set aside just for taxes. If you expect to make way more this year, up the percentage accordingly.

This is not a vacation fund or a Christmas-gift fund or an I-really-need-those-new-shoes fund! Resist the temptation to dip into your tax savings account.

Tracking Your Clients

No, we don't mean heading off after your clients with bloodhounds. We *do* mean that you need to document all sorts of information about your clients to help you create the best programs for them (and also to help you remember who's doing what).

Creating client forms

These forms are the ones you need to run your personal training business well:

- Prospect lead sheet
- Initial consultation form
- Medical history form
- Fitness assessment form
- Workout log
- Session log
- Exercise prescription form
- Activity log

Visit www.wiley.com/go/personaltrainer for sample client forms you use, or create forms on your computer that fit your way of doing business.

Putting together a client file

The client file will include all the forms listed in the preceding section. This way, you'll have the client's contact information and medical information, plus be able to track her fitness status and progress through the personal training sessions.

Keep the files consistent from client to client. For example, if the first page in one client's file is the prospect interest lead sheet and the second page is the initial consultation form, it should be that way for every client file. This setup makes it easier for you to find what you need pronto — and if you ever hire employees, they'll all be on the same page (pardon the pun).

Maintaining client files

Maintaining client files entails more than sticking them in carefully labeled, alphabetical folders. After all, what good are the files if they have clients' old addresses or don't note new injuries or other medical issues?

Go through your files quarterly and update the information. Make sure the clients' phone numbers and addresses are up-to-date and that you have their most current medical information. The files should also specify the date of the last fitness assessment, when you need to do a follow-up, and so on.

Chapter 8

Flexing Your Marketing Muscles

In This Chapter

▶ Figuring out who your clients are

▶ Generating good PR

▶ Reaching your clients through referrals

▶ Marketing on a shoestring

*I*f you want to get clients, you have to let them know you exist. That's where marketing comes in. Marketing sounds like something that requires a lot of money and maybe a specialized college degree, but that's not the case — most independent professionals and small-business owners do their own marketing.

In this chapter, we show you how to identify the people you should be marketing to, land your name in the press, get new clients through referrals, and successfully market your business when your marketing budget is small.

This chapter is just one chapter on marketing — for a whole book dedicated to the topic, check out *Small Business Marketing For Dummies* by Barbara Findlay Schenck with Linda English and *Advertising For Dummies* by Gary Dahl (both published by Wiley).

Ready, Aim . . .: Focusing on Your Target

In marketing-speak, the people you want to target with your marketing efforts are called your *target market*.

Figuring out who your target market is will save you bundles of money. For example, if your target market is seniors who want to prevent heart disease, sending brochures to teenagers would be a waste of money. If young women with kids are your target market, dropping a load of money on an ad in a men's magazine wouldn't make much sense.

Developing a specialty

Pinpointing a specialty within the personal training industry will help you identify your target market — and will make you stand out in people's minds to boot. For example, maybe you want to be known as the trainer who can work wonders for clients' bad backs, or the trainer who helps women get in shape after having babies.

In Chapter 2, we discuss the primary client populations that you can work with as a personal trainer: seniors, kids and teens, healthy adults, pregnant women, and athletes. Knowing which client population you want to work with will help you target your marketing efforts, so if you haven't already figured out which client population you want to work with, that's a good place to start.

Part of your specialty is your persona. Some clients will want you to stand on the sidelines and cheer them on — "Great, you're doing great! Just one more set! I know you can do it!" Others will prefer the drill-sergeant approach — "Okay, drop and give me 50. Move, move, move!" Which fits your personality? And which group of people do you think would most appreciate that approach?

Which of the following is your personal training personality:

- ✔ **Drill sergeant:** If your teaching style is to yell, "Faster! C'mon, you wimp!" you're a drill sergeant. You may be best off training athletes and healthy, gung-ho adults.

- ✔ **Cheerleader:** If your favorite phrase is, "Woo-hoo! You can do it!", the cheerleader is your type. You'll be great with everyone except those clients who expect to be whipped into shape.

- ✔ **Teacher:** If you're a patient soul who can handle a barrage of questions from your client, you're a teacher. You would be great as a trainer of kids or for adults who are new to exercise.

Whatever your "personality," it needs to mesh with your market. For example, the senior population may need more of a cheerleader personality rather than drill sergeant, whereas an athlete may need the drill sergeant rather than a cheerleader. Though women may prefer the teacher personality, what really matters is what *you're* most comfortable being. Clients who like your persona will find their way to you — just be yourself!

Don't worry, you won't have to try too hard — after a few clients, when the nervousness goes away, you'll find your style.

Targeting your market

The next step is to delve deep into the psyches of the people you want to work with to figure out who your target market is, what makes them tick, and how you can get them interested in your services. Ask yourself the following questions about your prospective clients.

What's their gender?

Do you want to work with men, women, both? For example, if you want to work with women only, you'll want to use female models in your advertising and market your services in places where women gather, such as day spas and at the YWCA.

How old are they?

If you chose a client population, you already know if you want to work with kids/teens, adults, or seniors. Within your chosen category, what age range do you prefer? Perhaps you want to focus on young men in their 20s, or women approaching 50, or kids between the ages of 7 and 12. If your focus is on older people, for example, you'll want to emphasize in your marketing materials how exercising helps the aging body, and do marketing in places where older people gather, such as senior centers.

What kind of income do they have?

Would your target market prefer less-expensive group classes, or do they expect pricier one-on-one sessions? If you plan to target people who are looking for low prices, your marketing materials need to emphasize the value you deliver. If you're targeting people who are willing to pay more, your marketing materials can focus on the high-end services you provide.

Where do they live?

Do they live in the city, suburbs, country? Do they live in houses, apartments, dorms? Knowing where your potential clients live helps you know where to concentrate your marketing efforts. Also, if you target people who tend to live in apartments or dorms, you can emphasize in your marketing materials that clients don't need to have a home gym to work with you.

What are their main concerns?

Are they concerned with money, family, aging, work, health? Are your clients interested in looking better, improving their basketball game, preventing cardiovascular disease? How can your personal training business help them with their concerns? Make sure you mention this in your marketing materials. For example, if your clients are people who put in a lot of time at work, you can stress your flexible hours in your marketing materials.

The Power of Publicity: Spreading the Word about Your Services

Want to get people talking about your personal training business? Then publicity is for you. In this section, we show you how to get your name in print, garner positive word of mouth, and turn your clients into walking billboards for your business.

Breaking the news

If you dream of seeing your name in print, success is only a press release away. A *press release* (sometimes referred to as a *news release*) is a document you send to members of your local media in the hopes that they'll print the information or call you for an interview. Even if members of the media don't use your press release, they may keep you on file as an expert they can call when they're writing an article about health or fitness — and that's just as good.

In the following sections, we give you some tips for writing a news release that will end up in print rather than in the circular file.

Be newsworthy

News releases are for news, not advertising — so don't try to pass off a self-serving ad as news. When an editor or producer reads such a release, he'll see that you're trying to get a free ad and toss it.

Here are some examples of real news:

- ✔ The opening of a new business (like yours!)
- ✔ Health stories, such as a new study linking exercise to longevity (you can quote yourself as an expert)
- ✔ An event, such as a seminar or demonstration (more on these topics later in this chapter)
- ✔ Community service (donating free sessions to at-risk youth, for example, or announcing that you'll be giving a percentage of a particular day's receipts to charity)
- ✔ A contest (for example, you can offer a week of free personal training sessions to the person who writes the best 300-word essay on why he wants to improve his health)

✔ A move to a new location

✔ A new product or service (but *only* if it's truly new and unique to your community, such as offering the first underwater bench-pressing class or being the first person in your area to use a new type of equipment)

Follow the proper format

A standard format is key to press-release success. Follow these guidelines to create a press release like the pros:

✔ **Print the release on your letterhead to clearly identify your business.**

✔ **In the upper-left-hand corner, write, "For Immediate Release," or, if the release has limited time value, "Hold Until XX/XX/XX" or "For Release During Lent."**

✔ **In the upper-right-hand corner, on the same line as the preceding bullet, tell the editors whom they can contact for further information.** For example, "Contact: Melyssa St. Michael, 800-123-4567."

✔ **Centered at the top of the page, put an eye-catching headline.** Editors and producers face looming stacks of news releases every day, and you want to make yours stand out. The headline is your first and sometimes only chance to hook the editor or producer and keep him reading. Make it newsy, clear, and interesting, such as "New Study Reports That Exercise Can Thwart Death." (Just don't overstate the story — you want the headline to accurately represent the story.)

✔ **The body of the news release should take the format of an inverted pyramid.** The critical information goes in the first paragraph, information of next highest importance in the second paragraph, and so on. Sometimes an editor will print a press release as is, and the inverted pyramid format allows him or her to slice off the last paragraphs if necessary, without sacrificing important information.

✔ **Use an easy-to-read typeface such as Times New Roman in 12-point size.**

✔ **Keep the press release to one page if possible.** If it does go over one page, end each running page with "–more–."

✔ **End with a short paragraph on your business, plus more-detailed contact information.**

✔ **After the last line of text, type "###" (without the quotes) centered at the bottom of the page.**

You could have a great news story on your hands, but if you don't follow the format that editors and producers are used to seeing, they'll likely ignore you.

Get it out there

After you've written a press release that will have editors panting with the desire to print it, it's time to send it out to the media. But who should you bless with this paragon of publicity perfection?

You don't need to spend a fortune to have someone distribute your release (though you can if you want); you can compile your own list of media outlets for nothing. Just be sure to make it targeted. If you want to get coverage for a new personal training service you're offering, for example, don't send a press release to *The Beekeepers' Journal.*

If you don't have the faintest idea what newspapers and magazines your target market reads, browse through *Bacon's Magazine & Newspaper Directory* or *Bacon's Publicity Checker,* both of which are available at your local library. Or pick up a copy of a magazine directory such as *Writer's Market,* which is available at most bookstores for under $30. The directory includes local and trade magazines that can be the perfect places for your release.

The newspaper doesn't have a lock on the news — send your release to the producers at all the radio and TV stations in your area as well. Local news outlets are often looking for interesting stories to tell.

Meet the press: Sitting for an interview

If you follow our instructions for creating a press release, you may actually have a journalist or even a local radio or TV station calling you to ask for an interview. What a scary thought!

Have no fear — the tips we provide in the following sections will turn you into a veteran media personality in no time.

If possible, have interviewers visit you in your workplace. This will help them get a better idea of what you do. Plus, you'll feel more comfortable if you're on your turf than you would on theirs.

Be prepared

Preparation is the key to success in any interview. To get yourself ready, think about some of the basic questions you can expect the reporter to ask. Make sure you have interesting, concise answers to these questions. Hone your answers by having a friend grill you like Mike Wallace.

If you're stumped for an answer, say, "That's a very good question." That response will buy you some time while you wrack your brain for an answer.

Melyssa is often in the news, providing insight into the latest fitness trends and whether they hold water. One time, she was live in the studio sharing a five-minute spot with a well-known surgeon in the area. Before they went on, the crew miked them up as they sat in one section of the studio, waiting for the anchor to come over. When they finally went on the air, Melyssa realized to her horror, that it was a call-in segment — and she didn't have the earpiece to hear the callers' questions! Every time the anchor turned to her and said, "And what do think about that, Melyssa?" she had to defer to the surgeon and let him answer it. Finally, ten questions later, the segment was over, and the anchor, whom Melyssa had worked with frequently, mentioned that she had been unusually quiet. Melyssa laughed and told the surgeon that she felt stupid, but the crew didn't give her an earpiece to hear the callers! You can never anticipate everything that may happen — but no matter what, don't panic, and keep your cool.

Don't stop with the basic queries. You want to be ready not just for the obvious questions, but also for the kinds of questions that give even seasoned press jockeys sweaty palms. For example, a reporter may ask you, "What do you think of all those bodybuilding supplements advertised in the backs of magazines and on late-night TV?"

As you may have discovered from watching political debates, what matters isn't so much *what* you say as *how* you say it. Distill your message into a few memorable words — what's called a *sound bite* — and practice saying it with conviction.

Answer the questions you're asked — and don't be afraid to admit when you don't know the answer

Despite all your preparation, you're bound to be asked a question that you don't have an answer to. When this happens, don't fake it. It's perfectly acceptable to say, "I'm not an expert on that, but I can tell you someone who is." You can also offer to get back to the reporter later with the information.

You were asked to sit for an interview for a reason, and you owe it to the reporter (and to your reputation) to answer the questions you're asked instead of viewing the interview as some kind of promotion for you or your business. If you sidestep all the reporter's questions and only talk about how wonderful you and your business are, you'll only make it difficult for the reporter to do her job — and not only won't you get any coverage, you'll blow your chances of being asked to for an interview by that reporter ever again.

Dress the way you normally do

That's right — *don't* dress for success. If you normally work in casual clothing, don't go pulling your lone suit out of its dry-cleaning bag and getting all gussied up for the TV reporter. If you feel uncomfortable, you'll look uncomfortable, and the audience won't take you seriously. For television, avoid pure white shirts or suits with stripes, checks, or small patterns, which don't mix well with the cameras.

Going to the head of the class: Giving free seminars

One way to get the word out about your business is to give free educational seminars, programs, and demonstrations. Potential clients get free information, and you get the chance to publicize your business, establish yourself as an expert, gain credibility — and even rake in some moolah to boot.

Picking your project

Here are some ideas for educational programs you can offer potential clients.

- Give a talk about how to prevent back pain, osteoporosis, or heart disease through exercise.

- Demonstrate how to use a body ball, dumbbells, or resistance bands.

- Give a seminar about the latest weight-loss techniques.

- Give a talk about starting an exercise program to a local business's employees.

Finding a venue

When you have an idea of what you want to offer potential clients, you need to find a place to do it in. Check out these possibilities:

- Browse the catalogs from local colleges and universities, or visit colleges online at College Board (www.collegeboard.org). Many colleges offer seminars and talks by local experts — like you!

- Call medium to large businesses in your area and ask if you can give your demonstration or seminar to their employees. Don't forget to mention that healthy employees work better and take fewer sick days!

- Contact a venue that your client population frequents — such as a senior center or high school — and offer your expertise.

- Contact your local hospital and ask whether they'd be interested in hosting your program. After all, hospitals have a vested interest in keeping people healthy!

Getting the word out

Let people know about your talk, seminar, or other program by sending a press release to your local newspapers, posting flyers on public bulletin boards, and leaving flyers at health-food stores, doctors' offices, and other places where your potential clients hang out.

Standing on your soapbox

Now's the time to brush up on your public speaking skills. Here are some tips that will give you the gift of gab:

- ✔ **Know your audience.** If you read Chapter 2, you know who your target audience is. Keep their concerns in mind when you're developing your presentation. Think about who they are and what they want to know.

- ✔ **Practice, practice, practice.** Grab a friend or family member and practice your presentation in front of them. Ask for feedback. Do you speak loudly enough? Is your presentation interesting? Ask them for honesty — and remember not to take criticism personally. (If you do, not only won't you learn anything, but they won't tell you the truth the next time you ask.)

- ✔ **Repeat yourself.** Adhere to the public speaking maxim "Tell 'em what you're gonna tell 'em, tell 'em, then tell 'em what you told 'em."

Public speaking is a huge topic — way too huge to cover in this chapter. Before you take the stage, pick up a book like *Public Speaking For Dummies,* 2nd Edition, by Malcolm Kushner (published by Wiley), and read up on public speaking tips on the Toastmasters Web site (www.toastmasters.org).

Reaching Your Clients through Referrals

The idea behind referrals is to get trustworthy people to give your business a little word of mouth. Referrals are a powerful — and free! — way to build your personal training business.

Happy clients are the best advertisement of all

No one can give your business better word of mouth than a happy client. Your role? To make your clients happy and keep them that way. Give your clients 100 percent, ask how you can make their personal training experiences better, and even give them the occasional survey asking what they enjoy and where you can improve your services. Give all your clients (or the happy ones, anyway) extra business cards that they can give out to their friends.

Say you have to choose between two hairdressers — one who has a Yellow Pages ad that says, "I rock!" and one who was recommended by a trusted friend (who also happens to have nice hair). Which would you pick? If you're like most people, you'd go with the hairdresser your friend referred you to. That's how referrals work.

Getting referrals

How do you get referrals? You ask for them! *Remember:* Now's not the time for modesty no matter how becoming it is. Ask for those referrals. But don't ask just anyone — ask the right people.

Be selective. Don't ask for referrals from a fast-food joint or a founding member of the Couch Potato Commission. You want to contact people and businesses that are credible and that attract the kind of clientele you're looking for.

From people in the medical profession

Physicians are the most important people you can approach for referrals, because they deal with weight-related issues and health problems that can be alleviated through exercise.

Giving to get

Sure, these people are great for getting the word out about your business — but what's in it for them? In this world you don't get somethin' for nothin', so try these tips:

✔ **Offer sessions — gratis.** Melyssa gives doctors 20 personal training sessions to show them the benefits of working with her. You can offer as many sessions as you like, but keep in mind that it takes four to six weeks to see results and for the client to develop enough trust in you to want to refer you to his patients or customers.

✔ **Offer to swap referrals.** For example, you'll give your clients coupons from the health-food store if the store will distribute your business cards to customers.

✔ **Be persistent.** The people and businesses you talk to may be uncomfortable referring you to their clients right away, so stay on their radar by sending occasional newsletters, flyers, and updates on your business and your accomplishments.

✔ **Say thanks.** Do the Miss Manners thing and make sure to send a thank-you note to people who have given you referrals. They'll remember your politeness when someone asks them for the name of a good personal trainer.

One way to ask for referrals is to call local physicians and ask for a ten-minute meeting to explain what you do and to develop a referral relationship. Start with your own doctor and the doctors of your friends and family. Scoring a meeting with a busy doctor will be easier if you have a connection! Find doctors in your area by looking in the Yellow Pages under "Physicians" or by using an online physician directory such as the American Medical Association's Doctor Finder at www.ama-assn.org/aps/amahg.htm.

You may not get to see the doctor herself, but an office manager or receptionist is just as good. Treat these gatekeepers well, and be sure to leave literature and business cards they can give to patients or leave in the waiting area.

Here are the doctors who are the most likely to give you referrals, plus the reasons they should do so. (Be sure to mention these reasons when you visit physicians!)

- **General practitioners (GPs):** These family doctors are the front line against disease for many people. Because excess weight can cause problems like diabetes and heart disease, GPs are likely to refer overweight patients to personal trainers.

  Why they should refer patients to you: Exercise can reduce high cholesterol and combat obesity.

- **Physical therapists:** Recovering from knee surgery? Suffering from back pain? Physical therapists help people reduce pain and regain function.

  Why they should refer patients to you: After a patient is well, exercise helps prevent reinjury.

- **Plastic surgeons:** You can generally bet that a person who opts for elective plastic surgery, such as a tummy tuck or breast enhancement, is concerned about her looks and is very physique-conscious to boot. What better clients for a personal trainer?

  Why they should refer patients to you: Plastic surgeons suggest exercise pre- and post-liposuction to help patients maintain the results of their surgery.

- **Endocrinologists:** Endocrinologists treat diseases that affect the endocrine system, including osteoporosis, diabetes, and thyroid disease.

  Why they should refer patients to you: Strength training can help prevent osteoporosis, which can be caused by hormone-replacement therapy.

- **Obstetricians/gynecologists (OB/GYNs):** OB/GYNs deal with women's medical issues, which may include excess weight.

  Why they should refer patients to you: Exercise can help control weight gain related to pregnancy and hormonal imbalances.

> ## Referrals: The best advertising of all
>
> In Melyssa's second year of business, an ad rep from a well-known direct-mail company that promoted high-end businesses contacted her to advertise in their circular. She hadn't done any advertising before and was hesitant about spending that much money. Reluctantly, she agreed to advertise with them.
>
> As she was signing the contract for quarterly ad placements, the rep reassured her that the ads would "pay for themselves," because the more people saw her ad, the more business it would bring in. Can you guess where this is going? The first ad brought in a good amount of business, and truly did pay for itself. However, the subsequent ones didn't bring in any business, and Melyssa ended up losing a great deal of money.
>
> Meanwhile, one of her very first clients had referred two of her best friends to Melyssa. They in turn referred a couple of their friends, who in turn referred a few people they knew. Before long, she had close to 30 referrals in a two-month period of time — and 26 of those referrals became paying clients. As a thank-you to each client who referred a *new* client, Melyssa gave a gift certificate for a free session — which they could use themselves or give to someone else as a gift. Thus, her referral program was born — and she hasn't advertised in circulars since.

When a doctor sends one of her patients to you, make sure you do the following:

- ✔ **Return the favor, and refer back!** As you become more established, your clients will start asking if you can recommend a doctor.
- ✔ **Make sure you're clear on the medical needs of your referral.** If you have any doubts, call and ask the doctor or nurse about your client's medical issues before beginning your sessions with them.
- ✔ **Send a thank-you note to the referring physician.**
- ✔ **Heed any exercise instructions sent along with the referral.**

From other people whose recommendations count

People talk — and you want to get them talking about your business in a favorable way. Doctors are great, but don't pass up these other opportunities for referrals:

- ✔ **Health-food stores:** People who shop at these stores tend to be concerned about their health — and you're just the person who can help them get fit. Ask the store manager if you can leave flyers or business cards at the register.
- ✔ **Weight-loss clubs:** Organizations such as Weight Watchers and Jenny Craig are full of people who are looking to pare pounds, and the clubs prescribe exercise as part of their weight-loss programs. Contact group leaders and ask if they'll pass out your info at their meetings.

✔ **Spas:** Clients of health and beauty spas want to look and feel their best — and they're not afraid to spend money to do it. Meet with the manager and ask if he'll refer clients to you.

✔ **Friends and family:** Who *better* to advertise your business than the people who already think you're the greatest thing since sliced multi-grain bread? Tell everyone you know about what you do, and they'll be sure to spread the word.

✔ **People you do business with:** Your hairdresser, your mechanic, your tax accountant — all these professionals come into contact with dozens of people each week who could be getting fitter with your help. Talk up your business with the people *you* do business with.

Turning referrals into clients

Congratulations! You've gotten your first referrals. Treat them right and watch your business boom. Here's how:

✔ **Offer the referral one free session.** This approach will give you a chance to show off what you can do for them.

✔ **Call each client who has been referred to you three times — one week, three weeks, and six weeks after your initial contact.** Call any more frequently than that, and you may be mistaken for a stalker. Ask the potential client if she has any questions and if you can do anything for her.

✔ **If you have no luck after three calls, take the potential clients off your calling list, but keep them on your mailing list so they get occasional updates, newsletters, and offers from you.** Melyssa had one person turn into a client *three years* after Melyssa first contacted her — so don't give up!

Marketing on a Shoestring

Coca-Cola, Microsoft, and Nike have multibillion dollar marketing budgets, and they spend it on billboards, multipage magazine spreads, and TV spots during the Super Bowl.

You? If you're just starting out as a personal trainer, chances are your marketing budget jingles when you shake it. But don't let your tiny budget get you down! Smart business owners know how to market on the cheap. The publicity tips we provide earlier in this chapter are a good start, but you have plenty more ways to get the word out without spending a mint.

Getting what you need through bartering

Long before the question "Cash, check, or charge?" became a part of every transaction, people "bought" their goods and services through barter. Need a new hammer? It'll cost you three chickens. Want someone to baby-sit little Glog? Your neighbor will do it — if you help her pick berries.

In these modern times, rather than trading chickens for hammers, you can trade personal training sessions for public-relations services, graphic design, copywriting, Web design, printing, and ad space. *Bonus:* The people who trade their services for personal training sessions may end up becoming your clients or referring their friends and business associates to you!

You can barter in two ways: You can join a retail barter exchange, or you can barter on your own with local businesses.

Retail barter exchanges

As a business owner, you can join a retail barter exchange , which is where you trade with other businesses and professionals. You can find retail barter exchanges online or in the Yellow Pages under "Barter and Trade Exchanges."

According to the International Reciprocal Trade Association, around 600 barter companies serve all parts of the U.S. and overseas markets. Here are some retail barter groups that operate across the U.S.:

- ✔ **TRADE USA,** 5019 McKinney Avenue, Suite 110, Dallas, TX 75205; phone: 214-528-6626; Web site: www.trade-usa.net; e-mail: tusa@trade-usa.net

- ✔ **VIP Barter,** 810 Emerald Street, San Diego, CA 92109; phone: 858-274-8600; Web site: www.vipbarter.com; e-mail: david@vipbarter.com

- ✔ **ATX: The Barter Company,** 8836 Tyler Boulevard, Mentor, OH 44060; phone: 440-205-9500; Web site: www.atxbarter.com; e-mail: anna@atxbarter.com

- ✔ **National Trade Association,** 7449 North Natchez Avenue, Niles, IL 60714; phone: 877-682-1234 (toll-free) or 847-588-1818; Web site: www.ntatrade.com; e-mail: info@ntatrade.com

The drawback: Barter exchanges can be pricey. National Trade Association, for example, charges $695 to join the organization. So before signing on the dotted line, do some sleuthing to ensure that you'll be able to recoup your investment through barter. Ask who the other members are and see if you're interested in what they have to offer.

To find a local group, visit the National Association of Trade Exchanges (www. nate.org) and click on Membership List. You can search for groups by state.

Solo swapping

Don't feel like shelling out a lot of cash to join a retail barter exchange? You can go solo. It's easy — just contact a printer or graphic designer or any business whose goods or services you need in order to market your business, and tell them that you're looking for X and are willing to barter Y. Explain how your offer will benefit them.

For example, let's say you need a graphic designer to create a flyer for your business. Tell him about your business and what you need (a flyer), and ask him if he'd be willing to design your brochure for you in exchange for personal training gift certificates that he can use himself or give out to his customers as a holiday gift or as a thank-you (be sure to point out to him that gift certificates buy him valuable goodwill with his customers).

Donating your services

Want to feel good about yourself and generate positive word of mouth at the same time? Of course you do! Then donate your services to charity.

One way is to offer a training package to be auctioned off at a fundraiser where the proceeds go to a charity. Your clients may ask you to participate in an auction, but if you want to be proactive, you can look up the head of a local charity organization and offer to donate your services. Call or e-mail to tell them who you are and how they can benefit from offering your personal training sessions in a fundraiser.

Bartering and taxes

Thought the tax man would turn a blind eye to your bartering? No dice. Products or services you obtain through bartering are considered income, so you must include their *fair market value* in your earnings at tax time. What's the fair market value of a service? If you and the other swapper have agreed ahead of time on the value of the services, the IRS will accept that value as fair-market value.

Generally, you report income from bartered services on Schedule C on your IRS Form 1040. Check with your accountant or take advantage of the IRS's Help page on www.irs.gov for more information.

Places like private schools, hospitals, and social groups often hold black-tie charity events with auctions. These events are the best places to donate your services, because the participants are usually affluent and can afford your services (which means they may become your clients). Also, the organizers typically include your company's information in their list of goods to be auctioned — so even if people don't win your donation, they'll at least see you're out there!

Consider donating a percentage of a day's (or a week's) income to a local charity, and send a press release about the offer to the local papers. (Make sure to notify the press in advance so they can get the word out in time for people to schedule appointments with you.) Or donate personal training sessions to at-risk youth, inhabitants of homeless shelters, patients in a hospital ward, or members of a senior center or youth center — and once again, send a press release to your local papers.

Putting it in print

For the cost of paper and a little time, you can create printed materials like newsletters, flyers, and brochures that will educate your clients and potential clients about your business.

Newsletters

Newsletters are a great way to gain credibility, put your name in front of potential clients on a regular basis, and spread the word about your product or service — but they won't do you any good if they get tossed rather than read.

Giving your spiel

Write down a description of your business and its benefits — a description you can recite in 30 seconds or less. This little spiel is called an *elevator speech,* because you can give it in the time it takes for the elevator you're riding in to reach your floor. Practice your speech until you've memorized it and until it sounds natural — not like a pitch. For example: "I run You Got Game Personal Training, which helps athletes get in shape and improve at their sport. I conduct training sessions at Gary's Gym on Main Street." Then whenever you meet someone, you're prepared to tell them who you are and what you do. *Remember:* Never miss an opportunity to spread the word about your services.

Here are some tips on how to create a newsletter that your prospective clients will look forward to receiving:

- ✔ **Collect the mailing addresses of your clients and of all the people who have shown an interest in your business, and use this as your mailing list.** Compatible businesses such as health-food stores and physical therapists may also give or rent you their own lists.

- ✔ **Decide how often you want to send out your newsletter.** A weekly newsletter sounds great, but will you really have time to write and mail a pithy piece every week, especially when your business picks up? Monthly, bimonthly, and quarterly newsletters are better solutions.

- ✔ **Come up with a name for your newsletter that will grab your readers' attention.** You want to start with a hook that keeps your audience reading. Don't make the mistake of sticking with your company's name — or you'll be throwing away prime newsletter real estate. For example, if your company's name is Perfect Personal Training, don't call your newsletter *Perfect Personal Training News.* A name like *The Health Success Guide* is more likely to pique the interest of all readers.

- ✔ **Share your knowledge.** Is there anything people like more than getting something for free? Filling your newsletter with free helpful information, tips, and resources will make you a valuable resource to your readers and create the kind of good will that all the ads in the world can't buy.

- ✔ **Include special offers like contests, coupons for a free session, or incentives like one free session to clients who get a friend to sign up.**

- ✔ **Give the heave-ho to the hard sell.** Studies show that newsletters have a 400 percent higher readership rate than standard sales materials, such as brochures and flyers. But a newsletter full of sales propaganda will get tossed in the round file just as fast as those other pitches. Concentrate on sharing information instead. If you make your newsletter a valuable resource rather than a boring sales tool, your audience will read it and maybe even file it away for future use. Can you say that much for an ad?

- ✔ **Tell them how to contact you.** Let your potential clients know how they can set up a consultation with you or become a client. Linda puts out an e-mail newsletter for one of the books she's written, and she spends lots of time finding information that will be helpful to her readers. After reading one issue, a reader commented to Linda that she might want to include information on how readers could order Linda's book. D'oh! Linda realized she'd been overlooking an important way to get her product out there. Always remember the purpose of the newsletter, and make it easy for clients to sign up with you.

✔ **Liven up your articles with quotes.** People love to hear what other people have to say. Quoting experts lends credibility, and quoting clients or the "man on the street" gives the newsletter a newsy, human-interest feel. Who can you quote in your newsletter?

- Your clients: If you're writing a newsletter article about weight loss, for example, you can quote a client who lost 50 pounds in six months. You can even include a different client success story in each issue. Clients love to see their names in print, and they're sure to show off your newsletter to others.

- Your suppliers (if you sell nutritional supplements, exercise equipment, or other products): These people would love to be included in your newsletter, because it means more exposure for their products.

- An expert in a related field such as a cardiologist or a physical therapist: Write an information piece on how exercise helps alleviate a certain condition, and quote the appropriate doctor. Or try writing about nutrition and interview a local nutritionist for quotes.

- Your employees: If you have employees, why not include a question-and-answer session with one of them in each issue, addressing their specialties.

- A local celebrity: Perhaps a popular restaurant owner serves up low-fat, organic cuisine — what a great idea for a short newsletter article! If someone in your area ran the Boston Marathon or won a power-lifting contest, he would also be perfect to interview.

Another bonus to using quotes: Instead of doing the hard sell, you can quote other people's great opinions of you or your product. It sounds less like hype if a third party is saying it for you. For her e-mail newsletter, Linda often interviews readers who have wonderful things to say about her book!

✔ **Make sure your newsletter has a clean, attractive layout with relevant and clear graphics or photos.** Follow these style tips for a newsletter that scores a home run:

- The most readable typefaces for newsletters are traditional typefaces such as Times, Palatino, and Roman.

- For headlines, use a type size two to three times larger than your regular text.

- Use subheads to break up long articles and keep the reader moving through the newsletter.

- Use *pull quotes* (quotes copied from the text and set in larger type elsewhere on the page) to attract your readers' attention and add a decorative touch to the page.

- Use white space to set off graphics, headlines, and pull quotes. Too little white space leads to a cluttered, confused look.

- Use a single large visual or photo rather than several small ones.

Newsletter news sources

If you'd like to include health news in your newsletter, check out EurekAlert (www.eurekalert.org), a science news site that includes press releases about health advancements, and PR Newswire (www.prnewswire.com), a media site that posts press releases on health-related topics.

You can also scan the magazine racks at the bookstore for health magazines like *Health, Fitness, Prevention, Oxygen, Men's Fitness, Men's Health,* and *Cooking Light.* You can use these magazines to find topics you'd like to include in your newsletter, but be aware that you can't publish the articles in your newsletter without getting permission from the copyright holder first.

Brochures

Brochures are multipage printed sales pieces that describe your offerings and how they can benefit clients. They're a great introduction to your business and they help open the lines of communication between you and a client. You can mail your brochures to potential clients, hand them out to people you meet, and leave them on bulletin boards and in compatible businesses such as doctors' offices and weight-loss clinics.

Don't make the mistake of thinking that, in order to be effective, brochures have to be glossy, 12-page affairs with a professional design and layout. You can create brochures that do the job with nothing but a word processing or desktop publishing program, some paper, an inkjet or laser printer, and a little time.

Take these steps to create a brochure that will entice your clients — but not break the bank:

- ✔ **Decide on a size that's right for the amount of information you have to convey.** A brochure can be one piece of paper folded in thirds (which gives you six panels), two pieces of paper folded in half and stapled in the middle (which gives you eight pages), or, really, any size and shape you want. Keep in mind that the less paper, the less expensive the brochure will be to produce. But don't skimp — you want to be able to include all your important information in the brochure.

- ✔ **Get creative with the paper you use.** You can find all sorts of attractive paper at your local copy shop or at an office-supply store. Or head to a business like Paper Direct (www.paperdirect.com), which offers attractive papers that are perfect for creating your own brochures (and business cards and letterhead) at home. Their papers come with decorative and professional borders and other graphics.

✔ **Push your benefits.** Brochures should stress benefits, not features. A *feature* is a new piece of equipment; a *benefit* is the fact that your new equipment can help clients lose their belly pooch.

✔ **Don't date yourself.** Instead of saying you've "been in business in the community for four years," say you've "been in business in the community since 2001." That way, your brochure never goes out of date and you won't have to keep reprinting it.

✔ **Quote your clients.** A nice idea is to include a list of testimonials from your happy clients. The best testimonials talk about results: "Jane Smith helped me lose 50 pounds!" or "Thanks to Mike Davis, I don't have to take blood pressure medication any more."

✔ **Be stylish.** Follow the style tips we listed in the "Newsletters" section, earlier in this chapter.

You are your best advertisement

The best marketing medium is also the cheapest, and the one you have the most control over — it's you. The way you look, talk, and act, and the things you say, can make a potential client drool over the prospect of working with you — or run the other way.

The last thing people want to see in the person who's supposed to get them healthy is bad skin, an outdated do, and clothes that were in style in the '80s. People go to personal trainers in part to improve the way they look, and they need you to serve as an example of good grooming and good looks.

You don't need to look like Brad Pitt or Jennifer Aniston, but you should be neat and stylish. Peruse magazines to get the scoop on fashionable (but not overly trendy) haircuts and clothing. When you go shopping for clothes, enlist the help of a personal shopper; many department stores offer this as a free service. (See more about dressing for success in Chapter 10.) Schedule a consultation with your hairdresser to talk about hairstyles that will flatter you, and if your skin leaves a lot to be desired, visit a dermatologist.

If you're healthy, if you're happy, if you love personal training, this will show through to prospective clients. After all, would you want to sign up with a personal trainer who has a depressed outlook and a hacking cough? Probably not.

Do everything you can to stay as healthy as possible, including eating well, taking vitamins as needed, getting regular check-ups, and getting adequate rest. Deep breathing and meditation can give you more get-up-and-go as well. When potential clients look at you, they should see a personal trainer who's glowing with health.

Love your job — if you don't, something has to change. Potential clients can tell if you're unhappy in your job. They'll figure you give your clients about as much attention as that kid flipping burgers gives to his customers. We hope the tips in this book help you build a career you adore!

Flyers

A *flyer* is a single sheet of paper printed on one or both sides. It's also sometimes called a *circular,* even though it's generally rectangular (ba-dum-bum). It contains less information than a brochure, but it's also less pricey.

Include this information on your flyer (much of which can be taken from your brochure):

- ✔ **A catchy headline:** For example, "Blast That Belly Flab!" or "Bathing Suit Season Is Coming — Are You Ready?"
- ✔ **The name of your business.**
- ✔ **A list of benefits of going to a personal trainer:** Some benefits you may want to include are more energy, more confidence, increased strength, better heart health, lowered risk of disease, a more attractive figure, and better sleep.
- ✔ **Any special offer you want to make:** For example, one free session or a discount on the first month's worth of sessions.
- ✔ **How people can reach you to schedule a personal training session.**

The point of a flyer is to produce it as cheaply as possible and spread it around like Donald Trump spreads hundred-dollar bills. Here are some places where you can put your flyers:

- ✔ **On the windshields of cars** — especially those parked at doctors' offices, outside of gyms, on university campuses (if college students are your target market), and outside of health-food stores
- ✔ **On bulletin boards** in these same places, plus in the supermarket and at the library
- ✔ **In flyer racks at the supermarket**
- ✔ **On the counter at the local bookstore, health-food store, and so on** (Be sure to get permission from the managers first!)
- ✔ **In lobbies of doctors' offices** (Be sure to ask first.)

Chapter 9

Retaining Your Clientele

*G*etting clients is easy. Keeping them — ah, there's the rub.

As a personal trainer, you have to use every trick in the book (this book!) to keep your clients happy, motivated, and on the track to fitness. The Yellow Pages are full of trainers like yourself, and if you don't make an effort to retain your clients, they just may let their fingers do the walking to your competitor down the street.

In this chapter, we give you the basics for keeping clients coming back, including how to motivate them, how to adjust your training sessions to their personalities, how to keep them excited about fitness, how to connect with them on a personal level, and how to resolve any conflicts that arise (alas, the road to true fitness never runs smoothly).

Keepin' It Real: Putting Fitness within Your Clients' Reach

Say you're using a computer for the first time. Your teacher tells you, "Okay, by next week I want you to write a ten-page document with tables and clip art in Microsoft Word, create a PowerPoint presentation, and, while you're at it, write a program that will control all the electronic appliances in your house." Chances are, you'd be so frustrated that you'd give up hope of ever becoming a computer whiz.

The same principle goes for personal training. If you tell a new client, "You need to overhaul your diet, stop smoking, exercise five times per week, and cut down on stress," she won't be a client for long. You need to get to know your client and develop a program that takes her abilities and personality into account so that she can tackle one step at a time.

Knowing who you're dealing with

In order to give your client what he needs, you have to know his goals, his likes and dislikes, his strengths and weaknesses, what he had for breakfast this morning. . . . Getting to know your client will create a bond between the two of you that will keep him coming back — and let you create a program that will help *him* reach his fitness goals at a pace he can handle.

But how do you get to know your clients without taking them out for dinner, going for long walks on the beach, or reading their memoirs? (Hey, who *doesn't* have a memoir these days?)

You start with your initial consultation, where your job is to ask question after question until you feel like a job interviewer for the CIA. (You can find out more on initial consultations in Chapter 10.) In the following sections, we show you how to take it beyond those first consultations and develop great relationships with your clients.

Getting to know you . . .: Personality typing

People tend to fall into distinct categories of personality types, and figuring out your clients' personalities will help you deal with them in the most effective way. Several different types of classification systems vie for shelf space in bookstores' Self Help sections. Here are a few:

- ✔ The **Myers-Briggs Type Indicator (MBTI)** divides people into 16 types of personalities, such as "The Scientist" and "The Executive," based on four main traits: introversion/extroversion, intuitiveness/sensing, thinking/feeling, and judging/perceiving. (The trait names have nothing to do with what career the person has; you may have a "Scientist" client who hasn't touched a Bunsen burner since high school.) Knowing the different types of personalities and how to recognize them is actually a lot of fun, and you can use this knowledge to communicate effectively with your clients. If your client is a "Scientist" type, for example, knowing how the exercises work and what muscles are involved can spur his enthusiasm. An "Executive" type of client, on the other hand, may be motivated more by research demonstrating that entrepreneurs who exercise daily are more likely to meet income goals. For an explanation of the 16 personality types and to take a test to find out *your* personality type, check out www.keirsey.com.

✔ The **Riso-Hudson Enneagram Type Indicator (RHETI)** divides people into nine categories, from "The Challenger" to "The Peacemaker." If your client is an Achiever, for example, you would want to break his fitness goals into smaller goals that he can achieve quickly, giving him a feeling of accomplishment that will keep him motivated. For more information, go to www.enneagraminstitute.com.

✔ Discovering whether your client is **Type A or Type B** will help you determine how much you can push him and how long you can spend on one exercise before moving on to the next. The Type A person is competitive, impatient, and goal oriented, and thrives on challenges. He'll probably expect you to change up his program frequently, and he'll want to achieve his fitness milestones quickly. The Type B person, on the other hand, is laid back, patient, noncompetitive, and not as productive as the Type A person. He'll want to take things nice and slow. Push him too hard, and he may quit in frustration, despite making progress.

When Melyssa was 18 and working at her first gym, the gym owners sent her to a personality training class where she learned to understand and sell to different personality types. Even though she wasn't actually pushing products, she *was* selling her clients on the idea of fitness. Knowing how to speak to them in their own "language" was the best way to get her message across.

Let me hear your body talk: Understanding body language

Think that what you say is more important than the way you say it? Not so. Fifty-five percent of the impact of what we say comes from our body language and other visual cues, 38 percent from the way we sound, and a piddling 7 percent of the meaning comes from our words.

You can use this fact to your advantage by reading your client's body language. Even if she keeps her mouth shut, you'll be able to tell whether she's bored, excited, angry, or happy — and whether you should give her some positive reinforcement, push her harder, or keep mum.

The cues in Table 9-1 will help you understand what your client is saying — even if she doesn't say a word.

Table 9-1	Understanding Body Language
Body Language	*What It Means*
Leaning forward	She's engaged in what's going on.
Standing with open arms	
Standing with her arms behind her back	She's paying attention to what's going on.
Moving backward	She's rejecting what you're saying.
Crossing her arms in front of her chest	
Tapping her fingers or foot	She's feeling combative.
Looking around	She's eager to leave.
Pointing her feet toward the door	
Blinking quickly	She's listening to what you're saying.
Tilting her head	
Clenching her hands	She's feeling defensive.

Mentoring your clients

Your clients look to you as a mentor — someone who can help them improve their lives by improving their health.

In business, a mentor helps his protégé learn the ropes of the industry and overcome obstacles that stand between the newbie and career success. In personal training, a mentor (that's you!) helps his client overcome obstacles that stand between the client and total fitness.

In a nutshell, mentoring is providing good advice and personal, thoughtful solutions — rather than textbook answers — to your clients' problems. For example, if a client tells you she doesn't eat breakfast, the true mentor doesn't start issuing commands from on high ("Well, starting tomorrow you are"). The mentor asks questions ("Why are you missing breakfast? Do you not like to eat in the morning? Do you not have enough time? Do you dislike certain breakfast foods?"), listens to the client's responses, and then comes up with tailored solutions, such as a list of healthy breakfasts that take less than ten minutes to prepare.

To make it easy for you, we've broken down the process into three key tips:

✔ Always listen — *really* listen — to your clients' questions and problems. Don't formulate a response in your head while your client is still talking.

✔ Don't interrupt, and don't jump in with your quick fix as soon as sounds cease to come out of your client's mouth.

✔ Take the time to formulate a customized solution, even if it means you have to get back to your client in a day or two.

Follow these tips and — voilà! — you're well on your way to successfully mentoring your clients.

Ensuring your clients' success

If your client loses those 20 extra pounds, lowers her blood pressure, or sees her belly go from beer gut to six-pack, she's sure to keep coming back. In other words, in order to retain clients, you need to help them succeed at their fitness goals.

Planning one step at a time

Nothing is more frustrating for a client than getting nowhere because the trainer has given her too much to do. Any program needs to be broken down into manageable steps. For example, if your client wants to start exercising but doesn't know how, you can start her exercising once a week as opposed to three times a week. After she's mastered that, she can go to two times per week; then three times per week. This strategy is much more effective than starting her off on a tough program that only leaves her feeling sore and discouraged.

Making the program livable and doable

If you've gotten close to your client as we suggested in the section "Knowing who you're dealing with" earlier in this chapter, then you understand her life-style and any constraints this puts on her schedule and her ability to follow a fitness program. For example, maybe your client has a high-powered career and is so busy that she can't eat five small meals per day or spend an hour every day running on the treadmill. You need to work within the confines of how your client lives her life and create her fitness program accordingly.

At the same time, you shouldn't allow a client to continually fall back on excuses for why she can't fit a 15-minute workout into her schedule. The longer you let your client slide by on excuses, the farther away she'll be from her goals — and rather than accept her failure as her own, she may turn the blame on you, losing you both a client and your reputation.

Tony Robbins Has Nothin' on You: Motivating Your Clients

Great motivational speakers (like Tony Robbins) make their audiences believe that they have the power to change their lives for the better. Great motivational trainers do the same for their clients. It's all about inspiring them with your example, keeping things interesting (people who are bored are rarely motivated), providing positive reinforcement, and substantiating their progress so that when they hit a low spot you can say, "Look how far you've come!"

Being a role model

You want clients to look at you and think, "Seeing this healthy, vibrant person motivates me to work hard to meet my fitness goals." You *don't* want them to look at you and think, "Those jelly donut stains on her polo shirt make me wonder what to have for dessert tonight." In other words, you need to be a good role model for your clients.

Do you rate?

Keeping track of your clients' satisfaction levels will let you make fixes when necessary to keep the love flowing in your direction. At the same time, telling your clients how they're doing will keep them motivated and on the right track.

Melyssa had her clients verbally rate their workout sessions on a scale of 1 to 10, where 1 was as easy as sitting in a chair and 10 was as hard as pushing a car uphill in the snow. If she and her trainers were consistently rated from 7 to 8, she knew they were doing okay.

Imagine going to college and never getting any grades. How would you know how you were doing? It's hard to improve if you don't know where your strengths and weaknesses lie. That's why it's a good idea to give your clients regular progress reports. Melyssa produced report cards

for her clients to let them know how they rated in terms of:

- ✔ Body fat
- ✔ Flexibility
- ✔ Strength
- ✔ Attendance (shades of high school!)
- ✔ Cardio endurance

If the client had improved in an area since the last report card, he would get a check-plus; if he hadn't lost any ground, he would get a check. Melyssa made it a point to always find something positive to say on the report card, such as, "When you started coming here, you could only do 10 minutes on the elliptical machine. Now you can do 30. Good job!"

It sounds like a lame cliché — okay, it *is* a lame cliché — but the reason people keep saying it is it's true. To be a good role model and keep your clients motivated, you have to practice what you preach. You need to:

- **Be fit.** You should look reasonably healthy. (Looks can be deceiving, but appearances do count. You want to project fitness to your clients so they can look to you for inspiration.)

- **Be strong.** Spotting clients, handing them weights, and putting plates on the machines takes a lot of strength. Make sure you have it.

- **Be a nonsmoker.** We can't think of anything worse than a trainer who teaches clients how to be healthy while he reeks of stale stogies — except maybe a trainer who bums cigarettes off a client as he conducts a session!

- **Eat healthfully.** Even though your clients may not see what you eat, it's the principle of the thing. You can't, in good conscience, tell your clients to deep-six their fave goodies while you eat fast food for every meal. As a bonus, eating well will give you that healthy look we mentioned at the top of this list.

Changing up the program

Would you want to eat toast with jelly for breakfast, a PB&J sandwich for lunch, and a grilled chicken breast for dinner *every day of your life?* Your clients feel the same way about their personal training sessions. Doing the exact same exercises in the exact same order on the exact same days of the week gets stale pretty fast. Not only that, but their progress will soon plateau, which can be discouraging.

To keep clients interested, motivated, and coming back for more, you can't stick with the same ol' same ol'. Throw them a few curveballs without changing the program so dramatically that they feel lost. Here are some ways to do this:

- **Up the weights.** Increase the weights as your client gains strength. She'll always be challenged and will be super-motivated when she sees that she can now bench-press way more weight than when she first started!

- **Decrease rest time.** If your client starts off with 1 minute of rest in between each set, decrease it to 45 seconds, then to 30 seconds as his fitness level improves.

- **Superset it.** It sounds like what you do in a fast-food joint when you upsize your fries and drink for a nickel, but *supersetting* is actually putting two exercises back to back without a rest period in between. This technique is for more-advanced clients. (Read more on advanced programming techniques in Chapter 15.)

✔ **Periodize it.** Talk with your clients about where you're taking them. Are you taking them from a fat-burning/endurance program lasting from three to six weeks, moving on to a hypertrophic phase for six weeks, and then going into a strength phase to give them that "hard look"? Periodizing — and telling them what they stand to gain from it — helps your clients set goals and look forward to new programming. Be sure to tell them whether they can expect to lose more weight during one period than in another. You can stick to a fat-burning/endurance phase for a good chunk of time, but shaking things up will help both mentally and physically.

✔ **Reschedule.** Even something as simple as changing your client's schedule can keep things interesting. For example, try changing the days of the week that you do strength training and cardio, or change the order of the exercises in a session.

Attaboy!: Providing positive reinforcement

When you're training a dog and the dog does something you want him to do, like sitting on command or not peeing on the floor, you reward him with pats and doggie treats. It works the same way with people (though you should refrain from patting their heads). When they're rewarded for a certain behavior, they want to do it more often.

Here are some ways to encourage and motivate your clients:

✔ **Make a comparison to her past performance.** For example, you can tell her, "You did five more reps than usual this time. Good going!"

✔ **Compliment her form when she's performing an exercise.** Focusing on form is a subtle reminder that it's not just about the end result — the journey matters just as much as the destination.

✔ **Incorporate encouraging comments into her progress report.** For example, you can write, "Good job on the cardio today!" or, "You're now lifting 15 more pounds than when you started!"

✔ **When you record her workouts in her exercise log, include friendly notes about her performance.**

✔ **Send her an occasional greeting card or e-mail, or give her a call, to let her know you're proud of her.** Everyone likes to get things in the mail or e-mail besides bills and spam (and phone calls from people who aren't trying to sell them something). A simple note or phone call with an encouraging message will help your client feel connected to you when she's away from the gym.

With new clients, do one of these things within the first four weeks, then again within two months. With clients you've worked with longer, you can do this less often — but don't forget to offer encouragement once in a while.

Don't overdo the gushing — clients can sense insincerity a mile off. And praise starts to lose its effectiveness if it comes in too fast and furious.

Be specific with your praise. If your client has excellent form on an exercise, don't just say, "Good form!" Tell her *why* it's good so she can benefit from your praise.

We all have days when we feel like we can't do anything right. If your client gets down on herself, try turning her negative comments into positive ones. For example, if she says, "I'm doing horribly today," you can remind her that, even though she doesn't feel at her best today, she's getting stronger with every session. Exercise logs can really help with occasional negativity — pointing out exactly how much she's improved since she started will help your client overcome the down days and keep focused on the long term.

Following up for follow-through

If you're a parent, you know that getting your kids to do their chores takes a lot of nagging. "Please take out the garbage." "When do you plan to take out the garbage?" "Have you taken out the garbage yet?"

Parenting a kid is good training for working with clients, except with clients, we don't call it *nagging* — we call it *following up*. Following up with your clients holds them accountable for following the plan you've laid out for them and gives them little motivational boosts.

Following up with your clients doesn't mean calling them every five minutes between sessions to ask if they've done their workout yet. Follow these tips for following up:

✔ **Lay out a plan.** Give the client specific directions, such as, "You will do exercises X, Y, and Z on these days, drink eight glasses of water per day, and eat five servings of vegetables every day."

✔ **Put it in writing.** Ask your client to record his exercises and progress in a log.

✔ **Check in once or twice while the client is between sessions (depending upon how many sessions you work with him per week).** A quick call or e-mail to make sure he's on track and to see if he has any questions is all you need.

✔ **Be a problem solver.** If your client reports that he hasn't been sticking to his plan, ask him what kept him from doing so and try to solve the problem. For example, if he feels crunched for time after work, you can suggest doing a workout before work or during his lunch break.

✔ **Schedule sessions.** Conduct sessions with the client at regular intervals to check his body fat, flexibility, and other measures of progress.

Getting Connected: Fostering Good Relationships with Your Clients

If you've ever been on a dud of a first date (and who hasn't?), you know that sometimes you just don't feel a connection with someone. Maybe he didn't share any personal information, or maybe she was argumentative. In any case, you probably didn't want to see that person again.

Your clients are trusting you with their most important possessions — their bodies — and you need to establish a connection with them based on trust, sharing, and rapport. Keeping a connection alive will keep your clients coming back.

Knowing when to talk and what to say

They say talk is cheap, but they're dead wrong. Saying the right thing at the right time (and knowing when not to say anything at all) will help you forge a connection with your clients that will keep them happy and motivated — not to mention paying.

Open up a little bit about yourself. When you do, you're telling your client, "I hear you, and I experience the same things as you." For example, if your client admits to a strong chocolate craving, you can say, "Yes, I go through the same thing myself."

Sometimes your client needs to vent, and you happen to be the person who's nearby at the time. You don't need to try to solve every problem unless she asks you to. If she starts complaining about her jerk of a boss, for example, don't tell her to quit her job. Just listen and let her know that you can relate.

If your client likes to complain about her job, be sure you don't commiserate too enthusiastically. You don't want to fall into the trap of complaining about your job — after all, you're at work when you're with your client, and no one likes a trainer who doesn't like her job.

If your client is normally talkative but is suddenly glaring at you and giving monosyllabic answers to your questions, don't take it personally. She's probably having a bad day and needs her space (and some silence). Take her reticence as a cue to clam up. Sometimes silence truly is golden.

Melyssa had a client who was an attorney with a high-stress job. Some days the client would come in and chat away, and other days she would barely mutter two words to Melyssa. Melyssa understood that the client's silence wasn't a personal slight — sometimes she just had a lot on her mind and didn't feel like talking.

Knowing what not to say

Certain words and phrases should never come out of a personal trainer's mouth (at least when the client is within hearing range). Naturally, you want to avoid cursing, talking smack about other clients, and insulting the client. But even such seemingly innocuous terms as *overweight* should be purged from your patois. Check out Table 9-2 to know what not to say, and for suggestions of what to say instead.

Table 9-2		What Not to Say to Your Clients
Instead of . . .	*Say . . .*	*The Reason*
Overweight	Overfat	Weight isn't always a good indication of a person's health status, but too much fat is too much fat. Focus on the fat, not on the weight.
Inflexible or not flexible	Shortened range range of motion	Inflexible sounds so . . . inflexible, as if the client can do nothing to fix it. Referring to it as a shortened range of motion lets the client know that the range of motion can be increased.
Weak	Not strong yet or not strong on this this exercise	Telling the client that she's not strong *yet* indicates that eventually she will be. Or perhaps she's not strong on a certain exercise because she's using a small body part — on the next exercise, she may be stronger.
No stamina	Low lung capacity	If you say that a client has no stamina, he may think this is just who he is, that he can't do anything to change that. If you tell him he has low lung capacity, you're telling him that he can improve this situation.
Out of shape	Deconditioned	No one likes hearing that she's out of shape. The word *deconditioned* tells her that her state of fitness is temporary, and with effort she'll be conditioned again.

Respecting your clients' privacy

Would you like it if your hairdresser told another of her clients exactly how natural your blond is? Or if the TV repairman told all your neighbors about your giant flat-screen TV? No? Then you understand why your clients' doings — even the positive ones — should be marked "Strictly Confidential" in your mind.

Recognizing the source of your clients' frustration

A normally cheery client snaps at you during a workout. What did you do wrong?

Maybe nothing. Sometimes people have a bad day, and they take it out on the people closest to them. Psychologists refer to this as *transference.* Your cranky client may have had a fight with his spouse, had a bad day at work, or been cut off by a rude driver, and he's taking out his anger on you.

The best way to deal with transference is to use simple words: "You're angry. I'm sorry. How can I fix this?" Chances are, he'll cool down.

If your client seems too angry to keep his mind on the session, ask if he'd like to reschedule, and stress that a good, hard workout mat be just what he needs to work out those negative feelings!

Remember: Just because you work in a gym doesn't mean you have to be your client's punching bag. You deserve to be treated with respect and civility; if your client can't grant you the minimum of human decency, you can — and should — ask him to leave and come back when he can.

Here are some suggestions for keeping the lid shut on your clients' private affairs:

- ✔ **During the initial consultation, assure the client that anything she says and does in her training sessions stays between the two of you.**

- ✔ **If you have employees, have them sign a nondisclosure agreement that states that they won't disclose information about clients to anyone.** You can have your lawyer draw one up for you.

- ✔ **If your client gets tight lipped about a subject, back off.** If she wants to talk about it, she will.

- ✔ **If you're in a client's home and you see or hear an argument or anything else the client would rather you didn't see, keep mum and don't pry.** Don't even share details about the client's belongings or decorating style. Even raving about the client's beautiful home isn't wise — if they hear you've talked about them in *any* way, they'll wonder what other things you've said about them.

- ✔ **Never talk about one client with another client.** If she hears you talk about others, she'll assume you talk about her as well.

- ✔ **If a client asks about another client, tell her that you're sorry, but you can't talk to her about your other clients.** She should feel reassured to know that you won't talk about *her* with other clients either!

Melyssa had a client who kept saying that she wanted her overweight daughter to come in for training sessions. Little did she know that her daughter was already training with Melyssa's company — the daughter just didn't want her mother to know. Melyssa's staff took pains to make sure that the two were never scheduled for the same time. Many months passed this way until the mother came in to buy supplements and saw her daughter working out. Instead of getting angry, she said, "That is the best professionalism I've ever seen." She appreciated that Melyssa and her staff were so good at respecting their clients' privacy.

Resolving Conflicts and Concerns

You know that you rock, and we know that you rock, but every once in a while a client will think that you do *not* rock — and you'll have to take action to make things right.

Figuring out what went wrong

The minute you sense something is wrong, start asking the client questions to dig up the root of the problem. You can come right out and say, "You seem upset — is anything bothering you that I can help you with?" Or you can ask questions that will help uncover the problem, such as, "Are you achieving your goals? Are you happy with my services?"

Why wrack your brains if you don't have to? If a client is unhappy with your services, ask what you can do to make them better. Often, the client will tell you exactly where you're going wrong and how to fix the situation.

Admitting to your mistakes

We all make mistakes. That's right, even the esteemed authors of this book have made mistakes. So you're not alone if you've made mistakes. In fact, you're alone if you *haven't!*

If you make a mistake, you have two choices: You can compound the mistake by denying it or blaming somewhere else, or you can do the right thing, fess up, and do what you can to make things right. You may feel that admitting to a mistake will lower you in the eyes of your client, but in truth she'll respect you for owning up to your actions.

Many trainers commit the faux pas in the following list. If you're aware of their mistakes, you have a better chance of avoiding them yourself:

✔ **Not following through:** For example, if you tell a client that you'll research a certain piece of equipment and then you don't do it because you were busy watching the season finale of your favorite reality show, apologize, then do what you promised ASAP.

✔ **Giving the client incorrect information:** For example, if you tell a client an exercise will work her biceps when it will really work her triceps, you can confuse your client. Correct yourself as soon as you discover the mistake.

✔ **Not admitting that you don't know the answer to a question:** When you don't know the answer, you're much better off telling your client that you'll have to find out and get back to her. She'll respect you for it in the long run — and even if she doesn't, you'll be able to respect yourself.

✔ **Showing up late:** Time is money — and this holds true not only for you, but also for your clients. If you're late to your appointments with your clients, the message you're communicating is that you don't care. And that's the last thing you want your clients to feel. If you can't avoid being late, call ahead of time to explain the situation, and make sure you extend the session to make up for the lost time.

✔ **Not showing up at all:** Worse than being late is not showing up. If you have an emergency and you have to cancel your appointment, be sure to call your client and explain the situation. And make sure you don't make a habit of it. Emergencies don't happen every day.

✔ **Not being prepared for your sessions:** For instance, if you were supposed to update your client's program but you didn't, the client may think that you're not concerned with her progress. Apologize and do what you promised — pronto.

Putting things right

If you make a mistake, the first thing to do is apologize. Then try to fix the problem. As we mention earlier, you can try asking the client what will make her happy. If you really messed up, a free session or two may be in order.

Melyssa once had a session with a client and forgot to record the next session in her logbook. On the day of the next session, the client was waiting at home like a jilted lover for Melyssa to show up — and she never did. To make amends, Melyssa offered the client two free sessions — one to make up for the missed one, and one just to say "I'm sorry."

"But you promised!": Guarantees and warranties

Sure, telling a client that he'll definitely lose 20 pounds in three months or that your plan will bring his blood pressure down to a healthy level will keep him coming to you. But is this a good tactic? Not really. You may offer the best workout sessions around, but you have no control over what the client does outside of the sessions. Maybe he goes home and downs two pints of Ben & Jerry's. Maybe he watches eight hours of TV every day. You simply can't guarantee that the client will lose weight, be free from back pain, or lower his cholesterol.

A better idea is to do what salespeople call "undersell and over-deliver." In other words, downplay what you can do for the client. For example, you can tell your client that your workouts will make him stronger and more flexible — you know this will happen if the client is working out with you regularly, even if he doesn't do it at home. If you give him exactly what you promised, he'll be happy. If you give him more — say, if he *does* lose 20 pounds or his back pain goes away — you're golden.

If you can't resolve the problem, the best option may be to refund the client's money for any unused sessions and refer him to another trainer. In fact, you should have a refund policy in place for such situations.

Many experts recommend a simple refund policy: 100 percent satisfaction or your money back. And why not? If you're good at what you do, you should be able to back it up with a strong refund policy. Of course, you should refund only for those sessions the client hasn't used yet. (See the nearby sidebar, "'But you promised!': Guarantees and warranties.")

When the Honeymoon Is Over: Recognizing When to Wean Your Client

Whoever said "All good things must come to an end" must have been talking about personal training. And the person who said "If you love something, set it free," well, he was talking about unicorns (if the posters bearing this slogan are any indication). But we can pretend he was talking about personal training, too. In other words, sometimes you have to let a client go.

If you like your client

Sometimes you can easily tell when it's time to set your client free — the client can work successfully on her own, and you don't think she needs you anymore. Or maybe she's gone as far as she can with you, and it's time to start working with another trainer (for example, maybe she wants to start doing sport-specific workouts and you can't accommodate her).

If you've determined that your client is ready to move on, and you've had a good relationship with your client, you can either suggest that she visit another trainer (you can refer her to a trainer you know) or that she start working out with you less often. For example, if you're seeing her three times a week, cut back to two times a week and give her homework to keep her motivated between sessions. Continue to taper off the sessions until you're seeing the client only once every couple of months to check on her progress and change her program if needed.

Staying in touch with clients after they've moved on

Y'know how you get notes in the mail from your dentist, your mechanic, and your cat's veterinarian reminding you that it's time for a checkup? Or how you changed from one long-distance provider to another, and now your old provider calls you up every once in a while (or every five minutes) with a new offer?

These companies know that staying in touch with your former clients is a good business practice. If you have clients who've moved on, shoot them an occasional phone call, letter, or e-mail to touch base and make sure they're on track. You never know — they may decide to come back to you!

Try these little reminders to keep former clients thinking about how wonderful you are:

✔ **Holiday cards:** Holiday cards are a great way to stay in touch. Just be sure they're non-denominational so you don't offend clients who don't celebrate a particular holiday.

Sending a "Happy New Year" card in the last week of December is a good approach — plus, you'll catch your former clients at a time when lots of people think about getting or staying in shape.

✔ **News clippings:** If a former client is a florist and you run across an article about new flower arranging techniques, clip it and send it along. This method drives home the importance of getting to know your clients.

✔ **Newsletters:** Turn to Chapter 8 for more information on creating winning newsletters.

✔ **Coupons or gift certificates:** Special offers like these may prompt your former clients to give you another try.

✔ **Thank-you notes:** Right after the client heads for other pastures, send her a thank-you note for doing business with you. She'll remember you for it.

If you don't like your client

Sometimes deciding to cut a client loose isn't so easy — you may be burned out on a client or you just don't click with her. If any of the items on the following list are true, it may be time to let go:

- ✔ The client has become increasingly noncompliant, refusing to stick to the plan you've agreed on.

- ✔ You find yourself ending workouts early, or you no longer have the passion to make the workouts as challenging as possible.

- ✔ The client has started to complain a lot (or a lot more than usual).

- ✔ You don't look forward to seeing the client.

Sound mean? Well, think of it this way: In order to give all your clients your best efforts, you need to love what you do. If you start feeling burned out because you're hanging on to a client who's not appropriate for you, everyone suffers.

Letting a client go requires an abundance of tact and grace. Try saying something like, "I sense that you're not getting as much as you can from our training sessions. I really think that Trainer X can offer you more than I can, and you'd enjoy working with him more." This puts the blame on your shoulders rather than the client's — you can't meet her needs — and eases the blow.

Part III
Putting the Personal into Personal Training

The 5th Wave   By Rich Tennant

"This readout shows your heart rate, blood pressure, bone density, skin hydration, plaque buildup, liver function, and expected lifetime."

In this part . . .

You're ready to meet your first client. Yipes! What to wear, what to do, what to say? No worries — we talk all about this in Chapter 10.

Next, Chapter 11 describes the fitness assessment, where you prepare the client for his first session and take baseline measurements like resting heart rate and range of motion.

And finally, starting with Chapter 12, we get to the good stuff — the actual training of clients! It's time to figure out how to plan your client's program, such as determining which exercises to prescribe, how intense they should be, and what order the client should do them in. We also tell you how to conduct the client's first session and how to advance your client when the time comes.

Chapter 10

Getting to Know You: Performing Initial Consultations

In This Chapter

▶ Honing your phone skills

▶ Meeting face-to-face for the first time

▶ Performing the consultation

▶ Wrapping it up

*H*ave you ever walked into a restaurant, sat down, and had a waitperson plop a plate in front of you without first asking what you wanted from the menu? We hope not! Waitpeople and personal trainers have similar jobs in that they have to find out what the customer wants and needs before they can help her.

How do you find out what a client needs (without stalking her)? Simple — you ask! Typically, in what's called an *initial consultation,* you sit down with the client before she hires you and talk to her about her needs, her goals, and her lifestyle. The information that you collect will enable you to help her safely, efficiently, and effectively.

But before you sit down with a prospective client to find out about her needs, she'll most likely call to find out about you and your services. We call this an *inquiry call* — your prospective client is calling to find out if you and your services are appropriate for her needs. Think of this as a job interview. If she likes what she hears, *then* she'll come in for an initial consultation, where you'll find out about how you can help her and sign her on as a new client.

In this chapter, we give you the scoop on how to sharpen your phone skills, sell your services (and yourself), and perform an initial consultation that will have the potential client signing on the dotted line.

Hello, My Name Is . . .

Before you meet with a potential client, you have to sell to him on the phone. Not sell to him in the sense of saying, "Hey, you can sign on with me for the low, low price of $49.99 per session, and you get a free set of Ginsu knives!" But sell to him in the sense that you want to educate him about your services enough to make him want to go to the next step — sitting down face-to-face for an initial consult.

"No sweat," you think. "Any bozo can talk on the phone!" Well, yes, picking up the receiver and issuing sounds into the mouthpiece is pretty easy. But convincing the person on the other end, within the span of one phone call, that you offer unparalleled service that will give him the results he's expecting — that's the hard part. And that's also why you don't want to try to close the sale over the phone. On an inquiry call, your objectives are:

✔ To develop rapport with your potential client

✔ To *qualify* your potential client (that is, to determine whether this person will be a good client for you — and whether he can afford you)

✔ To schedule an initial consultation with your potential client

TIP

Polishing your phone etiquette

Imagine this. You're home, it's 7 p.m., you have a load of laundry in, dinner's cooking on the stove, you're elbow-deep in dish suds, your dog is barking to go out — and the phone rings with a potential client inquiring about your services. What do you do?

Do you:

A. Yell "No hablo Inglés!" and hang up.

B. Pretend you're the babysitter and take a message.

C. Breathlessly tick off the many reasons that you're the best personal trainer in the Northern Hemisphere — while letting out the dog and removing your burned dinner from the stove.

D. Politely let her know that you're interested in talking with her, but you'd like to do so at a time that is mutually convenient for both you and her.

Sure, it seems funny now, but this can (and probably will) happen! Like it or not, being a personal trainer means your hours of availability are other people's nonworking hours — that is, anytime between 5 a.m. and 10 a.m. and after 4 p.m. This means that you may have to be available at unusual times of the day — possibly Saturdays and Sundays as well.

Oh, and in case you're wondering, the correct answer is D.

Figuring out what you're going to say

In order to know what you want to say, having a phone script helps. A *phone script* is a prepared dialogue, similar to those used by long-distance services when they beg you to switch providers. The phone script is a series of well-thought-out statements about your services that answer commonly asked questions. The script guides the conversation toward the goal of scheduling an initial consultation.

A phone script is more than a piece of paper from which you recite lines — it's your mantra. And how effective it is depends on how well you know it and how comfortable you are with your dialogue.

Start by grabbing a piece of paper and a pen or sitting down at your computer. Write out what you would say if someone asked you to describe who you are and what you do.

If you've created a marketing plan (see Chapter 8), refer to it. You want to include in a phone script all the items from your marketing plan that differentiate you from your competitors.

Some common questions prospective clients ask are:

- ✔ What type of services do you offer?
- ✔ How can you help me?
- ✔ How long have you been in business?
- ✔ Are you certified?
- ✔ Are you insured?
- ✔ How much are your services?
- ✔ Do you travel?
- ✔ Do you offer group discounts?
- ✔ Do you have references?
- ✔ What's your background?

Write out the answers to these questions — they'll be part of your phone script — and practice, practice, practice. When you're doing this, try to paint pictures with words for your caller. You want the caller to connect to your message.

When you're writing your script (and talking on the phone), avoid using weak phrases like "I think" or "I feel." No need to replace these words; just eliminate them from your vocabulary and your message will be much stronger. Convey confidence and success in your vocal tone, and be concise and definitive in your answers. Strong answers lead to strong sales!

Writing out an example phone call will pin down the right words that communicate your message clearly. Having a script like this in front of you during an inquiry call will also keep you on track and the conversation moving in the right direction — that is, toward an initial consultation. Here's an example script to get you started:

> **Crissy:** Hi, this is Crissy.
>
> **Jack:** Hi, my name's Jack. I'm looking for a personal trainer.
>
> **Crissy:** I'm a certified personal trainer. How can I help you today, Jack?
>
> **Jack:** I need to lose weight and bring my blood pressure down, or else my doctor is going to put me on medication, and I don't want that.
>
> **Crissy:** I totally understand. Before we go any farther, I need to ask a couple of questions to help me determine if I'm the right trainer for you. Is that okay?
>
> **Jack:** Sure.
>
> **Crissy:** Great! First, how did you hear about me, Jack?
>
> **Jack:** My friend Kenny trains with you. He said you were great.
>
> **Crissy:** Kenny's a great guy! Good to know — thank you! Have you ever worked out before?
>
> **Jack:** I've tried a few times, but I haven't been able to keep it going consistently.
>
> **Crissy:** Yes — it can be difficult! Do you currently have a gym membership?
>
> **Jack:** No, not right now.
>
> **Crissy:** Were you planning on working out at home or going to a gym?
>
> **Jack:** I was hoping you could help me learn to work out at home. I think the reason I haven't been successful is that it takes me too long to get to the gym.
>
> **Crissy:** No problem! I do travel to clients' homes. Where do you live?
>
> **Jack:** I live on the west side.
>
> **Crissy:** You're right within my driving range. That's perfect! Do you have any workout equipment at home?
>
> **Jack:** No, that was something else I was hoping you could help me with.

Crissy: You really don't need a lot — just a few key pieces such as a body ball and a couple of pairs of dumbbells, and you're good to go.

Jack: Great!

Crissy: Jack, have you gotten clearance from your doctor to start an exercise program?

Jack: Absolutely. I'm not quite sure exactly what you do or how much your services are. How does your pricing work?

Crissy: I show people how to exercise properly so they can achieve their fitness goals. I'm certified to prescribe exercise programs and work one-on-one with clients. This means that I work with each client individually. I can come to your home or meet you at your gym. When I work with new clients, the first step is an initial consultation. To create a safe workout for you, we need to meet before starting a working relationship. During this appointment, we'll discuss your medical history, your previous exercise experiences, your lifestyle, and, of course, your goals. This conversation helps me get a handle on what I need to do to help you achieve your goals safely, efficiently, and effectively. It also gives you a chance to get to know me. After all, you need to feel comfortable with me because we'll be working very closely together.

Jack: Is there a charge for the first appointment?

Crissy: No, it's free. After we cover all your information, I'll be able to determine the best way for us to work together so that you can achieve your goals. I'll also give you all my background information and cover how I typically work with clients — from my refund policy to how I like to handle cancellations and everything in between. Would you like to schedule an initial consultation with me?

Jack: Can you see me this Saturday at 10 a.m.?

Crissy: I certainly can! Can you come to my office for the first appointment? Then after that, I'll meet you at your house.

Jack: No problem.

Crissy: Great! Let me get your mailing address and phone number. I'll send you an appointment card and directions, and I'll call you the day before to confirm.

Jack: I look forward to meeting you!

You may think that reciting from a prepared script will kill any chance of having a true conversation with the prospective client, but the opposite is actually true. By practicing answers in advance, you'll develop a free-flowing dialogue with your caller, allowing the focus of the call to center around your prospect's needs. Not stumbling over your words or pausing to search for the right answer will give your prospect the sense that you're confident in what you do — and that enables her to be confident in you and your services.

Letting the client lead the way

If you find the caller reluctant to provide information, ask if she'd like to set up an appointment for a free consultation instead. If she does, great — you're on to Chapter 11. If she doesn't want an initial consultation just yet, give her an overview of your services and pricing, then offer to send more information in the mail. Sometimes letting the caller dictate the flow of the conversation is best — if she's interested, she'll be back in touch when she's ready.

Building credibility . . . fast!

Your potential client is calling you to feel you out. She has some interest in your services, but she needs to know more about you. She also needs to feel confident that you're credible and that you know your biceps from your triceps before she commits to hiring you.

You need to use this phone call to gain credibility and build a rapport with your caller — and you have to do it quickly, because if the caller doesn't feel that rapport with you right off the bat, she'll go elsewhere. She should view you as an expert and trust you enough to disclose vital information about herself without knowing you well. After all, would you feel comfortable telling some stranger about your lifestyle and health woes?

You can build credibility and rapport by:

- ✔ **Using your wonderful sense of humor.** Don't feel you have to stifle yourself — people appreciate humor, and it will put your potential client at ease. So go ahead, make a joke about the weather!

- ✔ **Not abusing your vast knowledge of industry terminology.** Using a slightly more advanced vocabulary shows your caller you know what you're talking about. But if a word is too technical for your caller, don't be afraid to define it in layperson's terms.

- ✔ **Using compelling quotes and facts from recent studies relevant to your callers' inquiry.** Foe example, "Mrs. Smith, did you know that strength training increases metabolic rate by 40 percent for up to four hours after a workout session? That means you burn more calories, even when you aren't exercising!"

- ✔ **Mentioning other respected experts (either by name or field) in your area whom you work with.** For example, "Yes, Mrs. Smith, I'm very familiar with tennis elbow. Dr. D'Angelo refers clients to us often and has taught me how to properly work around common tendonitis."

- ✔ **Using descriptive words that compare and contrast.** For example, "Personal training is like having a tutor, where it's one-on-one, unlike an aerobics class, where one instructor watches many participants." This strategy gives your caller something tangible to associate your services with.

- ✔ **Sharing your firsthand experience.** Your caller wants to hear personal stories to let her know that you understand where she's coming from.

Presenting your services

It would be nice if a potential client said, "I like the sound of your voice. I don't care what you do or how much you cost. Sign me up!" But in real life, no matter how well your phone conversation goes, the question of price and services will come up.

Instead of offering a blow-by-blow breakdown of your service plans and pricing, give an *overview* of what you do, with a range of prices for the different plans. This overview gives the caller an idea of whether she can afford you. Also, by not giving the entire sales spiel over the phone, you don't pressure the caller into feeling that she has to decide that second.

Your services are intangible and the caller can't fairly evaluate them until she meets you in person. Stress the importance of meeting your caller for a full, *free* consultation so you can best assess how to help her. Explain that you'll be able to provide her with pricing and packaging that will be most effective for her when you fully know her needs.

Qualifying a potential client

Sometimes a potential client just isn't a good fit for your business. Maybe she can't afford you, she lives too far away, or she wants something you can't offer. As hungry as you may be for business, you need to ask *qualifying questions* (questions that let you know whether the client is right for you) before scheduling an initial consultation. Qualifying your caller beforehand saves you time and energy — after all, you don't want to take the time to do a free initial consultation with a prospective client only to find out that she wants a type of training that you don't offer or she can't afford your rates.

Some qualifying questions you can ask are:

- ✔ **Where do you live?** (Is she within driving distance for you?)

- ✔ **What type of training are you looking for?** (Is it something you can provide?)

- ✔ **My rates range from X to Y. Does that work for you?** (Can she afford you?)

Knowing what to say before you hang up

You've been through your entire script, discovered what your caller is looking for, found out how she heard about you, and discussed your services and how you can help her. Now what?

Don't say adieu yet! You need to schedule an initial consultation with the caller, even if she's itching to get started right away.

Using the notes you took during the conversation, summarize the key points and tell the caller that the next step is scheduling a free initial consultation. If the caller asks to skip this step and start working out with you immediately, explain that you must meet before engaging in any work together, because, if you aren't fully informed, you can hurt her as easily as help her. Tell her that you need to get pertinent information about her medical history, lifestyle, needs, and goals, as well as cover administrative details such as your pricing/ packaging structure, refund policy, cancellation policy, and liability waiver.

If the caller isn't ready to go the next step with you, she'll let you know. Ask if she'd like you to send literature that she can check out on her own time. If you aren't able to schedule an initial consultation, make a note in your to-do list to follow up with the caller in a week or so.

Getting to Know You: Preparing to Meet for the First Time

Remember your first day of school — yes, we're asking you to remember *way* back. The night before, you had books packed in your school bag along with all the pertinent accessories (pencils, an eraser, a zillion highlighters), clothes laid out neatly, lunch waiting downstairs in the fridge — all in anticipation of meeting your new classmates and teachers for the first time. You wanted to make sure that you made a good impression and that everyone liked you.

That's just what you need to do before meeting a potential client for the first time. Taking a little time beforehand to make sure you have your ducks in a row will give you the extra boost of confidence of knowing that you're well prepared for anything that may happen.

Don't skip the initial consultation! Melyssa has known of trainers who skip this step, eager to show their clients how great they are, and it has come back to haunt them. Either the client gets injured because the trainer wasn't aware of previous injuries, or the client heads for the door early on because the trainer wasn't clear about what the client needed and expected from him.

The time, energy, and effort you devote up front to learning everything you can about your client will benefit you in the long run. The more you know about the client, the better you'll be able to help him and the more effective you'll be — which means your client will get the results he wants.

Making a good first impression

Good or bad, the first impression is the one that lasts. Either you're going to wow the prospective client with your amazing professionalism and knowledge, or you're going to completely underwhelm her with your lack thereof.

Do not despair, grasshopper! Whether this consultation is your 1st or your 50th, we have time-tested tips that are sure to leave your new client all aglow afterward. These tips are simple and easy, with no studying involved.

Practice punctuality

Always be on time. Better yet, plan to be ten minutes early, even if you risk sitting in your car in front of the prospective client's house for nine of those ten minutes. Besides, you can do a lot during those nine minutes. You can:

- Review the notes from your earlier phone conversation with the prospect.
- Make sure you have your paperwork in order.
- Mentally rehearse your presentation.

Planning to arrive early allows time for the unexpected — a traffic jam or a lost client form — to happen without causing you to be late. Nothing is worse than greeting a potential client with, "Hi! Sorry I'm late! The funniest thing happened to me on the way over here. . . ."

In her early days of personal training, Melyssa traveled between various gyms and clients' houses. One day, while coming off an interstate ramp on her way to an initial consultation, a uniformed police officer stepped out of the bushes and flagged her over. With no cellphone to call her consult, Melyssa arrived 40 minutes late. Thankfully, the potential client was understanding and knew of the speed trap that caught Melyssa. She did become a client, and Melyssa gave her a free session to make up for her lateness. Melyssa was lucky — a mistake like that could have easily cost her a client!

Dress for success

Granted, personal training lends itself to uniforms consisting of Lycra and cotton, but you should still strive to look professional. Is it possible to look professional in sweats? Of course! Whether you're working solo or planning to have a whole fleet of trainers, picking the right attire can set the tone for how potential clients perceive you.

Keep these tips in mind when choosing your personal training uniform:

✔ **Choose fabrics that have some stretch to them.** This will allow the garment to retain its shape in an active environment. (No saggy knees and baggy butts!)

✔ **Opt for collared polo shirts.** You can easily have them embroidered with your logo, and the collar helps to give a more business-oriented look than a T-shirt does.

✔ **Make sure your clothes fit well.** You want your clothing to accentuate your physique, but you also don't want to intimidate or offend anyone with a uniform that looks more like it belongs on Britney Spears than on a professional trainer.

✔ **Make sure you don't have any rips or stains (like sweat) on your clothes or shoes.** Save your old workout clothes for mowing the lawn or cleaning the house. Just as you wouldn't wear torn or stained clothes if you worked in an office, you shouldn't wear them when you meet with clients. *Remember:* If you work in a gym, and you're working out in your off-hours, clients may still see you. Look your best *whenever* you're around potential clients, even if you're not officially on the clock.

The trainer in Figure 10-1 is dressed professionally and appropriately when she arrives at her client's home.

Be enthusiastic

Smile, smile, and smile some more! Your smile is your best asset, and is the best way to put your consult at ease. Naturally, he's going to be nervous about meeting a new person (and sharing his personal health information), but your enthusiasm will help him be enthusiastic as well.

Smiling can help *you,* too! If you're feeling nervous about performing your initial consultation, just smile, crack a joke, make fun of yourself, throw some levity into your conversation. Sometimes you have to fake it 'til you make it.

Being prepared

The Boy Scouts had it right when they picked their motto: "Be prepared." Being prepared can save you headaches and embarrassment while you're presenting your services to a potential client. The more organized you are, the more smoothly the whole consultation will go. Knowing you have everything in place ahead of time lets you concentrate solely on your consult.

Figure 10-1:
A polished appearance makes for a professional presentation.

Before setting out for the initial consultation, you may want to put together a *consult packet* to give to your prospective client. This packet will contain information about you and your services that the prospect can keep after the consultation is over. Your packet can include copies of your:

- Company overview or personal bio
- Résumé
- Training philosophy
- Personal training certifications
- Current CPR certification
- Letters of recommendation from other clientele
- Liability insurance policy
- Media appearances
- Client policies

Remember when you put reports in plastic folders to score brownie points with your high-school teacher? You can do the same with your consult packet. Put the copies in a folder that has a slot for your business card, or you can take the copies to an office-supply store and have them spiral-bound with a clear cover. Professional presentations help establish your credibility.

In addition to your consult packet, before leaving for the consultation, make sure you have the following items in your attaché (yes, you should carry a briefcase or similar bag, not a duffel bag like the one you throw your gym clothes in):

✔ Forms and information on your prices and policies (such as your liability policy, your cancellation policy, and your refund policy), as well as information on what to expect during the client's first training session

✔ Forms you use to record information on your prospective client, such as his medical history and his exercise history

✔ Clipboard

✔ Notepaper

✔ Pens and pencils

✔ Business cards

Check out our sample forms to get started with at www.wiley.com/go/personaltrainer!

Arrange your paperwork in a clipboard in the order in which you'll be referring to it. Typically, after you have your consult fill out the initial consultation sheet, you then fill out the rest of the forms for him, using the forms as a guide for obtaining the correct information. The order of your paperwork (and your consultation) should be:

1. Initial consultation sheet

2. Medical history form

3. Typical day sheet

4. Exercise history sheet

5. Packages and pricing sheet

6. Client agreement form

7. Waiver of liability

8. Cancellation policy

9. Refund policy

10. What to Expect During Your First Session sheet

Note: You can find all these forms at www.wiley.com/go/personaltrainer.

Grab ahold of one of your friends, sit down with him, and using your initial consultation forms as your guide, have him role-play with you — no, we don't mean playing Dungeons & Dragons. For instance, your friend can play the part of a new client who has never worked out before and is very timid about stepping foot in the gym. Or your friend can pretend he's a busy CEO who travels a lot and needs a travel workout program. Check your certification book for other practice scenarios. (All certification bodies offer a certification book; if you've lost or sold yours and need another, you can order and pay for it through your certifying body.)

No matter how good you are, you need to put aside your ego during an initial consultation. You're trying to find out about your prospective client, which means asking insightful questions and being a good listener. The last thing you want to do is yap on about the wonderfulness that is you. If your potential client wants to hear more about your background, give him a brief overview, but then gently tell him that you need to know important information about *him* that will help you to be a better trainer for him.

Performing the Consultation

You've packed your briefcase, gotten to your prospective client's house ten minutes early (sans speeding ticket), and are about to ring the bell dressed in full personal training garb. Take a deep breath, relax, and go for it! You've done most of the hard work already. Now is the time to relax and enjoy finding out all about your client-to-be.

Setting the tone

Say you meet someone at a party, and before you can even say, "So, come here often?" he launches into an interrogation about your health problems and sleeping habits. Makes you want to bolt for the door, right? That's why setting the tone with a potential client is so important.

Upon greeting your consult, shake hands and make small talk about the weather or driving conditions to break the ice. Settle yourself in a position where you can look him directly in the eyes while you're speaking. You want to be close enough that you can share your clipboard with him when you're doing your packaging presentation at the end, but not so close that you invade his personal space.

Start out by placing the clipboard in his hands with your initial consult sheet on top. This form has blank spaces for his contact information, date of birth, current physician, and how he heard about you, plus a place for him to list his goals. Tell him to fill out the entire sheet, and after he's done you'll take the clipboard from him and do the other sheets.

While he's filling out the form, keep quiet unless he has questions. Being silent shows that you respect him, and it allows you a chance to gather your thoughts before proceeding to the next step.

Reviewing the client's medical history

After your prospective client has finished filling out the initial consultation form, take the clipboard from him and flip to the next page — the medical history sheet. The medical history sheet contains important medical information that will determine how you'll train the client and note how exercise will affect him.

Medications

Some medications affect heart rate or respiration rate, or can make a person dizzy from exertion, among other side effects. That's why you need to know the type of medications your potential client is taking.

If you don't know what a medication does, or what the side effects are, call your local pharmacist or doctor after you leave the client. You can also purchase the *Physicians' Desk Reference* (PDR) to keep in your reference library, or check out the PDR's consumer site to look up drug interactions online at www.pdrhealth.com/drug_info/index.html.

Previous surgeries

You want to know whether your client has been through surgery — especially if the surgery involved a joint, muscle, tendon, or cartilage. If you're unsure of the training parameters for a client who has had a surgery involving *soft tissue* (muscle, ligament, or tendon), ask for his surgeon's name and number.

Don't hesitate to call the surgeon's office and ask for training parameters — it will show your prospective client that you care about him enough to make sure you have the right information to work with him. And, as a bonus, you may also develop a new source of referrals from the surgeon.

Muscle aches, strains, and pulls

When asking your potential client about any aches, strains, or muscle pulls he experiences frequently, pause and give him a chance to think about it. If he says he doesn't have any, ask about each joint specifically (each joint is listed on the medical history form).

Often, in doing consultations, Melyssa's prospective clients said they didn't have any aches, strains, or pulls. Then, as she read through each joint, it would trigger their memories and they would remember waking up with a stiff back or having knee pain walking down stairs.

Be sure to make a note of which side the prospective client is experiencing pain or soreness on and how frequently he experiences it. Use this part of your consultation to flag any movements that may cause problems for him during the actual workout (plus write down any corrective exercises or stretches you may want to prescribe).

Finding out about a day in the life of your potential client

You need to know about your potential client's daily lifestyle, from his sleeping habits to his stress levels. Using the typical day sheet, ask the consult to verbally take you through a day in his life. Have him start from the time he wakes up, and have him explain in detail everything he does until the time he goes to bed.

Questions that are most important to you as a trainer are the following:

- Is he still tired when he wakes? Or does he feel refreshed and ready to start the day?

- Does he eat breakfast on a regular basis? If so, what does he eat?

- Does he feel that he performs well throughout the day? Or does he feel that his energy levels could be better?

- Does he eat lunch on a regular basis? If yes, what does he eat?

- Is he feeling stressed throughout the day?

- How many hours of sleep does he average per night?

- What kind of job does he have? Is it active, or is he sitting in a chair all day?

- Does he snack? If yes, what types of foods does he snack on?

These types of questions will help you determine exactly where your client is in terms of his lifestyle. Knowing how busy your consult is and whether he's performing well throughout the day will help you determine how to get him started making healthy lifestyle changes that are in alignment with his goals.

Identifying your client's goals

After you've completed the typical day sheet with your consult, revisit the first page your consult filled out — the initial consultation sheet. On it, your consult has listed his goals. If something about his goals is unclear, ask specific questions to get to the root of what he wants. When you feel like you understand his goals, repeat in your own words what you feel his goals are. Doing this will ensure that you've understood what your potential client is saying. If he corrects you, make a note of what he says and talk about it with him until you're sure you're on the same page.

Discussing your client's exercise history

After you've identified your prospective client's goals, move on to the exercise history sheet. This will allow you to find out what your prospect's experience has been with exercise, what he liked or didn't like about it, and other information that will help you determine his exercise prescription should he become one of your clients.

Before You Say Goodbye

You now know everything there is to know about your consult, down to what brand of toothpaste she uses (okay, maybe not that). Before you head for the door (or show your prospective client out), summarize everything you've discussed with your prospect and show her how you can help her with your services.

Outlining solutions that will meet your prospect's goals

Propose a plan to get the potential client to her goals, and using her goals as your objectives, outline how you intend to help her achieve them. (This is where all that stuff you studied for in your certification comes in handy!) For example, you might say:

> Mrs. Smith, I believe that if we start you working out twice a week, we can steadily progress to your goal of training three times a week in four to six weeks. I wouldn't want to start you working out three times a week immediately, because you haven't exercised consistently before and your body needs time to become conditioned.

Knowing when to back off: Letting the client think about it

When you go car shopping, you don't open your wallet for the first car you look at — you tell the salesperson you'll think about it, then head out to look at other options. In the same way, some prospective clients would rather think about all the information you've gone over with them before signing on the dotted line. If your client seems unsure or combative, give her the space she needs to make up her mind.

Remember: Your time is limited and precious — you want clients who are champing at the bit to get in shape, not ones whose arms you have to twist. Leave your consult packet with the potential client to peruse on her own time, and let her know that you'll follow up in a few days to answer any questions she may have.

If she isn't interested, don't push the issue. Personal training is a service that clients will buy when they're good and ready. By being gracious and professional and respecting the potential client's space, you'll create a good relationship with her — and when she's ready, you'll probably be the first one she calls.

Your plan isn't set in stone, because you can't predict how the client will respond to a program until she tries it. You can tell her, "I don't know you or your body yet, but if you respond well to your fitness assessment, this is what I envision for you. . . ." Then lay out the plan.

Explaining your prospect's options

After you propose your solution, hand the prospective client your pricing and packaging sheet. Point to the service plan that will best suit her needs, and explain how your services work — from the very first session that you will have with her to the last.

Sample forms are available at www.wiley.com/go/personaltrainer.

Requiring a physician's release

Occasionally, you'll run into a prospective client for whom you'll want to get permission from her doctor before she starts working with you. This *physician's release* is important both for her safety and yours. Examples of such clients include those with elevated blood pressure or an erratic heart rate, as well as anyone who has experienced dizziness or sharp chest pain within the past 30 days.

If your prospective client has any of these symptoms, gently let her know that, as much as you'd like to work with her, you'll need to have her doctor provide her with a release before you get started together. Leave her with a physician's release form to take to her doctor.

Setting the stage for the first appointment

If all has gone well, the next step is to set up your first appointment with the client. Explain that the first session is a fitness assessment, where you'll be measuring your client's baseline fitness levels.

After you've set the appointment, you'll need to collect payment based on your payment policy. Typically, if she has set an appointment in your book, she's reserving your time, so you need to collect your fee for at least that session up front. *Remember:* You're not charging her for the initial consultation (which you're just wrapping up); you're charging her for the first appointment.

After you've set up your first appointment and collected your fee, make sure before you leave that you have your new client sign your:

- ✔ Client agreement form
- ✔ Waiver of liability
- ✔ Cancellation policy
- ✔ Refund policy

Before the client signs each one, briefly explain the purpose of each policy and answer any questions she may have. Have her sign two copies — one for your records and one for hers.

You're almost done! The last step is to explain to your new client what happens next. Clarify what she should wear to the first session, whether she needs to eat beforehand, and whether she needs to purchase anything. This helps to alleviate anxiety the new client may have before starting with you. It also ensures a great first session — one that will leave a positive impression in your client's mind. Let her know that everything you covered is also in her consult packet on the What to Expect During Your First Session sheet.

Chapter 11

The First Session: Performing the Fitness Assessment

*B*efore you make like Michelangelo and mold your client a peak physique, you need to take a closer look at the raw materials you have to work with. That's where the client assessment comes in. The client assessment is where you record baseline measurements and safe working ranges for the client's starting sessions. The baseline measurements provide an excellent motivational tool to use when showing your client his progress, and the safe working ranges ensure that your client doesn't try to do too much.

You can measure baseline fitness levels in many different ways, and some methods are easier than others. Some require expensive equipment that's not all that portable, while others call for a PhD in exercise physiology to interpret the results. In this chapter, we cover the most practical assessment methods — ones that you can administer safely and effectively with little equipment (and without a PhD).

Prepping the Client

When your client arrives for her appointment, before you jump into the assessment, take a few minutes to sit down with her and show her your fitness assessment forms. Thoroughly explain each section of the form, detailing what the client will be doing in this initial session, what you're looking for, and how the numbers are relevant to her workout. Having your client sit for a few minutes before getting started should help to lower her heart rate and blood pressure, as well as calm any jittery nerves before she starts her fitness assessment.

Introducing the tools of your trade

After you've fully explained how the session is going to work, it's time to break out all the fun toys that you'll be using with your client!

You don't have to own the most expensive gadgets to be a good trainer! Start with the bare essentials, and as you build profits you can upgrade your equipment if you want.

When purchasing equipment, consider factors such as warranties, portability, durability, and cost. Ask other professionals in your area what they recommend — you don't need to reinvent the wheel.

The following list includes some low-budget tools that can increase your professionalism and profitability. Explain what each of the following tools does and when and where you'll be using it:

- ✔ **Tape measure:** You won't believe how handy a tape measure is. You can measure girth, range of motion, flexibility, distance — and the stacks of money you'll earn as a personal trainer. Inexpensive and portable, tape measures with a *lanyard* (a string so you can hang it around your neck) and a self-retracting wheel will work best for you. (You don't want to spend all your time rolling and unrolling it!) You can find them for as little $2 or $3 in the arts-and-crafts departments of major discount stores, or you can check your local craft, sewing, or hobby store.

- ✔ **Body-fat calipers:** Calipers range in price from $20 to $450, but unless you have spare buckets of loot, your best bet is to stick with a durable, nondigital one that can withstand the rigors of everyday use. We recommend The Slim Guide, a lightweight but heavy-duty caliper that costs about $20. You can order it from BodyTrends Health & Fitness (Web: www.bodytrends.com, phone: 800-549-1667).

- ✔ **Body-weight scale:** In addition to having a durable set of calipers, you'll need a scale to complete your tool set for measuring body fat and body weight. When purchasing a scale, you need to ask yourself these questions:

  - How portable is the scale?

  - Is it thin and flat or big and bulky?

  - Is it solar powered with battery backup, or just one or the other?

  - What's the maximum poundage it can measure (and will I someday take clients who weigh more than that)?

Scales can range from $30 to $200, with the more expensive models being marketed to the medical community. We highly recommend scales made by Tanita, which are available online at www.tanita.com and at your local home store.

✔ **Heart-rate monitors:** Taking a heart rate manually can be tedious and time consuming, especially if you're trying to get an active heart rate! Buying a heart-rate monitor to use with your clients is a good investment — the reading you get from it is immediate and accurate. Prices range from $50 to $350. Check out your local fitness-equipment stores for pricing, or do an online search for "heart-rate monitor." The most popular manufacturer is Polar, and you can check out their products at www.polarusa.com or call them at 800-227-1314.

✔ **Blood-pressure cuffs and stethoscopes:** With prices ranging from $30 to $300 for a stethoscope and $20 to $80 for a blood-pressure cuff, you have a lot of options. Your best bet is to call a medical-supply company like Quick Medical (Web: www.quickmedical.com, phone: 888-345-4858), and talk with one of the customer-service personnel. Explain to them what you want, and they can offer you a complete education on what product is best suited for you and your needs.

While you're explaining the tools, go ahead and put your heart-rate monitor on your client. Have her sit down to relax, because your first step in the fitness assessment will be to get her resting heart rate and you want her calm and relaxed for that reading.

Setting the bar low

While your client rests for his heart-rate reading, let him know that the assessment isn't meant to test the limits of his physical ability. You're not looking for him to Hulk-out and pop veins in his forehead as he juggles dumbbells. You want to discover what he can do *comfortably*.

Playing down the assessment is critical because many clients will try to impress you with how much they can do, sometimes going above and beyond their safe working limits. If your client isn't conditioned properly — and because he's hiring you, you can probably assume that he's not — he can hurt himself by straining unnecessarily.

A client who pushes himself too hard puts you at risk as well. If you interpret his abilities as being greater than what they actually are, you may set his program at an elevated level, possibly hurting him and almost certainly discouraging him with an initial program that's too difficult. Let him know that the only way you can help him is if he portrays his current capabilities accurately — you're not expecting him to perform like an elite athlete.

Using the perceived-rate-of-exertion scale

A good way to check in with your client to see how he's feeling is to ask how hard he feels like he's working. This method of letting your client evaluate his own working intensity is called *perceived rate of exertion*. (Ring a bell? This is one of the basic training principles taught in most certification courses.) Pair this technique with a heart-rate monitor, and you have a great method for showing your client how to evaluate workout intensity.

Teaching your client up front — at the initial fitness assessment — about perceived rate of exertion will help you later on, because he'll be able to provide accurate feedback as to how hard he *thinks* he's working. This information will, in turn, let you know whether you're on track with your programming. You can also set intensity levels for him by using the same method when he's not with you (for instance, "When you're performing your circuit sets, you should be working around a level 6").

You may want to prepare something like the chart in Table 11-1 that you can use with each new client.

Table 11-1		The Perceived-Rate-of-Exertion Scale	
Cardio-respiratory Conditioning Level	*Perceived Exertion Rating Level*	*Workout Intensity*	*Similar to . . .*
No Effort	0	Not exercising	Sitting down and relaxing
Very little effort	1	Very easy	Standing up
Warm-up or recovery effort	2	Somewhat easy	Walking
Warm-up or recovery effort	3	Moderate	Walking moderately
Aerobic effort	4	Somewhat hard	Walking uphill moderately
Aerobic effort	5	Moderately hard	Jogging slowly
Aerobic effort	6	Hard	Jogging fast
Anaerobic effort	7	Hard	Running moderately
Anaerobic effort	8	Very hard	Running
Anaerobic effort	9	Very, very hard	Sprinting
Anaerobic effort	10	Maximal	Sprinting maximally

Recording Baseline Measurements

All-righty then! You have your client relaxed and ready to begin, your assessment tools are laid out and ready to be put into action, your pencil is sharpened, and your clipboard is at the ready. What are you waiting for? Let's get started!

Taking your client's resting heart rate

You can use either one of two easy methods for measuring heart rate — the palpation method or the heart-rate-monitor method. We cover each of these in the following sections.

Palpation method

Palpation is the most common method for taking heart rate. It's also the least expensive — all you need are your index and middle fingers and a stopwatch. Here's how you do it:

1. **Using the tips of your index and middle fingers, locate the brachial, carotid, or radial artery.**

   Avoid using your thumb, because it has its own pulse and may confuse your count.

   Keep in mind that most people, especially during the first session, are uncomfortable with the trainer putting his hands on their neck, because the neck is a very vulnerable area.

2. **Using your stopwatch or the second hand on your watch, keep time while counting the beats for a full minute.**

   If you start your stopwatch simultaneously with a beat, count that beat as 0. If your stopwatch or secondhand is already running, count the first beat you start your time measure on as 1.

When measuring heart rate, make sure your client is calm and still (see Figure 11-1), and remember that the *white-coat effect* (elevated heart rate due to nervousness from being around an analyst) may skew the results.

Heart-rate-monitor method

Heart-rate monitoring is easy and painless — the equipment does all the work for you! A monitor is always on, giving you continuous feedback. To use a chest-strap monitor, read the instructions in the following section and see Figure 11-2.

1. **Attach the transmitter to the elastic strap.**

2. **Moisten the two grooved electrodes.**

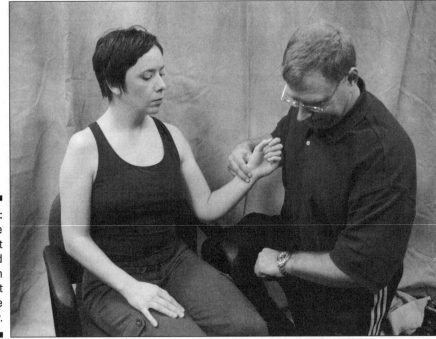

Figure 11-1:
Be sure
your client
is calm and
still when
taking heart
rate
manually.

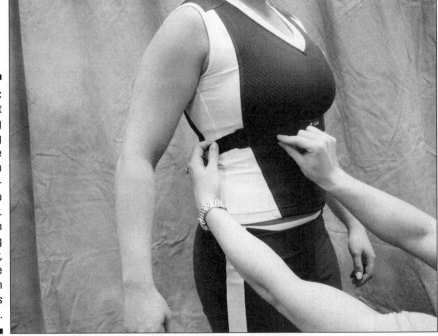

Figure 11-2:
Client
getting
resting
heart rate
taken with
a chest-
strap
monitor.
When
attaching
the monitor,
make sure
to moisten
the contacts
well.

3. Adjust the strap length to fit snugly and comfortably.

4. Secure the strap around your client's chest, just below the chest muscles at the *zyphoid process* (the area where the two halves of your rib cage meet at the bottom of your breastbone), and buckle it.

5. Make sure the area under the electrodes are wet as well, or that the transmitter has snug contact with the wet fabric/skin.

6. Check the specific manufacturer's directions on the interaction of the watch (receiver) and the chest strap (transmitter).

Measuring your client's blood pressure

Measure blood pressure when your client is in a resting state. High blood pressure is denoted as a reading greater than 140 systolic and 90 diastolic (140/90). However, if your client's reading is above 120 systolic and 80 diastolic (120/80), you may want her to get a physician's clearance before working with her further.

Follow these tips to take your client's blood pressure:

1. Have your client sit upright in a chair that supports her back, with either her left or right arm exposed, palm facing up and supported at heart level.

2. Select the appropriate cuff size for your client.

   The large adult cuff size is for people whose arm circumference is 13 to 16½ inches (33 to 42 cm). The adult standard cuff size is for people whose arm circumference is 9½ to 12½ inches (24 to 32 cm).

3. Place the cuff on your client's arm so that the *air bladder* (the cuff that goes around your clients arm) is directly over the *brachial artery* (the large pulse point on the inside of the arm) and the edge of the cuff is 1 inch above the *antecubital space* (the crease where your arm bends on the inside of the elbow), as shown in Figure 11-3.

4. With your client's palm facing up, place the stethoscope directly over the antecubital space, as shown in Figure 11-4.

   Do not press so hard that the stethoscope indents the skin.

5. Position the *sphygmomanometer* (the dial on the cuff you use to measure blood pressure) so that the center of the dial is at eye level.

   Be sure that all tubing is free and not in contact with anything else.

6. When everything is in place, quickly inflate the air bladder to 160 mmHg.

7. **Upon maximum inflation, turn the air-release screw counterclockwise to release the pressure slowly, at a rate of 2 mmHg per second.**

8. **Mentally note the mmHg at which you hear the first *Korotkoff sound* (a heartbeat-like sound).**

   This is your systolic number.

9. **Mentally note the mmHg where the Korotkoff sounds disappear.**

   This is your diastolic number.

10. **Continue to observe the manometer to ensure the sounds stay disappeared.**

11. **When you've confirmed the absence of sound, rapidly release the pressure and remove the cuff.**

If you feel uncomfortable using these tools, buy an automatic blood-pressure cuff similar to the ones used in drugstores. Use it until you get more practice with the sphygmomanometer.

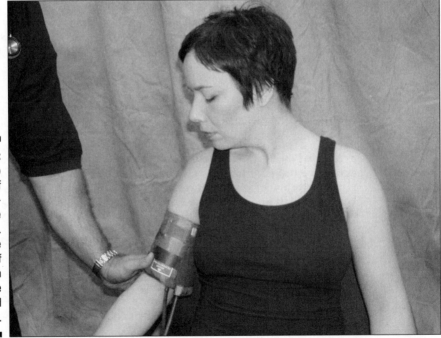

Figure 11-3:
Where to put the cuff for blood-pressure reading. Make sure the cuff ends 1 inch above the antecubital space.

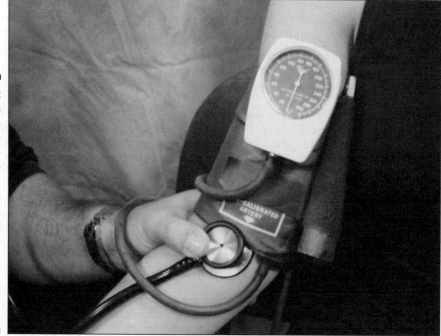

Figure 11-4:
Where to put the stethoscope for blood-pressure reading. Make sure to place the bell of the scope directly over the antecubital space.

Fit or fat?: Measuring body composition

Because body weight consists of muscle, fat, and fluids, having a client keep track of only her weight can be a very disheartening and misleading assessment tool for monitoring change. A client's body weight can fluctuate up to 6 pounds a day — and it's not very motivating if your client steps on the scale when she's at the high point of those 6 pounds! A more accurate way to measure your client's progress is to take an initial body-composition reading. Body composition can tell your client exactly how many pounds of fat versus lean mass she has on her frame. You can take body-composition measurements via the skinfold (caliper) method as well as the anthroprometric (tape) method.

Skinfold measurements

Body fat can be measured in several different ways:

- ✔ **Hydrostatic weighing:** In this method, the client is dunked in a tank and made to blow out all her air. Technicians measure the difference in the water volume displacement.

- ✔ **Bioelectrical impedance analysis:** In this method, a safe electrical signal is sent through your body via a machine, the machine measures the amount of time it takes for the signal to return to it. (Fat doesn't conduct the signal as fast as muscle does because there is less water in fat than there is in muscle.)

✔ **Infrared technology:** In this method, a fiber-optic gun is placed over the biceps and an infrared light is emitted, passing through subcutaneous fat and muscle, bouncing back to the gun).

The least expensive and most reasonably accurate method for use in the field is the *caliper method.* The calipers "pinch" the skin, indirectly measuring the thickness of subcutaneous fat tissue that lies underneath. When administered properly, skinfold testing can be highly correlated to the gold standard of body-composition measurement — hydrostatic weighing.

Several formulas for analyzing body fat exist, from three-site methods to nine-site methods. The more sites that you're able to read from, the more accurate a picture you're going to get. Check out `www.wiley.com/go/personaltrainer` for all the formulas and forms for body-fat analysis.

Follow these tips for skinfold testing:

✔ **Take all skinfold measurements on the right side of the body.**

✔ **Take all measurements pre-exercise, when the client's skin is dry and free of lotions or oils.** Exercise causes hydration changes in the skin that significantly affect skin thickness, therefore affecting the skinfold reading.

To measure your client's body fat:

1. **Carefully locate, measure, and mark your skinfold site with an erasable marker (see Figures 11-5 and 11-6).**

   After you become practiced at locating skinfold sites, you'll be able to "eyeball" the site, and you won't need to mark it!

   Depending on the method you use for measuring body fat, the number of locations and site locations themselves vary. Refer to your certification manual for the specifics on how to locate, measure, and mark each site based on the formula you will be using.

2. **Grasp the skinfold firmly between your thumb and forefinger, gently lifting the skin and subcutaneous fat up and away from the firm muscle underneath.**

   Make sure you have at least 1 cm between your grip and the area to be measured. Also be sure your grip is not too hard.

3. **Keeping the skinfold elevated, place the jaws of the calipers perpendicular to the line of the fold (see Figure 11-7).**

4. **Release the tension of the jaws and, after waiting 2 to 3 seconds, record the site to the nearest 0.5 mm.**

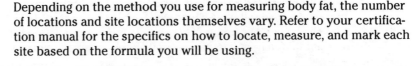

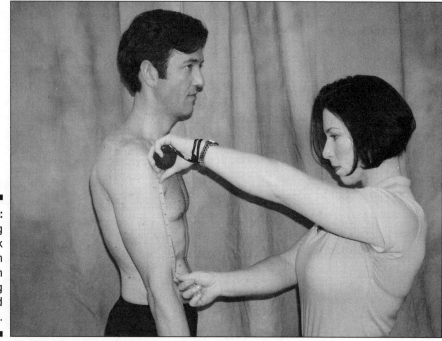

Figure 11-5:
Measuring
a landmark
site in
preparation
for taking
a skinfold
reading.

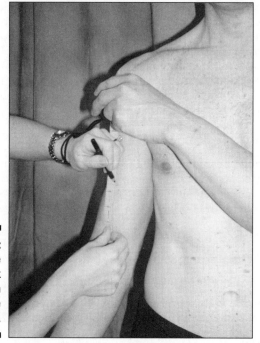

Figure 11-6:
Marking the
landmark
site with an
erasable
marker.

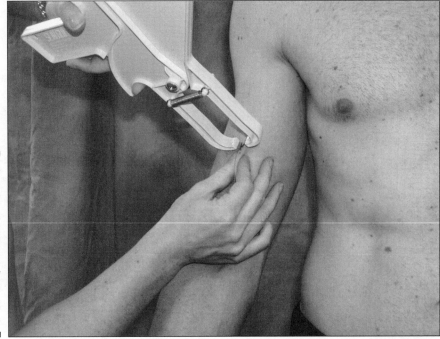

Figure 11-7:
Taking the skinfold reading. Pinch and lift the skinfold away from the underlying muscle.

Keep in mind that measuring body fat on everyone may not be a good idea. If you have a client who is seriously overfat, taking a body-fat measurement is just another slap in the face. Not only that but it's much more likely that you'll take an unreliable measurement due to the large size of the pinch and the inability to pull the skin away from muscle. Try a few random pinches on different areas of the body that may be thin enough to measure correctly so you can establish some sort of baseline. Or try to find a formula that may work with the pinches you can take on that person.

Girth measurements

In addition to measuring body composition with calipers, you can measure *anthroprometric* (body circumference) change with a nonelasticized tape measure. Providing both skinfold and anthroprometric measurements can give your client a total picture of her body's physical state. Here's how:

1. **Have your client stand in the correct anatomical position.**

   Your client should be standing so her arms are relaxed and at her sides.

2. **Have her relax the area to be measured — no flexing!**

3. **Making sure the tape is flat and in full contact with her body, pull the tape tight, but not so tight you indent her skin (see Figure 11-8).**

4. **Take the measurement where the tape meets itself.**

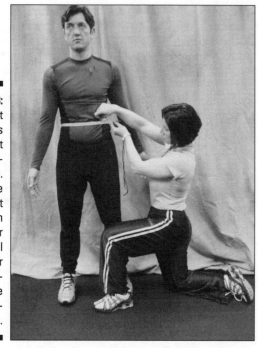

Figure 11-8:
Client having his waist measurement taken. Make sure your client stands in the proper anatomical position for circumference measurements.

Testing Your Client's Fitness

Imagine taking an English class and being tested on, say, how to dissect a frog or how to solve a quadratic equation. You would likely fail the test — and feel pretty rotten to boot.

In the same way, you have to make sure that the tests you give your client won't demotivate or even hurt her. For instance, you may have a 55-year-old female with weak knees whose only recent exercise has been changing the channel on her TV. Knowing that she's deconditioned and has some possible joint problems with her knees, would you administer a step test? Most likely not. How about a walk-run test? No again.

What you *can* do, however, is take what you've learned from the clinical aspects of testing and create your own individualized cardiovascular test just for your client. When you retest her, you'll need to re-create the test exactly as you did it the first time — but that's okay, because the whole purpose of testing with most of your clients is merely to show that they're improving and getting healthier.

Most clients won't know what VO$_2$ max is — and they won't really care. What they *will* care about, however, is how much easier it is for them to perform a five-minute march, how quickly their heart rate comes down, and how they now consider a certain exercise to be a perceived rate of exertion level 3, whereas the first time they did it they rated it a 6.

When testing your client, apply only the tests that are going to be the most useful and beneficial for you and your client — even if you have to create them yourself.

Run, don't walk: Testing cardiovascular endurance

A key component to any exercise prescription is aerobic conditioning. Most clients will be concerned about their heart health and overall cardiovascular endurance, and the tests in the following sections will show them where they stand (or walk, or run).

The walk-run test

The walk-run test is a great field test to measure a client's cardiovascular capacity. All you'll need is a stopwatch and a measured mile. Here's how to make it work:

1. **Mark off a 1-mile route.**

2. **Have your client warm up for three to five minutes prior to starting the course.**

   Your client can warm up by walking at a pace that is comfortable and easy to her.

3. **Instruct the client to finish the course as quickly as she can — walking, jogging, running, whatever she can do.**

4. **Give the client a countdown for her start, and start your stopwatch when she begins.**

5. **After the client finishes the course, either immediately take her pulse for 10 seconds, or use her heart-rate monitor to record her exercise heart rate.**

6. **One minute after she stops exercising, record the client's heart rate again.**

   This is her recovery heart rate.

You can also perform this test on a treadmill, or with a shorter distance if 1 mile is too long. Just follow the same testing procedures.

The step test

Another great field test, the step test can be done with an actual 12-inch platform step or with any step available — such as a stair in your client's home, an aerobic step, or an outside step (as long as the step is no higher than 12 inches). Here's how to do it:

1. **Explain to your client that she is going to be stepping "up, up, down, down" (up with one leg, up with the other, down with one leg, down with the other) at a pace a little faster than 1 second per step.**

2. **Have her step to a cadence of 96 beats per minute (or more slowly if necessary) for 3 minutes.**

   You can count cadence for her if you have a stopwatch by counting on the seconds: "up, up, down, down, up, up, down, down . . ."). You can also set a metronome so that you don't have to worry about counting at the right pace.

3. **When the client has stepped for 3 minutes, take her heart rate manually for 10 seconds or read her heart-rate monitor.**

   This is her exercise heart rate.

4. **One minute after she stops exercising, take her heart rate again.**

   This will be her recovery heart rate.

Stretch marks: Testing flexibility

A long muscle is a strong muscle — so testing flexibility is important in evaluating your client's overall fitness. Because hamstrings are the most commonly understretched muscle and have a direct impact on the health of the back, it's a good test to include in your fitness assessment.

The sit-and-reach test

For most starting clients, touching their toes is out of the question. Although fitness experts have recently debated the usefulness of the sit-and-reach test, it's an easy test to administer in the field. The only equipment you need is a nonelasticized tape measure and your client. Be sure to perform this test only after you've thoroughly warmed up your client (for example, after performing her cardiovascular test). Conducting the flexibility test after your client is warmed up ensures that she won't pull any muscles.

Follow these guidelines for performing a sit-and-reach test:

1. **Have your client sit on the floor with her legs extended in front of her.**

2. **Place the beginning of your tape measure at the tops of her toes.**

3. Hold the tape measure out in a straight line away from her body.

4. Instruct your client to slowly reach as far forward past her toes as she can, to just where it becomes uncomfortable.

5. Measure where her fingers touch the tape (see Figure 11-9).

The modified hamstring flexibility assessment

For certain clients, administering the sit-and-reach test may not be appropriate. For instance, if your client has back or hip issues, you may want to perform a modified hamstring flexibility assessment. Follow these guidelines:

1. Have your client lie flat on her back with both knees bent and feet flat on the floor.

2. Have her extend one leg until her leg is straight (or as straight as possible) and close to 90 degrees at the hip.

3. Visually determine how close the client's leg is to 90 degrees (see Figure 11-10).

4. Have her slowly return her leg to the starting position.

Figure 11-9: The sit-and-reach test can be performed anywhere.

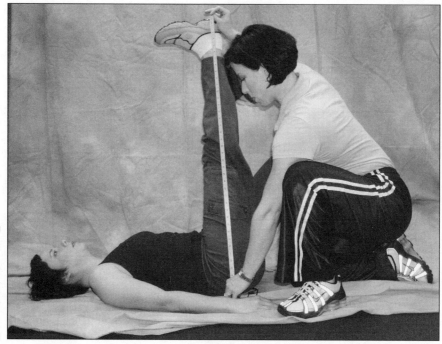

Figure 11-10:
The modified hamstring flexibility assessment.

Testing muscular strength and endurance

Let's face it — a lot of personal training is about building muscles, or as Hans and Franz said on *Saturday Night Live,* "We vant [clap!] to pump you up." As a personal trainer, much of your time will be spent dealing with your client's muscular strength and endurance, which is why it's really important to put some serious time into this portion of the fitness assessment.

Explaining the difference between muscular strength and muscular endurance as you demonstrate each test will be helpful to your client — and the more you educate her, the more she'll feel she's getting her money's worth!

Muscular *endurance* is the body's ability to exert a submaximal force for a sustained period of time. Muscular *strength* is the body's ability to exert a maximal force for a very short period of time.

The push-up test

The push-up test is frequently used in the field, because it requires no equipment. Plus, for some clients who aren't strong enough to do sustained repetitions, it can be used as a measure of strength rather than endurance. Here's how to perform a push-up test:

1. **Have the client assume either the standard (see Figure 11-11) or modified (see Figure 11-12) push-up position.**

2. **Lightly place your hands in the proper spotting position.**

3. **Have the client start lowering her body until her elbow angle is 90 degrees.**

4. **Have the client return to her start position.**

5. **Count how many repetitions the client can do without interruption.**

The crunch test

The crunch test is also frequently used in the field, because, like the push-up test, it requires no strength equipment. Where the push-up test measures upper-body endurance/strength, this test measure the muscular endurance of the abdominals.

1. **Have the client lie on her back with her feet flat on the floor and her knees at 90 degrees.**

2. **Have her cross her hands and place them flat on her chest.**

3. **Set your metronome to 40 beats per minute.**

4. **Lightly place your hands in the proper spotting position.**

5. **Have your client "curl up" so her shoulder blades lift off the mat, her trunk making a 30-degree angle with the floor or mat.**

6. **Have her perform her movements in a controlled manner, in time with the metronome.**

7. **Record the number of crunches she can perform at one time without pausing.**

When deciding which muscular strength and endurance tests to administer, use only what is practical, safe, and useful. For example, testing one exercise for muscular strength and endurance will not give you enough information to safely design a proper strength program for a client.

Don't hesitate to use this part of the assessment to "test" starting weights for exercises you're planning on using with the client. After each test set of 10 to 12 reps, ask your client for a rating of relative perceived exertion. When your client rates the set a 6 or 7, you've found your working weight for that exercise.

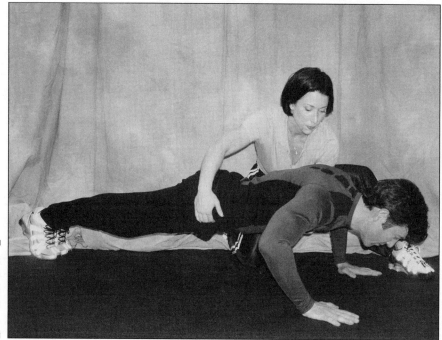

Figure 11-11:
The
standard
push-up
position.

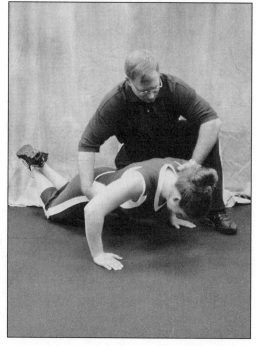

Figure 11-12:
The
modified
push-up
position.

Discussing the Results with Your Client

After you're done with your fitness assessment, take the time to review your client's results with him. Set realistic goals for him to achieve within a one-month period of time. If you reassess the client's fitness level at the beginning of every month, he'll know when to expect it — and he'll be excited to see the gains he can make in four weeks!

Give your client accurate assessments of normal ranges for someone of his body type, age, and conditioning level. The next time you assess him, measure his progress in percentages improved rather than against the norms.

Chapter 12

Before We Meet Again: Planning the Program

*W*hen planning out your client's program, you need to consider not only how you're going to help your client achieve her fitness goals, but also how to make reaching her goals realistic — and that means making her program fun, livable, doable, and achievable.

Before you try to create a program for your client, you need to have the initial consultation and do the initial fitness assessment, covered in Chapters 10 and 11.

Now it's time for the fun stuff — planning your client's program, which means deciding what exercises your client will do, how many of them, and for how long — the stuff that personal training is all about. So get ready to make your client's fitness dreams a reality!

Get with the Program: Considering Your Client's Programming Needs

If creating an exercise program were based solely on the results of a fitness assessment, prescribing exercises wouldn't be so challenging — in fact, it most likely would be the easiest part of a personal trainer's job.

Unfortunately, mi amigo, this is not the case! You need to consider many other factors besides the results of your client's fitness assessment. Issues such as time availability, where and when your client is planning to exercise, what equipment she'll have available to her, and what equipment she may need are important parameters to consider. Also, you need to consider intangible aspects like your client's lifestyle, personality, exercise likes and dislikes, motivation levels, and commitment to train.

When you have a strong grasp of all these important parts, you'll be able to successfully piece together a sound (and successful!) fitness formula for your client.

Knowing your client's goals

It's the reason your client came to you in the first place — a motivating desire to make a change in her lifestyle. Your client's goals become *your* goals when you're programming for her — that's why understanding what your client's goals are, and, more important, programming specifically to attain those goals, is key.

Your client's goal is her "fuel" — it's the driving force that feeds her mentally, keeping her motivated and on track. Your job is to sustain that fuel by prescribing exercise and activities that directly correlate to her goal.

For example, if a client came to you saying that she wanted to run a marathon, would you have her bench-pressing one and a half times her body weight? Probably not. To do so would be discouraging for her, because that style of training doesn't lend itself to enhancing endurance-based exercise and isn't especially helpful in training for a marathon.

As you're planning your client's prescription, think of ways that you can explain to her how each exercise or activity contributes to her success in reaching her goal. The more educated your client is about the why's of her program, the more compliant and dedicated she'll be!

Location, location, location: Knowing where your client will be exercising

When you sit down to plan your client's exercise program, knowing where she'll be exercising is very important. Each location — such as the gym, home, office, or outdoors — has its own unique set of variables that you need to consider when prescribing exercise. When you know where your client will be training, you can set her program accordingly.

Table 12-1 provides a quick overview of the pros and cons of different training locations.

Table 12-1	The Pros and Cons of Different Locations	
Location	**Pros**	**Cons**
Gym	Optimal environment for strength training	May be difficult to travel to
	Large variety and selection of equipment	Client may not feel "ready" to train in a gym
		Can be crowded during peak hours, requiring you to wait for equipment
Home	Can exercise any time	May not be enough space to exercise
	Easy and convenient to get to	Limited equipment availability
	Clients can exercise in the comfort of their own homes	Clients may find exercise easy to put off because of other household responsibilities
Office	Allows clients to exercise during their working hours without having to leave work	Clients may find exercise easy to put off because of work-related responsibilities
		May not be enough space to exercise
		Limited equipment availability
		The client may not be comfortable exercising at work
Outside	Optimal environment to train for aerobic endurance	Pollution, bugs, potential safety issues
	Fresh air, nice views	Very limited equipment availability
		Weather constraints

Knowing what equipment your client will (or won't) be using

After determining your client's exercise location, the next step is to determine what she currently has for equipment and what she may need access to.

If your client is training in a gym

Gyms typically have the largest selection of equipment — be sure to know beforehand what brand of equipment they carry and what pieces are available. A good rule of thumb is to be sure you can cover each body part with at least one piece of equipment or dumbbell movement.

If your client has hired you to create a program for her in a gym you aren't familiar with, visit the gym ahead of time to see what type of equipment they have and how it operates. If you can, work out there yourself — it'll help you to get a feel for the equipment and make your job a lot easier when it comes time to train your client there. Also, you'll know where everything is and how it works, which will make you look very polished and professional. Your client will appreciate the fact that you took time to do research to give her the best possible program!

If your client is training at home or the office

You can give a very effective workout with very little space and very little equipment. If your client doesn't have any equipment to start, you may want to recommend a few key pieces such as:

- One or two pairs of dumbbells
- Resistance tubing
- Weighted body bar
- Weighted medicine ball
- Body ball
- Exercise mat

Your client doesn't need to have all these goodies to start — you can actually do a full routine with everyday objects like chairs and stairs and bodyweight exercises. However, these items aren't expensive. You can start with one or two pieces, and, as your client's conditioning improves, you can add to her collection and diversify her program with new equipment.

If your client is exercising in the great outdoors

Equipment here varies greatly depending on the type of program you're looking to set your client up on — the outdoors *is* one big piece of equipment! You're limited only by your imagination — from walking/running a hilly course to obstacle-coursing it through the local park. Be sure to remind your client of the safety equipment she'll need when she's exercising on her own, such as a cellphone, sunblock, and a water bottle.

We've got your number: Considering how many sessions your client has purchased

Another very important factor to consider in your initial program-planning stage is how many sessions your client has purchased. If your client has purchased a small number of sessions (one to three), you need to determine what you can realistically teach her in that amount of time. Start thinking about the progression of your sessions with her — this will help you to determine which exercises you can safely teach her to do on her own within that time frame.

The same holds true if your client has purchased a large number of sessions. Even though you have more time to work with her, you still need to determine ahead of time at what points you'll progress her and how much information you can give her each session.

Be sure not to overwhelm your client with too much information at once. By knowing how many sessions you have to work with each client, you'll be able to break down the exercise progression you're teaching into stages, allowing you to deliver your information in small, easy-to-understand "bites" that allow your client to "digest" the information before moving on to the next session.

Just as you wouldn't crush your client under bucketloads of weight the first session — to do so would probably lose you a client — the same applies with how much information and education you unload on your client the first time through. Overeducating your client can be as much of a turnoff as overtraining her! Educate her as you would train her — give her just enough information to teach her about what she's doing that day, and leave her excited and invigorated, wanting to learn a little bit more the next time.

Keeping injuries and medical issues in mind

When planning out your client's exercise program, be sure to remember all her little aches and pains, as well as any major physiological issues that you covered with her during your initial consultation. When beginning to plan each exercise, double-check against her medical history to make sure that you aren't setting her up for pain or reinjury. Remember to take into account the stabilizing and assisting muscles of each exercise as well; even though these muscles aren't being worked directly, they still contract through movement and can easily inflame tissues that have been previously injured or strained.

If you aren't sure what impact a particular exercise will have on an injury, put a call in to the physical therapist or rehab specialist your client worked with, or one of your medical advisors, who can help you decide which exercises are appropriate.

Using assessment results to create a baseline program

You've really already done the work on this one (and if you haven't, you need to). By using your client's fitness assessment results, you have baseline starting weights, as well as sets and reps for your client's prescription (more on sets and reps later in this chapter).

It's All in the Planning!

Before you start madly concocting the best gosh-darn exercise program in the universe, you need to determine the order of operations for your client's exercise plan. These factors include the following:

- Type of exercises for the program
- Order of exercises for the program
- Working exercise intensity
- Session duration
- Exercise frequency

As you know, a balanced exercise program covers three core components: cardiovascular conditioning, muscular conditioning, and flexibility. Choosing the right type of exercises for your client will rely primarily on your client's:

- Specific goals and objectives
- Likes and dislikes of certain cardiovascular activities
- Availability of equipment
- Availability of time
- Conditioning level

A good time to discuss your client's exercise preferences is during your initial consultation with him. Ask him what type of exercise experience he has, as well as what type of exercise and activities he prefers. Be sure to take detailed notes — they'll come in handy for this part of the process!

Creating an aerobic workout

Aerobic exercise can come in many different forms. In personal-training-speak, any type of activity that uses the body's large muscle groups in a sustained, movement-oriented manner that increases respiration for a prolonged period of time can be considered *aerobic,* and can contribute to increasing your client's cardiovascular endurance and health. You can offer your client many options for cardiovascular exercise — from traditional pieces of cardiovascular equipment, such as a bike or rower, to nontraditional methods, such as running bleachers at the local gym stadium (when there's no game on, that is).

However, prescribing aerobic activity for your client is more than deciding whether he should use a treadmill or walk outdoors, though that is an important part of it. You need to be able to decide his:

- ✔ **Training mode:** Which activity will he perform? Will it be equipment-based (such as the treadmill), or will he simply go for a walk outside?

- ✔ **Training method:** What type of training method will he perform while he's exercising? Will it be continuous training (CT), where he maintains a steady heart rate for a sustained period of time, or will it be interval training (IT), where he alternates short bursts of high intensity effort with longer, slower bursts of less maximal effort?

- ✔ **Working intensity:** Exactly how hard will he work during his session? Will he be able to gab with his friend on the neighboring treadmill, or will he barely be able to carry on a conversation?

- ✔ **Exercise frequency:** How often will he exercise over a predetermined time period? Will it be four times a month, three times a week, every other day?

- ✔ **Exercise duration:** How long will he perform his activity per session? Will he exercise for 20 minutes? An hour?

We cover each of these key questions in the following sections.

Choosing the proper training mode

The *mode* (or type) of exercise you prescribe for your client should be easily accessible and convenient for him (so extreme skydiving is probably out). It should be an activity that your client likes and a mode that is *progressable —*

the factors contributing to the workload (typically resistance, speed, and/or incline) can be incrementally increased to provide greater exercise intensity as your client's conditioning level increases.

On a broad spectrum, equipment-based aerobic activity is preferable for most clients for multiple reasons — primarily because of the ease of use and high enjoyment factor. You may know a few people who *absolutely love* to do cardio, but they are few and far between. The advent of cardio machines such as treadmills, steppers, and bikes have made the boring task of getting healthy only semiboring. Whereas, back in the olden days, if you wanted to get healthy, you had to worry about getting struck by lightning, tripping over a pothole, or swallowing a bug, now clients can read, watch TV, listen to their favorite music, *and* exercise without fear of being run over! Imagine that!

Table 12-2 provides a quick reference chart of the most common aerobic training modes, all of which can be done in any location.

Table 12-2		Common Aerobic Training Modes	
Activity/ Equipment	*Client Level*	*Pros*	*Cons*
Walking or running	Beginning to advanced	On machine, multivariable speed and resistance settings can accommodate all fitness levels.	Can be difficult or unsafe for clients with balance problems or hip/knee/ankle/foot issues.
Optional equipment: Treadmill or elliptical machine		The client can control his movements easily — he will be working on a fixed plane of movement, so he has no choice but to push the machine where it is designed to go.	Can be difficult or unsafe if performed outside in unfamiliar territory.
		Walking has a low perceived exertion value, meaning clients don't think of it as a hard workout.	
		The activity can be intensified easily.	
		Walking or running outside gives the client a dose of fresh air and nice scenery.	

Activity/ Equipment	Client Level	Pros	Cons
Stair climbing *Optional equipment:* Stair stepper	Intermediate to advanced	Equipment doesn't take up much room. More demanding exercise mode with higher perceived exertion value, meaning the client thinks of stair climbing as a harder workout. If performed outside, without a machine, the client can easily control the intensity of the workout.	Continuous same-plane movement on a machine, which can place a strain on the lower back, knees, ankles, and feet.
Bicycle riding *Optional equipment:* Upright bike or *recumbent bike* (where your feet are out in front of you, rather than underneath you)	Beginning to advanced	Low perceived value of exertion, meaning the client doesn't perceive bicycle riding as a hard workout. Moderately inexpensive equipment to own. Recumbent position takes stress off lower back and hips.	Upright model can place stress on lower back in some people.
Rowing Optional equipment: Rowing machine or upper-body ergometer (bicycle for the upper body)	Beginning to advanced	Offers clients an upper-body aerobic workout. Very challenging.	Clients with neck, shoulder, or bicep problems should be very careful on this machine.

Choosing the proper aerobic training method

When you've chosen what mode of aerobic exercise your client will be performing, the next step is determining what type of aerobic training method he'll be using. You have a choice of two types of training methods for cardiovascular conditioning: continuous training (CT) and interval training (IT). Both methods have been proven to increase cardiovascular capacity and endurance. You can determine which method is best suited for your client by looking at his current conditioning level and his specific fitness goals.

Continuous aerobic training

Continuous training (CT) is a method of aerobic training that maintains a moderately elevated heart rate for a sustained period of time. As implied by its name, continuous training does not allow for a rest period during the working phase. Continuous training is well suited for all types of clients — from beginners to elite athletes.

The work is performed at a moderate intensity level (60 to 80 percent of the client's maximum heart rate). Because of its lower intensity level, it can be done every day and for a longer period of time.

Continuous training is less physically and mentally taxing than other methods of aerobic training.

Clients who benefit most from continuous training are those who:

- ✔ Are just starting to exercise aerobically on a regular basis
- ✔ Have cardiovascular disease
- ✔ Are older and have joint issues
- ✔ Want to lose weight
- ✔ Want to lower their cholesterol levels
- ✔ Want to increase their cardiovascular endurance and stamina

Interval training

Interval training (IT) is a method of aerobic training that intersperses short, high-intensity bursts of maximal effort with slower, longer periods of submaximal work.

Interval training is best suited for:

- ✔ Clients who can no longer elevate their heart rate into a satisfactory working zone with continuous training.
- ✔ Clients who are more conditioned and who want to increase their maximal oxygen consumption capacity (lung capacity).

✔ Athletes who need to train at a maximum aerobic capacity for their sport or competition.

✔ Clients who can't sustain moderate cardiovascular activity for long periods of time. Working hard for short periods of time followed by a long recovery period allows them to perform a greater total volume of work.

We cover the various ways to implement interval training methods in more detail in Chapter 15.

Determining working intensity

To the client, *working intensity* is how hard she'll work during her aerobic session. To you, it means the heart-rate training zone that the client will maintain during an aerobic session.

Several methods are available for formulating working intensity. The most common is the *Karvohnen formula,* which is a mathematical formula that uses an estimate of maximal heart rate based on a client's age and actual resting heart rate to determine optimal lower and upper aerobic training ranges.

Calculating the appropriate working intensity is important to prevent under-training or overtraining your client. The right range will ensure that your client will reach his goal safely and efficiently.

During your client's fitness assessment, you had him relax for a minute or so. After he was relaxed and destressed, you took his resting heart rate either manually or with a heart-rate monitor. You'll now use that information plus his age to determine his appropriate training zone. (Don't worry — we help you with the math.)

Let's say you have a 41-year-old client named Steve, who has a resting heart rate of 68.

1. **Subtract Steve's age (41) from 220. So, 220 – 41 = 179.**

   This is his age-predicted maximum heart rate.

2. **Subtract Steve's resting heart rate (68) from Steve's age-predicted maximum heart rate (179), which you got in Step 1. So, 179 – 68 = 111.**

   This is his *heart-rate reserve.*

3. **Multiply the heart-rate reserve, which you got in Step 2, by the percent of maximum heart rate you want Steve to minimally achieve while he's training, and then add that to Steve's resting heart rate. Let's say you want Steve to exert at least 60 percent. So, first, 111 × 0.60 = 67. Then 67 + 68 (his resting heart rate) = 134.**

   This is the minimum target heart rate.

4. **Multiply the heart-rate reserve, which you got in Step 2, by the percent of maximum heart rate you want Steve to maximally achieve while he's training, and then add that to Steve's resting heart rate. Let's say you want Steve to exert no more than 80 percent. So, first, $111 \times 0.80 = 89$. Then $89 + 68$ (his resting heart rate) = 157.**

This is the maximum target heart rate.

Achieving working intensity is the net result of how long the session itself lasts and at what pace the session occurs. Other factors, such as resistance and training method type, as well as frequency of exercise, also play a large part in how intensity is delivered and perceived aerobically.

Unless Steve has a heart-rate monitor, accurately gauging whether he's working in the right training zone is going to be difficult. This is where the perceived rate of exertion scale comes into play (more on the perceived rate of exertion scale is in Chapter 11). After you've set his target training limits, also determine a perceived exertion level he should be working at that correlates to his actual target heart-rate range and help him understand how to gauge his own exertion levels.

Specifying exercise frequency

Exercise frequency (or how often your client exercises) is dependent on your client's time constraints. You'll find that some clients will have no problems training three times a week, and others will be lucky if they can get in three times a month. The trick here is to make your recommendations work for your client.

All too often, trainers tell their clients, "You need to be exercising three times a week," when the client clearly isn't able to do that. Telling a client what he *should* be doing is easy — but if he *could* do what he *should* be doing, he wouldn't have hired you in the first place. You're a professional fitness troubleshooter — your job is to look at and evaluate each client's unique fitness needs and come up with a customized solution that fits his lifestyle. Okay, so John can't exercise three times a week because he travels every week. But he *is* home on the weekends and can do an intense cardio session once a week. So if that's what he *can* do, that's what you prescribe. It's not the textbook three times a week, but at least it's some exercise — and some exercise is better than no exercise.

That said, the American College of Sports Medicine recommends a minimum of two days a week (and up to five days a week) to obtain general fitness goals. Here are some sample weekly exercise frequency goals, based on client conditioning levels:

- ✔ **Beginner:** Every third day per week, or two times per week
- ✔ **Advanced beginner:** Every second day per week, or three times per week

- **Intermediate:** Four times per week
- **Advanced intermediate:** Five times per week
- **Advanced:** Six times per week

Taking into account how many other activities your client is participating in outside of his prescribed exercise time is important. Your client needs rest and recovery to get the most out of his aerobic sessions. Be sure to build in rest days so your client doesn't become overtrained.

Designating duration

The *duration* of your client's session, or how long he will perform his exercise at one time, is ultimately determined by his personal fitness goals, the intensity level you have prescribed for him, and how often he's required to do it. On average, you want to aim to have your clients exercising between 20 and 40 minutes per session.

The higher the intensity level of a cardio session, the less time a client will be able to perform it. If your goal is to build your client's cardiovascular endurance, lower the intensity level so he can perform for a longer duration.

Creating a strength program

Putting together a strength program involves more than slapping some plates on the weight machine. As with the aerobics program, you need to consider several factors before putting pen to paper and creating the ultimate weight workout for your client.

Choosing the exercises

The first step in setting up a weight-training program is choosing which exercises your client is going to perform. You can choose from a multitude of equipment and methods; determining the best one for your client is the tough part.

To figure out which exercises are best for your client, consider the following:

- **Your client's specific training goals:** Generally, you train your client in a specific way to produce a specific change or result to meet his specific goals. This approach is called the *Specificity Principle.* (Did we mention that all this should be specific?) For example, if you were training a swimmer who wanted to increase his lap time, you would choose upper-body movements that strengthen his back, chest, shoulders, and arms to increase his stroke power in the water.

✔ **Location of training:** Knowing where your client will be training will let you determine which exercises he can realistically and safely perform in his training environment.

✔ **Available equipment:** Weight training is an activity that absolutely requires some type of specialized equipment — whether it's a pair of dumbbells, a *selectorized weight machine* (a machine that has a stack of plates, where you select the weight by sticking a pin into the plate), or a plate-loaded weight machine. Knowing what type of equipment the client can use will help you determine which exercises he can perform.

✔ **Previous exercise experience:** Knowing how much exercise experience your client has behind him can save time and frustration during your sessions. Your number-one goal is to ensure that your client understands the exercise and can perform it safely and correctly on his own. If you have a beginning client with no weight-training experience, you may choose to start him on machines rather than free weights, because mastering the exercise motion through a fixed-plane mechanism such as a selectorized machine is easier than using free weights, which require a lot more skill and control.

✔ **How much time he has available to train:** The amount of time the client has to train greatly affects your choice of exercise. If the client is time-strapped, you probably aren't going to include exercises such as alternating dumbbell curls or single-arm kickbacks — they simply take too long to perform and are not optimal for a limited-time program.

Specifying how often your client will work out

Training frequency refers to the number of times a client will work out in one week. Training frequency is determined by the client's personal fitness goals, available training time, and other activities such as sports or aerobic activities.

Here are the suggested guidelines for strength-training frequency:

✔ **Beginner:** Two to three times per week

✔ **Intermediate:** Three to four times per week

✔ **Advanced:** Four to six times per week

Less-conditioned clients need more rest between their workout sessions than more-conditioned clients, who can work more frequently within the week with fewer rest days in between.

Always make sure to allow at least one full day of rest before training the same muscle groups again — no matter how conditioned the client is.

Determining the order of the exercises

Deciding in which order your client will do the exercises goes hand in hand with selecting the exercises themselves. You need to keep in mind your client's training goals, previous training experience, and conditioning level.

Choosing the best exercise order for your client is important. Your goal is to arrange the exercises you're prescribing so that you don't fatigue their small muscle groups first; your client will need them to help his large muscle groups perform the exercises!

For example, if Jeri wanted to increase her upper-body strength, you most likely wouldn't prescribe tricep extensions as her primary movement. To exhaust her triceps first would be counterproductive, because the tricep is the *assisting,* or secondary, muscle for multijoint movements such as the chest press or overhead press. These compound movements are more goal-specific for Jeri because they involve the larger muscle groups of the upper body, and lend themselves to developing upper-body strength — exactly what Jeri wants! If Jeri *did* perform tricep extensions first and completely fatigued those muscles; then when she moved on to perform the chest press or overhead press, not only would she be at risk for injury (because her triceps provide important stabilization and power to the movement), but also her triceps would be too fatigued to perform the exercises correctly. Jeri would become frustrated because it would appear to her that she was too weak to make substantial progress with the exercise — when it's really because her triceps were too tired to assist properly!

Table 12-3 provides some suggested guidelines for choosing exercise order based on client goals.

Table 12-3	Choosing Exercise Orders
Exercise Order	*Benefit*
Multijoint movements first, then single-joint movements, working from largest muscle groups down to small muscle groups	Helps to prevent injury, because larger muscle groups need assistance from smaller muscles to perform the exercise correctly. Great for beginning clients.
Alternating push and pull exercises (for example, chest press [push]; then seated row [pull])	Allows for adequate muscle-group recovery by not allowing the same muscle groups to be used consecutively, reducing muscular fatigue. Good for clients who are deconditioned and can't sustain a progressive multijoint to single-joint method.

(continued)

Table 12-3 *(continued)*

Exercise Order	Benefit
Alternating upper-body exercises with lower-body exercises (for example, chest press [upper body]; then leg press [lower body])	Allows clients who can't sustain consecutive upper-body or lower-body work to perform more total work volume by completely resting the upper body while lower-body work is being performed, and vice versa.
	Great for clients with minimal muscular endurance.

Check out Chapter 15 for advanced programming techniques. There we provide examples of these types of workouts.

Planning sets, reps, and rest

Okay, you've decided where your client is going to train, which exercises she's going to perform, what equipment she'll use to perform her exercises, and in what order she'll work her muscles. Next, you need to determine how much work she's going to perform — also known as *volume* — during her weight-training session.

Volume is the number of sets and reps you prescribe for your client. A *repetition* (or *rep,* for short) is a single-movement count that, when performed consecutively, makes up a *set* of repetitions. For example, if you perform a squat one time, then rest, that is one rep, making it a one-rep set. If you perform a squat 15 times before resting, that is considered one set of 15 reps. If you perform a squat for 15 reps, rest, then perform 15 squats again, you will have completed two sets of 15 reps each.

Sets and reps depend on your client's specific training goals, training frequency, conditioning level, and recovery between exercises. As a general rule, the training volume directly correlates to the client's conditioning level (see Table 12-4).

Table 12-4   Sets and Reps based on Fitness Level and Goals

Client Level	Goal	Reps	Sets (per exercise)	Rest (between sets)
Beginner	General fitness	12 to 15	2 to 3	1 to 2 minutes
Intermediate	Muscular endurance	12 to 15	3 to 4	45 seconds

Client Level	Goal	Reps	Sets (per exercise)	Rest (between sets)
Intermediate	Muscular size	10 to 12	3 to 4	45 to 90 seconds
Intermediate	Muscular strength	8 to 10	3 to 4	1 to 2 minutes
Advanced	Muscular endurance	12 to 20	4 to 6	30 to 45 seconds
Advanced	Muscular size	8 to 12	4 to 6	30 to 90 seconds
Advanced	Muscular strength	6 to 8	3 to 6	2 to 5 minutes

Setting the starting weight

After you've determined the total training volume for your client, you need to whip out the initial fitness assessment you took her through. Use the assessment exercises to provide baseline starting points for weights in her new exercise prescription.

Looking at your client's perceived exertion rate for each exercise will help you to determine a starting weight for your client. As you go through the actual session with your client, you can adjust the starting weights and following weight sets based on your client's response to the program.

Chapter 13

The Second Session: Taking Your Client through the First Workout

*F*inally! It's the moment you've been waiting for. You're up and running as a personal trainer. You've gotten your first client, done his fitness assessment, written out his program, and now and you're ready to do the thing that brings in the dough — take your client through his first full-fledged workout with you.

If you've studied for your certification exam already (see Chapter 2), you probably already know about the elements of a workout session: the warm-up, the stretch, the cardio and strength exercises, and the cool-down. However, this chapter is a handy reference that gives you options for each part of the workout. Here, we also tell you how to communicate with your client during the session and how to keep him motivated and moving along toward his fitness goals.

Checking Up So Your Client Doesn't Check Out

Before you hand your client that 20-pound dumbbell, ask him a few quick questions to check in with him. The way he responds will let you know how ready he is to work with you today.

Asking the right questions

In the following sections, we provide some sample questions that can help determine your client's readiness.

How are you feeling today?

If your client has slept well and has had a normal day so far, he'll tell you "good."

Be watchful for clients who answer otherwise — you may need to do a little digging to determine if your client is feeling poorly because of physical reasons (for example, he hasn't gotten enough sleep, he's not feeling well) or because of mental reasons (for example, he's had a bad day at work, he's feeling stressed). If he isn't feeling well physically, ask him if he feels capable of performing the workout today. Remind him that rescheduling is in his best interest if he's running a fever, if he feels achy, or if he has any type of head cold, congestion, sore throat, or cough.

If your client is determined to work out even though he's feeling poorly, try explaining that his body only has one immune system — and when he strength-trains, he makes little microscopic tears in his muscles, which the body has to heal with the same antibodies that it's using right now to fight off the cold. Although you appreciate his diligence and enthusiasm, not only does working out while under the weather result in a poor workout (because his body isn't capable of performing at full capacity) but also your client may end up not feeling well for a longer period of time than if he had let his body rest before he worked out with you.

How did you feel after our last session?

This question is good to ask *every* session, especially if you haven't called to check up on your client in between her last session and now. If your client says, "I was sore for days!" you may want to temper this workout. On the other hand, if she comes back with "I felt great — it didn't even feel like I worked out!" you may decide it's time to push up the intensity a notch.

Even when your client tells you "I felt awesome after our last workout! You rock!" you may want to ask some direct questions, such as, "Did you experience any usual pain in your joints and muscles other than some soreness?" Or if she has an injury, you may want to ask a question about that injury — for example, "Did you have any problems with your rotator cuff after the workout?" Double-checking may trigger your client to remember that, yes, she did experience something unusual after the last workout, and then it passed and she simply forgot about it. By asking again in another way, you can ensure that you're delivering the right type of programming for your client, as well as show her that you're concerned with her well-being *after* the workout, too!

When was the last time you ate today, and what did you have to eat?

This question is *tres importante!* If your client hasn't had anything to eat within the last three hours, chances are he's going to experience a weak workout. Worse yet, he can become dizzy, nauseated, or even faint if he trains too hard without enough fuel!

Remind your client that he needs to eat consistently throughout the day, and he especially should have a small meal that includes protein, unprocessed carbs, and a small amount of healthy fat two to three hours before the workout. This will keep his motor running strong through the entire session!

Another great question to ask is, "How much have you had to eat today?" Clients sometimes go all day without eating; then remembering that they have to work out, they grab a quick bite to eat before going to the training session. If you just ask your client, "When was the last time you ate?" he'll say, "Oh, about an hour ago." But if he's just grabbed something quick an hour before the workout, there's a good chance that, halfway into the workout, he'll end up on the floor with his head between his knees and a cold towel on the back of his neck, dizzy and nauseated from not eating enough to sustain his workout.

Keep a sports-recovery drink on hand to help get some quick sugar back into your client's system if he ends up nauseated or dizzy. Energy bars also work very well to help your client recover. If this happens to your client repeatedly, you may need to refer him to his doctor.

On a scale of 1 to 10, how hard was your last workout?

By asking your client to rate his last workout's overall intensity by using perceived rate of exertion, you'll have a good idea of exactly how hard your client thought you worked him. You'll also be able to use this information when you think about this session's intensity level and where you'll begin.

Explaining what will happen during the first session

Imagine that it's your first time, say, taking a martial arts class. You don't know how to tie your belt. You don't know when and how to bow. You certainly don't know how to block, punch, or kick. You don't even know how to put on your uniform (yes, there is a right way to put on your uniform)! You feel lost — and a little scared.

That's how your client may feel at his first real training session. Sure, *you* know those exercise machines as well as the back of your hand, and you automatically know which machines work which muscles. But your client is clueless (that's why he hired you in the first place). He may not know how to step on a treadmill, much less what to expect during your session with him. That's why providing your client an overview of what will happen during the session, before it actually occurs, is important. This approach will eliminate any anxieties he may have, and also prevent misconceptions as to how your client may feel he needs to act or perform during the session.

In the following sections, we cover the types of things you should explain to your client the first time you do them.

What activities will occur, and the order they will occur in

For example, you might say something like the following:

> Today, you're going to start your training session warming up on the treadmill. After you're warm, we're going to lightly stretch all your muscles to help prepare them for the work we're going to do with the weights and also to help prevent them from being injured. After you're fully stretched out, you'll be ready to start your strength exercises, which I'll demonstrate to you before you actually perform them. We're doing a full-body workout today, which means you'll do one strength exercise for each muscle group. After you complete your strength training, we'll end the workout with some abdominal work and lower-body stretches that will serve as your cool-down, which will help prevent any muscle cramping and breathing problems. Cooling down helps to return your body to the way it normally breathes — the way it was when you first walked in here, before you started exercising.

What he can expect to feel like while he's training

For example, you might tell your client:

> While you're exercising, your heart rate will increase slightly, and your body will become warm — you may start sweating. During your warm-up, your breathing will become faster and heavier, but you shouldn't feel uncomfortable and you should still be able to hold a conversation with me. If you do feel uncomfortable, don't be afraid to let me know. During the strength exercises, you may experience a very warm and/or light "burning " sensation in the muscle group we're working. Don't be alarmed — this is completely normal. When you're through with your entire workout, your body will feel slightly fatigued, but not to the point of being exhausted.

What he can expect from you

For example, you might say:

> During your workout, I'll demonstrate every movement first, giving you verbal and visual instruction of how to do it. After I've demonstrated what you'll be doing, you'll perform the movement with me spotting you through

the entire movement. I'll be giving you pointers as you go through the exercise to help you get the form right, as well as guiding you with my hands. I'm here to help you learn the exercise correctly so eventually you can do it on your own. When I spot you, I'm not helping you lift the weight — I'm just making sure that nothing unsafe happens.

What you expect from him

You may say something like the following:

> While you're training, I'll be asking you to rate how hard you feel you're working during an exercise by using a scale of 1 to 10. A rating of 1 would be equivalent to you sitting down in a chair, whereas a rating of 10 would be the way you'd feel if you were pushing your car uphill in the middle of winter. During this first workout, I *don't* want you trying to perform at a level of 10. That's all-out, maximal exertion and effort, which at this point isn't necessary to reach your fitness goals. Also, this is my first time working with you, and I'm still learning your body and what you're capable of doing. As we work together longer, I'll know you and your body better, and I'll be able to push you harder in a safer manner. For today, the intensity level of your workout will be slightly lower than your normal working intensity. I do expect, however, that if at any point you feel dizzy, nauseated, or uncomfortable in any way, you'll let me know immediately. Also, please don't hesitate to interrupt me or stop me at any time to ask questions. My goal is to make sure that you completely understand what you're doing, and that you do it well.

So Hot It's Cool: Warming Up the Client

Now that your client is clear on what's going to happen during the session, it's time to warm up!

Sometimes clients want to skip the warm-up and get right into the fun stuff. You don't want your client injured during her very first session — that's not exactly motivating! So explain to your eager-beaver client that warming up is very important (and necessary!). If she doesn't warm up, her muscles will need a lot more time to get the greater blood flow they need. Cold muscles with less blood flow don't move as well as warm muscles with increased blood flow — which means she'll have a much greater chance of pulling or straining a muscle.

If your eager beaver is still persistent in wanting to skip the warm-up, you can always negotiate — say, by letting her warm up for five minutes rather than ten. But do keep stressing how important the warm-up is.

Cardio equipment can be scary for a new client. So you need to use several teaching techniques to get her up and running (or walking or stepping).

To keep your client interested, try warming her up on a different piece of equipment each time she works with you. If you're training her at home, try a different method each time.

Showing her what's what

Unless you enjoy seeing your client perplexed, you need to show her how the machines work — making her figure it out on her own isn't cool!

For the warm-up, your client will be on the equipment for only a short period of time. Use this time to train her well — the lessons you convey here extend far beyond the warm-up, well into your client's cardiovascular prescription, where she'll be spending a greater amount of time on the equipment you're teaching her to use. Use the warm-up time to make sure you cover *every* detail of how to use the equipment.

You'll want to show your client:

- ✔ How to safely get on the machine
- ✔ How to turn the machine on
- ✔ How to increase and decrease the intensity
- ✔ How to use the features, such as the calories-burned counter and the heart-rate readout
- ✔ How to slow down, turn the machine off, and safely dismount

Believe it or not, Melyssa *has* seen people fall off the treadmill because they started it while standing on it, instead of straddling the machine, turning it on, holding the hand rails, and then hopping on.

When putting a client on a piece of cardio equipment for the first time, show her how to use the machine by first hopping on yourself. Explain what all the buttons do, and where to place her hands and feet. Be sure to show her what the proper form is on that machine — and also be sure to show her what *isn't* proper form.

You can't possibly be *too* obvious when explaining cardio exercises — after all, what's obvious to you is probably totally new to your client.

Lay out each action as a set of steps, and verbally describe the action as you're demonstrating it. Most clients will need to hear you say it and see you do it to learn how to do the activity properly themselves.

Here's an example script for teaching your client how to use the treadmill:

1. **Walk up to the console on the side tracks that run the length of the tread.**

   At this point you'll be straddling the tread.

2. **Start the treadmill.**

3. **As the treadmill slowly starts, put both hands on the side rails or front hand bar for balance.**

4. **Lightly step onto the tread, still holding on to the machine for balance.**

5. **When you're comfortable matching your walking stride to the pace of the machine, take one hand off the treadmill and press the up arrow to increase the treadmill's speed so that the machine mimics your natural walking pace.**

6. **When you're comfortable walking at that pace, let go of the handrails.**

   Make sure that, as you walk, you pick up your foot and extend your leg, swinging your leg from your hip. As your leg lowers and your foot comes down, be sure to land heel-first. Also, be sure to swing your arms in a normal walking motion.

7. **To decrease your speed, put both hands back onto the handrails.**

8. **Holding on with one hand, use the other hand to depress the down arrow, which will decrease your speed.**

9. **When the treadmill slows down, press the stop button.**

10. **When the treadmill has come to a complete stop, get off the machine.**

    Be sure to wait for the treadmill to come to a complete stop. As you dismount the treadmill, be sure to hold onto the handrail as you step down. Your body may feel a little strange walking on a nonmoving floor after being on the treadmill.

Correcting your client's mistakes

Don't hesitate to correct your client's movements if she's performing the activity incorrectly. (Clients always *think* they're doing it right, because they've never done it before!)

On the treadmill

Table 13-1 outlines the most common form mistakes made by clients using treadmills — along with solutions to all these problems.

Table 13-1	Solutions to Common Mistakes Made on a Treadmill	
Form Issue	*Reason*	*Solution*
The client is dragging her feet.	The pace may be too slow or too fast.	Adjust the speed to match the client's walking pace.
		Instruct the client to raise her knees higher when she steps and walk lightly on top of the tread.
The client is leaning forward onto the hand bar and pushing the tread with her feet, trying to make it go faster.	The speed of the tread is too slow.	Adjust the speed to match the client's walking pace.
		Instruct the client to walk lightly on top of the tread.
The client is gripping the hand bar and straining her upper body trying to hold on.	The incline is too high.	Lower the speed and/or incline until the client can walk without holding on.
	The speed is too fast.	

On the stair machine

Most form snafus on the stair machine occur when the resistance is too light or the pace is too fast. This may be the case if the client continues to:

- Hit the floor at the end of his downstroke
- Lean forward on the rails, unable to maintain an upright position
- Hold onto the forward rail while leaning back, unable to maintain an upright position

If any of these form problems occur, increase the resistance or decrease the speed until your client's form is corrected.

Letting your client do it herself

Just as with strength-training exercises, you'll eventually have to let the client fly on her own. Ask her to turn the machine on and off by herself, and let her use the machine while you stand close by.

Sometimes newbie clients panic and forget how to slow down or turn off a cardio machine. Stay with your client if it's her first time using a piece of cardio equipment so you can walk her through all the steps. She'll feel much more comfortable with you there.

Clients differ in the amount of time they need to get their bodies warm; some clients may be warm in 5 minutes, while others may take as long as 15 or 20 minutes to increase their core temperature. It doesn't matter how long it takes your client to warm up, as long as he gets warm!

If your client isn't sure whether he's warm yet, place your hand on his back between his shoulder blades. If his clothing feels unusually warm and slightly damp to the touch, he's most likely warmed up. If the client will be working on his own between sessions, tell him that he'll know he's warmed up when he breaks a light sweat on his brow or the small of his back.

After your client is warm, the next step is to lightly stretch all your client's muscles, preparing him for the exertive work ahead. (We cover preworkout stretching later in this chapter.)

When performing trainer-assisted stretches (see the section on stretching later in the chapter), make sure your client is relaxed. Tell her to breathe in on the easiest part of the stretch and breathe out on the hardest part of the stretch — this will help to get her endorphins going as well as focus her mind on the strength work she's about to do.

Home is where the warm-up is

If you're training your client at his home, you can warm her up in several ways. You can have her:

✔ **Walk up and down the stairs three to four times; then walk outside for five minutes.**

✔ **March in place for five to ten minutes.** To keep your client on pace, try using a metronome, or you can just snap your fingers (this is great exercise for your thumbs!). Counting beats works well, too: "left, right, up, down, left, right. . . ." (Know a good marching song, anyone?)

✔ **Do jumping jacks.** Doing a bunch of jumping jacks all at once may raise your client's heart rate too quickly. Instead, have her alternate 20 jumping jacks with 30 marches in place; repeat this sequence once.

✔ **Do step-ups on a bench for five to ten minutes.** You can time this the same way you time marching in place.

✔ **Jog in place at a moderate pace for five to ten minutes.**

✔ **If the client has cardio equipment, you can have her bike, walk, or step for five to ten minutes.**

Going for the Stretch

One of Melyssa's mentors, a physical therapist named Dr. David, taught her that "a long muscle is a strong muscle." Shortened muscles are weaker, are more prone to injury, and limit the range of motion of a joint, interfering with workout performance — which is why stretching your client is so important. You want to ensure that she receives the maximum benefit of her workout.

Before the workout

Prior to strength-training your client, a gentle, full-body static stretch routine is appropriate. After you're done with the workout, a more concentrated stretching segment is recommended, because your client is as warm as she's going to be at that point, which is the safest and most effective time to stretch her.

The preworkout stretch typically is a light, quick, full-body stretch routine consisting of no more than three to four stretches for the entire body. For this part of the session, you want to use static stretches. *Static stretching* is the most commonly used stretching technique, and is what clients usually envision when they think of stretching. When your client performs a static stretch, she will assume each stretching position slowly until she feels tension, then hold it for ten seconds or longer.

Choose static stretches that focus on the muscles as groups, such as hamstring/lower-back stretches, arm/shoulder stretches, and chest/shoulder stretches. By lightly stretching these muscle groups preworkout, you prime your client's muscles for activity by helping to kick-start her mind-muscle connection and get the endorphins flowing (*endorphins* are a natural painkilling chemical released by the body during vigorous exercise). After the workout, when your client is at her warmest, you'll be able to work on her flexibility and concentrate fully on each muscle group itself by performing an in-depth stretch incorporating some of the different stretching techniques listed in the following section.

Most of your clients will like stretching about as much as they like a nasty cold. The good news: Because there are so many different ways to stretch, one of them is bound to appeal to you and your client.

After the workout

Here are a few tried-and-true techniques that are excellent for postworkout stretching; they'll effectively stretch your clients above and beyond the static stretching that you do preworkout:

- ✔ **Proprioceptive neuromuscular facilitation (PNF):** This type of stretching is commonly called PNF because the name that PNF stands for — proprioceptive neuromuscular facilitation — is pretty much unpronounceable. In English, this technique consists of tightening a muscle as hard as you can before stretching it. The theory is that tightening the muscle exhausts it so that it's more receptive to the stretch. As an example, to stretch a client's hamstrings, have her lie on her back with her heel on your shoulder. Have her press her heel into your shoulder while you resist for five to ten seconds. Then have her relax and hold the stretch for 15 seconds.

- ✔ **Active isolated stretching:** Some experts say that, when you stretch a muscle too hard or too long, it rebounds like a rubber band, becoming even tighter. Active isolated stretching is meant to avoid this rebound reflex. To do active isolated stretching, the client tightens the muscle opposite to the one that is to be stretched, then stretches the targeted muscle for about two seconds. The client does this stretch 8 to 20 times. The idea is that, when you contract a muscle, the opposite muscle has to relax and elongate, making it more receptive to a stretch and less likely to rebound. For example, to stretch your client's hamstrings, have the client lies on her back, bend her leg, and wrap a special AI rope or a towel around her foot. Then have her straighten her leg by tightening the quadriceps. With the leg still straight, have her pull it into a hamstring stretch. (You can buy an AI rope — or Active Isolated Stretch Rope — from exercise-equipment stores, including Wharton Performance at www.mpi.bigstep.com/catalog.jhtml or 800-240-9805.)

- ✔ **Contract, relax, and contract (CRAC):** Want the best of both worlds? CRAC (which stands for *contract, relax, and contract*) involves stretching a muscle, tightening it, and then tightening the muscle directly opposite. To stretch your client's hamstrings, for example, have her sit on the floor with one leg straight in front of her and the other leg either bent or straight. Have her reach for her toes and hold for ten seconds, then have her squeeze her hamstrings for the next ten seconds, then relax her hamstrings as she tightens her quads for ten seconds.

When stretching your client, keep in mind the following tips:

- ✔ **While stretching, your client should feel tension, *not* pain.**

- ✔ **Don't be afraid to help your client with a stretch (see Figure 13-1).** When assisting your client in a stretch, be sure to be aware of your hand placement — if your hand is putting pressure on the tendons that are being stretched, that can create an uncomfortable burning sensation for your client.

- ✔ **Don't let your client bounce when stretching.** Bouncing can cause muscle pulls or tears.

- ✔ **Take advantage of tools your client can use to assist with stretching (see Figure 13-2).** For example, you can use towels, bands, or bars to help the client increase flexibility.

✔ **Tell the client to breathe in through her nose and out through her mouth.**

✔ **Stretch all the client's muscles.** The muscle groups to stretch are the:

- lower back
- upper back
- chest
- shoulders
- rear thighs
- front thighs
- hip flexors
- calves
- shins
- neck
- arms
- wrists

Figure 13-1:
When assisting a client with a stretch, be aware of hand placement.

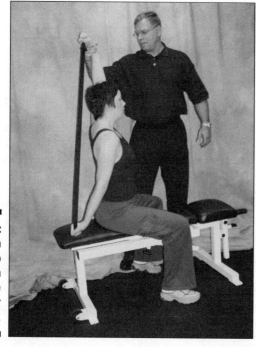

Figure 13-2:
Clients can
use tools to
help them
increase
their
flexibility.

For some great stretches your client can do on her own, check out *Fitness For Dummies,* 2nd Edition, by Suzanne Schlosberg and Liz Neporent, MA (published by Wiley).

Now for the Main Event: Exercising Your Client

You've probably already decided which exercises you want your client to do based on her fitness assessment (see Chapter 11). However, just as important as the exercises you give your client is how you present them. After all, when you were in high school, your math teacher didn't teach you algebra by tossing you a book or barking orders, did he? Great teachers make great students (and happy clients).

Strong but not silent: Teaching strength exercises

If you could toss your client an Olympic bar, tell her to do a chest press, and collect your $50, your job would be simple. But because each client is different and learns in different ways, you need to modify your teaching techniques for each client.

Here are some tactics for teaching your clients strength exercises. Use whichever techniques work best for the client you're working with:

✔ **Use analogies.** Some clients need to have a mental image of the exercise, so try using analogies. For example, when explaining a chest fly, you can tell the client to imagine that she's hugging a big tree and can't quite get her arms around it.

✔ **Demonstrate what you're looking for.** Your client may learn visually, which means you should show her how to do the exercise by doing it yourself, instead of simply by describing it.

✔ **Keep her from looking in the mirror.** Sometimes looking in the mirror while doing a move can confuse a client — she may not be able to mentally reverse what she's seeing in the mirror. Have her close her eyes; then you touch the muscle you want her to contract.

✔ **Ask your client to do a move while looking in the mirror, and then while turned away from the mirror.** That way she gets to see how the move looks, and then she uses her muscle memory to do the move again.

✔ **Try saying the same thing several different ways until the client grasps the concept.** For example, you can say, "During a seated chest press or a lying dumbbell press, you're working your chest, so keep your elbows at 90 degrees." Then you can say, "To keep your elbows at 90 degrees, you have to keep your shoulders down." That way you're drilling into the client's mind that the elbows need to be kept at — guess what? — 90 degrees.

During the first few workouts, you hands should never leave your spot for the client. If you always have your hands on your client, you can be in control of what happens — for example, if she drops a weight. After a few sessions, you can start taking your hands away more and more as the client becomes more conditioned.

You'll find spotting techniques in Chapter 14, but here are some tips to keep in mind during your client's first workout:

- ✔ **Keep your eyes on the client — not on the pretty girl or hot guy across the room.**

- ✔ **Be smooth.** Don't jerk the weight around while your client is lifting it.

- ✔ **Don't try to spot more weight than you can handle.**

- ✔ **Provide only as much effort as the client needs from you (see Figure 13-3).** In other words, don't lift the weight yourself! *Remember:* As sad as it may seem, your goal is to get rid of your client. In other words, you want her to become so proficient and so fit that she doesn't need you anymore. And how can that happen if you don't let the client do the exercises herself?

- ✔ **Offer encouragement.** An "atta girl!" can help the client squeeze out a few more reps.

When the client seems comfortable with an exercise, let her know that she's graduated, and you won't need to spot her all the time anymore. Then don't — unless she clearly needs it.

Be as verbal and descriptive as possible while you talk your client through each exercise. Use action verbs such as *stop, push, pull,* and *lift.* Tell her what to do, how to do it, and how much energy to put into it.

Figure 13-3:
Always spot your client from a position of strength — but don't do her work for her.

Getting feedback

During your session, feedback from your client is very important to you as a trainer. It lets you know how well the session is going, how well the client thinks the session is going, how hard your client is working, and whether your programming is on track. Feedback can come in a variety of forms, but here are the two main types:

- **Verbal feedback:** Grunts, groans, and the always beloved "I can't believe you're making me do this!" let you know your client feels like she's working — and working hard! On the other hand, if you get more than the occasional "Do I have to?" or a flat out "No!" you may want to rethink your intensity with the client.

- **Physical feedback:** If your client is breathing hard and perspiring, you're doing something right. Also, look for signs of flushed cheeks and quivering muscles to let you know you're on track.

Your client's body will tell you how hard she's working. If your client's face suddenly drains of color or if your client starts to feel clammy to the touch, she may be working *too* hard and could potentially be experiencing low blood sugar. Slow down your intensity or even stop the workout to prevent your client from becoming dizzy, nauseated, or even faint.

Although you can guess how hard your client is working by watching and listening to her, you can ask your client to rate her exertion by using the perceived-rate-of-exertion scale, to confirm your educated guess. During the course of your session, be sure to keep checking in with your client to see where she's at by asking her, "On a scale of 1 to 10, how hard was that exercise?" or "On a scale of 1 to 10, how hard are you working right now?" (For more on perceived rate of exertion, turn to Chapter 11.) When your client identifies how hard she's working, you'll be able to promptly adjust the workout to the intensity level you intend.

Don't hesitate to keep asking your client how she's feeling during the session. Constant communication during the session is vital, because your client can go from feeling great to not feeling good at all in a matter of minutes. Keep checking in with her — she'll appreciate that you care!

Cooling Down and Recovering from the Workout

Cooling down is a period of time after strength training that involves activities that are nonexertive and that allows your client's blood pressure, heart rate, and breathing to slowly return to normal levels before stopping exercise altogether.

You can effectively cool down your client in several ways:

✔ **Do abdominal exercises.**

✔ **Do low-intensity, steady-state cardiovascular work.** *Steady-state* means keeping intensity, pace, and heart rate all at one level — not changing throughout the program.

✔ **Perform trainer-assisted stretches.**

Cooling down takes roughly 10 to 15 minutes for the average client. Be sure to maintain these cool-down activities as *low*-exertion activities to enforce the cooling down period.

Melyssa's favorite way of cooling down a client is to stretch her — especially using the PNF technique described earlier in this chapter. Stretching is a great way to get the client's mind and body refreshed after an exertive work-out, while helping to safely get her respiration levels back to normal. Clients have told Melyssa time and time again that the stretching segment has become their favorite aspect of the session, too. They didn't realize how good stretching would make them feel!

After the session, you may want to ask your client to sit for a while before leaving your company. This just allows you to monitor how long it takes her to recover, and also to keep a watchful eye on her in case anything unforeseen happens. After she recovers fully, you'll be able to make a note in her file that it takes her a little longer to recover, and adjust her workouts accordingly.

Melyssa learned this lesson the hard way. One time, after a particularly hard leg session with a client, both she and her client were leaving the gym. Her client had been laughing about how hard it was to walk — until his leg buck-led underneath him as he took his first step down the stairs outside the gym! He fell down the stairs, completely taken by surprise. He didn't expect his legs not to be able to carry him down the stairs after the workout — and nei-ther did Melyssa!

Chapter 14

Teaching Your Beginning Client Beginning Exercises

In This Chapter

▶ Introducing your client to upper-body, lower-body, and core exercises

▶ Drawing out the program

▶ Including progressions

*O*ver time, you'll find that beginning clients tend to start out with the same set of exercises. Typically, for a client who hasn't weight-trained before, you need to condition all his muscles groups in a slow and safe manner before progressing him to more-advanced exercise routines with higher working intensities.

We call this method *developing base-level conditioning*. To accomplish this successfully, you typically prescribe a full-body workout with one exercise dedicated to each body part. In this chapter, we cover our top picks for beginning exercises.

With the multitude of exercises out there, this is only a tiny sampling of beginning exercises for your client. We picked these because they rely mostly on bodyweight and can be done in the home or gym.

Upper-Body Exercises

For men, the upper body is typically their favorite half of the body to train; they're reasonably strong, and they see improvements in this area quickly. For women, though, the upper body is usually the least-favorite half of the body to train; women aren't as strong here as men are, and they're often afraid of their upper bodies getting "too big." They don't want to look like Ah-nuld!

The following exercises are great starting exercises for either gender. They allow your clients to see progress without compromising their form, and you can have your client do them in a gym or at home.

Push-up

Muscles worked: Chest, shoulders, and triceps

Equipment needed: None

The movement:

1. **The client starts in the kneeling position and then leans forward, placing her hands flat on the ground so that her arms are shoulder-width out to sides, slightly in front of her shoulder line.**

2. **The client leans forward, putting her weight on her upper body.**

3. **The client walks her legs and feet back so that she's no longer kneeling and is now on her toes and hands, facing the floor, with straight arms and legs.**

4. **The client slowly bends her arms to allow her body to descend toward the floor.**

   Her knees, hips, and shoulders should remain aligned — they should look flat, like a board.

5. **When the client's shoulders and elbows make a 90-degree angle, the client stops her descent and starts to push back up to her start position.**

6. **When the client reaches her original position with straight arms, that counts as one full rep and she begins again.**

The correct spot for this movement is either to:

✔ Straddle your client, placing one hand underneath each hipbone.

✔ Kneel beside your client, placing one hand on her sternum and the other hand around her opposite side, on her hipbone.

Clients who have the following injuries should not do this exercise:

✔ Shoulder injuries or tendonitis (rotator cuff, anterior deltoid)

✔ Elbow injuries

✔ Wrist injuries or pain (carpal tunnel)

If your client cannot do a standard push-up, have her try to:

✔ Do a modified push-up, leaving her legs in a kneeling position rather than extending them into a standard push-up position.

✔ Perform only the descent to where she feels strain, with you helping her return to the start position.

✔ Do both of the preceding together.

One-arm row

Muscles worked: Latissimus dorsi, rhomboids, rear deltoid, trapezius, and bicep

Equipment needed: Dumbbell, plus bench or chair

The movement (using a bench):

1. **Standing on the side of the bench, feet pointing the length of the bench, the client puts the knee that's closest to the bench on the bench.**

2. **The client moves his standing leg out so that he forms a broad stance of support between the bent knee on the bench and the straightened leg standing on the floor.**

3. **The client leans over and places his hand (the same side as the foot that's on the bench) flat on the bench with a straight arm so that he's facing the floor with a straight back.**

   His hip and shoulder should be in line; he should look like a tabletop.

4. **With his free arm, the client takes the dumbbell and lets his arm hang with it straight from the shoulder.**

   This is the start position.

5. **The client lifts the dumbbell up and back, brushing his elbow and arm by his side, as if he were going to elbow someone behind him.**

6. **When the client reaches the top of the movement, he slowly returns to his starting position.**

The movement (using a chair):

1. **The client stands facing the back of a chair, with his feet shoulder-width apart.**

   Make sure the chair is far enough in front of your client so he can lean forward and place one hand on the back of the chair. You want him to have a 45- to 65-degree angle from his hip.

2. **With his free arm, the client takes the dumbbell and lets his arm hang with it straight from the shoulder.**

   This is his start position.

3. **The client lifts the dumbbell up and back, brushing his elbow and arm by his side, as if he were going to elbow someone behind him.**

4. **When the client reaches the top of the movement, he slowly returns to his starting position.**

The correct spot for this movement is to place one hand under the dumbbell and your free hand on the client's shoulder blade. Spot from the dumbbell and, with your other hand, lightly keep his shoulder down (keep his torso from opening up and from using momentum when rowing) to show him proper form.

Clients who have the following injuries should not do this exercise:

- ✔ Bicipidal tendonitis
- ✔ Rotator cuff injuries (depending on the weight used and the angle of the upper arm in relation to the torso)
- ✔ Any spinal injury that's aggravated by rotation or by doing a unilateral movement requiring core stabilization
- ✔ Neck injuries or strain

Beware of the following form problems:

- ✔ Rounded or hunched-over upper back
- ✔ Jerking of the weight
- ✔ Rowing with the biceps with little to no scapular retraction
- ✔ "Opening" the hips and torso when rowing
- ✔ Throwing the shoulder back

Dip

Muscles worked: Triceps, deltoids, and pectorals

Equipment needed: Bench or chair

The movement (using a bench):

1. **Sitting on the side of the bench, feet pointing away from the length of the bench, the client grips the side of the bench with her hands.**

   Hand placement should be right next to either leg.

2. **With straight arms and still gripping the bench, the client walks her legs forward so her hips come forward and off the bench.**

3. **The client stops when her hips are 3 to 4 inches past the edge of the bench.**

4. **With feet flat on the floor and knees at a 90-degree angle, the client slowly bends her elbows, placing her weight on the heels of her hands, and slowly descends to dip her torso below the bench line.**

5. **When her elbows reach 90 degrees, she starts pressing against the bench to raise her torso back up to the start position.**

The movement (using a chair):

1. **Sitting on a chair, the client grips the front of the chair with her hands.**

   Hand placement should be right next to either leg.

2. **With straight arms and still gripping the chair, the client walks her legs forward so her hips come forward and off the chair.**

3. **The client stops when her hips are 3 to 4 inches past the edge of the chair.**

4. **With feet flat on the floor and knees at a 90-degree angle, the client slowly bends her elbows, placing her weight on the heels of her hands, and slowly descends to dip her torso below the chair line.**

5. **When her elbows reach 90 degrees, she starts pressing against the chair to raise her torso back up to the start position.**

Spotting this exercise is difficult — the best way to spot is to straddle your client's legs, face her, and spot by grasping her torso on her rib cage.

Be careful if your client has:

- ✔ Wrist strain
- ✔ Elbow strain
- ✔ Shoulder injuries including rotator cuff issues
- ✔ Neck injuries

Beware of the following form problems:

- ✔ Using the legs rather than the arms
- ✔ Hunching forward
- ✔ Going too deep (beyond a 90-degree shoulder angle)

Bicep curl

Muscles worked: Biceps and forearms

Equipment needed: Dumbbells

The movement (standing or seated):

1. **With feet shoulder-width apart, the client stands with his hands at his sides, palms facing forward.**

   He should have a slight bend in the knees to relieve lower-back stress, his scapulae retracted and depressed (to isolate his biceps and prevent swinging), and his elbows in line with his torso or slightly forward to keep tension on his biceps.

2. **The client raises his arms so that he lifts the dumbbells in front of him, bringing the dumbbells up as far as the arms will bend, keeping his elbows close to but not touching his sides.**

3. **When the dumbbells are close to his shoulders, the client slowly lowers the dumbbells so that he returns to the start position of fully straightened arms by his side.**

To spot this exercise, stand in front of your client, place your hands under the back of his hands, mimicking the movement with him.

Be careful if your client has:

- ✔ Wrist strain
- ✔ Bicipital tendonitis
- ✔ Tennis elbow

Beware of the following form problems:

- ✔ Swinging his arms up
- ✔ Leaning back to lift the weight

Lateral raise

Muscles worked: Deltoids and trapezius

Equipment needed: Dumbbells

The movement (standing or seated):

1. **With feet shoulder-width apart, the client stands with her hands at her sides, palms facing her thighs. Similar stance as bicep curl but leaning slightly (10 degrees or so) forward in order to isolate the lateral head.**

   Standing vertically tends to involve the anterior as well as the lateral heads, so leaning forward a little remedies this problem. Make sure she keeps her scapulae depressed in order to isolate the deltoids over the trapezius. Those with poor strength and/or neurological control tend to activate the trapezius before the deltoids.

2. **The client bends her elbows slightly, cocks her wrists slightly, and raises her dumbbells out to the side until they're shoulder level.**

3. **After the dumbbells are shoulder level, the client slowly lowers the dumbbells to her start position of fully straightened arms by her side.**

To spot this exercise, stand behind your client and place your hands under her wrists, mimicking the movement with her.

Be careful if your client has:

✔ Wrist strain

✔ Tennis elbow

✔ Neck strain

Beware of the following form problems:

✔ Swinging the arms up

✔ Shortening at the elbow (not completing the full movement)

✔ Leaning back to lift the weight.

Lower-Body Exercises

The beautiful thing about the following lower-body exercises is that, usually, the client's own body weight is sufficient to fatigue the muscles. You typically don't need additional weight — although you can have the client hold dumbbells while performing these if you want to move the intensity up a notch! Your clients may grow to love these exercises.

Wall squat

Muscles worked: Glutes, quads, hamstrings, erector spinae, and abdominals

Equipment needed: Dumbbells (optional)

The movement:

1. The client stands with his back against a wall, feet together.
2. Keeping his legs straight and hips and back against the wall, the client walks his feet out from the wall 12 to 18 inches.
3. Keeping his feet in a neutral position, the client bends his knees so that he slides his body down the wall until he reaches a 90-degree angle with his knees.
4. He holds this position anywhere from 10 to 60 seconds.
5. The client pushes against the wall to raise his torso back up to the starting position.

Standing in front of your client, straddle his legs. Have your client hold his arms out straight (if he isn't holding dumbbells). Hold his hands and follow him down into the squat position with your arms. He will tense his arms and use your arms to help him get back up if he needs to.

Be careful if your client has:

- ✔ Knee pain
- ✔ Sciatica
- ✔ Pregnancy past the second trimester
- ✔ Arthritic hip(s)

Beware of the following form problems:

- ✔ Feet not far enough away from the wall
- ✔ Knees buckling in
- ✔ Client leaning forward off the wall

Shoulder-width squat

Muscles worked: Glutes, quads, hamstrings, erector spinae, and abdominals

Equipment needed: Dumbbells (optional)

The movement:

1. **The client stands with her feet shoulder-width apart, slightly turned out.**

2. **Keeping her legs straight, she puts her arms straight out in front of her for balance (if she's not holding dumbbells) and leans slightly forward from her hips. Scapula depressed and retracted, belly button drawn in.**

3. **Keeping her torso in the forward position, she looks ahead and slowly bends her knees, sitting back as she lowers her body until she reaches a 90-degree angle with her legs.**

4. **The client returns immediately to her start position and repeats.**

Depending on the comfort level of your client, you can spot this movement in two ways:

✔ **From behind:** Standing behind your client, place your hands on her hips. As your client descends, move your hands with her. This position allows you to control the rate at which she descends, as well as stabilize her torso if she falls forward or backward, and provide help if she needs it when getting back up.

✔ **From in front:** Standing in front of your client, have her place her palms on your hands. Act as a "bar" for her, providing balance and support through the amount of tension you provide by your spot.

Be careful if your client has:

✔ Knee pain

✔ Sciatica

✔ Arthritic hip(s)

✔ Pregnancy past second trimester

✔ Lower-back pain

Beware of the following form problems:

✔ Only lowering the torso and not sitting back into the squat

✔ Leaning too far forward

✔ Knees passing too far in front of toes

✔ Rolling knees and legs in during movement

Split squat

Muscles worked: Glutes, quads, hamstrings, erector spinae, and abdominals

Equipment needed: Dumbbells (optional)

The movement:

1. **The client stands with a split stance, one foot 18 inches in front of him, and the opposite foot 12 inches behind him, both feet facing forward.**

2. **Keeping his legs straight, he puts his arms on his hips for balance (if he isn't holding dumbbells).**

3. **Keeping his torso upright, he looks ahead and slowly drops his back knee straight down toward the floor, lowering his torso.**

   As he drops his back knee, his front knee will bend as well, enabling his torso to lower.

4. **When both knees reach 90 degrees, he pushes against the floor to return to his upright start position.**

To spot this exercise, stay on one side and face your client. Grasp him underneath the upper arm with the hand farthest from him. Place the hand closest to him on his sternum to keep his torso upright and prevent him from falling forward. Another simple way to spot is to straddle the back leg and spot like a traditional squat.

Be careful if your client has:

- Knee pain
- Lower-back pain

Beware of the following form problems:

- Going too deep
- Leaning too far forward (front knee passing over the front toe)
- Sitting back too far

Core Exercises

Clients love to hate their ab and lower-back work! These exercises are necessary components of any proper fitness regime, so here are two that are easy to teach and very effective.

Abdominal crunch

Muscles worked: Abdominals

Equipment needed: None

The movement:

1. **The client lies flat on the floor on her back, with knees bent and feet flat.**

2. **She places her hands behind her head so that her elbows are pointing forward.**

3. **Have her slowly curl her torso so that her shoulder blades come off the floor and her elbows are pointing at her knees.**

4. **After she's in a fully curled position, she slowly returns to her start position to perform the crunch again.**

To spot this exercise, kneel next to your client's head, and gently place one hand behind her neck so you can assist her curl if necessary.

Be careful if your client has:

- ✔ Neck strain
- ✔ Lower-back injury

Beware of the following form problems:

- ✔ Swinging with the arms to pull the torso forward
- ✔ Just moving the head and not the upper body
- ✔ Pulling on the neck with the arms

Back extension

Muscles worked: Erector spinae

Equipment needed: None

The movement:

1. **The client lies flat on the floor on his stomach.**

2. **He places his hands behind his head so that his elbows are out to the side.**

3. **Keeping his toes and legs in contact with the floor, he slowly arches his back so his chest lifts up off the floor.**

4. **After he has lifted his chest up off the floor, he slowly returns to his start position to perform the extension again.**

To spot this exercise, kneel next to your client's torso, and gently place one hand on his sternum so you can assist the lift if necessary.

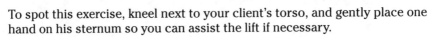

Be careful if your client has:

- ✔ Neck strain
- ✔ Lower-back injury

Beware of the following form problems:

- ✔ Swinging with the arms to pull the torso back
- ✔ Just moving the head and not the upper body
- ✔ Rocking from the hips rather than arching the back to lift

Drawing Out the Program

No, that's not a typo. In order to teach your client effectively, you have to do more than give him verbal instructions. You need to visually instruct him through demonstration, and physically instruct him through spotting. But you should draw the movement for him as well so when he isn't with you he'll have a visual reminder of what the movement is supposed to look like.

Sharpen your pencil and get ready, Picasso! Today you're going to master the drawing of stick figures. Yes, you heard us right — stick figures. Believe it or not, stick figures are the best way to represent a movement visually to your client. Trust us: When you aren't around to holler, "Turn your thumbs up!" your client will be glad he has his stick figures to refer to.

Here are some key points to keep in mind when drawing stick figures for your clients:

- ✔ Draw figures in the starting position.
- ✔ Use arrows to indicate the direction of movement to the midpoint.
- ✔ Draw which way the dumbbell heads should be facing.
- ✔ Use dotted lines for limb position to indicate the midpoint of a position.
- ✔ Don't be afraid to label if something isn't clear.

Figures 14-1 through 14-10 are stick figures we've drawn for the ten exercises that we outline earlier in this chapter. These drawings (obviously) don't have to be perfect, and you don't have to be an artist to create them. Just make sure you practice them before you draw them for your client.

Figure 14-1:
Stick-figure drawing of push-up.

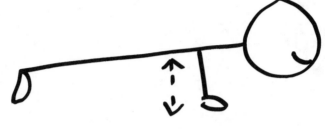

Figure 14-2:
Stick-figure drawing of one-arm row.

Figure 14-3:
Stick-figure drawing of dip.

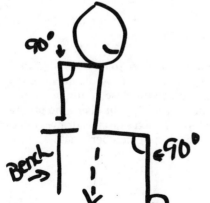

Figure 14-4:
Stick-figure
drawing of
bicep curl.

Figure 14-5:
Stick-figure
drawing of
lateral raise.

Check out www.wiley.com/go/personaltrainer for client program charts
with spaces on it for drawing your stick figures.

When you draw your stick figures, the place to do so is right next to the exercise sets, reps, and weights on your client's program sheet or in his exercise
workbook. Dedicate one page solely to the description of the program — a
place where, after you're through teaching your client the program, both you
and he can walk through the steps of each exercise, drawing out the movement and writing keywords to help him remember what he needs to do when
you aren't there.

Figure 14-6:
Stick-figure
drawing of
wall squat.

Figure 14-7:
Stick-figure
drawing of
shoulder-
width squat.

You can draw stick figures for stretches, too!

Figure 14-8:
Stick-figure
drawing of
split squat.

Figure 14-9:
Stick-figure
drawing of
abdominal
curl.

Figure 14-10:
Stick-figure
drawing
of back
extension.

Chapter 15

Taking Your Client to the Next Level

In This Chapter

▶ Helping your client take his training up a notch

▶ Knowing what techniques will get your client where he wants to go

According to the SAID principle (short for *Specific Adaptations to Imposed Demands*), the body will adapt to overcome a demand that is greater than what it is capable of performing at that time. What does this mean in plain English? Your client may not be able to perform 15 repetitions of a bicep curl with a 10-pound dumbbell *today* — but with repeated training, her body will continually grow stronger until it can achieve that workload. At some point, your client's once-slightly-weak muscles will inevitably become stronger. And when they do become stronger, the initial programming you've done for her will no longer seems as strenuous or challenging.

So, true to the SAID principle, you need to change your client's program to increase the demand on her body so she continues to be challenged, and she can continue progressing. The question is, how do you know *when* to progress your client, and exactly *how much* do you progress her by?

You may be tired of hearing this by now, but it's true: Each program you create is unique to that particular client's current level of conditioning and specific training goals. So it only stands to reason that the ways in which you help your client advance in her training depends on the client — what works for one person may not work for the next. In this chapter, we fill you in on some different methods and techniques you can use to take your clients' programs up a notch.

Taking the Next Step

Progressing your client is a skill and an art — one that's polished over time and with lots of client experience. Each client will respond in his own way to program change. As you gain working knowledge of your client's physiological responses to different workload scenarios, you'll soon be able to masterfully manipulate his exercise prescriptions to keep him continually progressing toward his goals.

Some techniques to create change in your client's program include the following:

- ✔ Increasing or decreasing rest time
- ✔ Increasing or decreasing repetitions
- ✔ Adding sets
- ✔ Adding exercises
- ✔ Changing the type of exercises
- ✔ Changing the order of exercises
- ✔ Adding weight
- ✔ Increasing exercise frequency

In the following section, we help you identify when the time is right to help your client advance, as well as come up with a plan to use for your client.

Ch-ch-ch-changes: Knowing when to change it up

If you go through a session with a client, only to have him look at you and say, "That's it?" that's a sign that he's ready for something a little more challenging.

Of course, the signs aren't always that obvious — not all clients love exercise, and not all clients will want to let you know that the workout was less than challenging. Most of the time, you're going to need to look for signs from your client — mostly nonverbal signs — that it's time to advance him.

Here are a few signs that it's time to advance your client:

- ✔ He talks through the entire set.
- ✔ He doesn't appear to be exerting much effort.

✔ His perceived exertion rate is under 6.

✔ His respiration doesn't increase.

✔ His heart rate doesn't elevate to his target training range during the set.

✔ He's no longer sore from his previous workout.

Taking it slowly

No matter how eager your client is, you need to advance him properly. Improper progression can result in injury, undue fatigue, and an overall unmotivating effect that can lead to your client saying, "No way, José," every time you ask him to do something. Your job is to manage your client's program progression so that his muscles, ligaments, tendons and cardiovascular system get stronger safely, before pushing him on to his next training level.

Here are some key points to remember when planning a program progression so that you end up with successful results (rather than a burned-out client):

✔ **Always put safety first.** If your client can't perform an exercise with acceptable form, you may want to introduce a different exercise rather than increase the weight or intensity for that one.

✔ **Change one aspect of the program per session.** If you were to change the weight, sets, reps, and rest periods for a client all in one session, you could end up injuring your client — and then you're not only not gaining ground, you're losing it. By changing one aspect of the program per session, you ensure that you allow enough time for your client's body to safely adapt to the new element.

✔ **Increase intensity, weight, or duration levels by no more than 10 percent.** For instance, you can increase his weight by 5 pounds for a few of his sets — not all of them. Or you can increase his reps for a few sets.

✔ **Allow a minimum of two weeks to elapse before increasing intensity, weight, or duration again.** For example, you may choose to increase his tempo of lifting after increasing his reps two weeks earlier.

✔ **When advancing a client's exercises, make sure you advance them logically.** You don't want to jump a beginning client who's never worked with free weights before from a machine-based program to a complete free-weight program. Institute change one exercise at a time over the course of a few sessions.

You can never progress a client too slowly!

Providing direction for clients you see less often

If your client has purchased a long-term package from you and you've been working with him on a frequent basis; then you have the luxury of knowing your client's capabilities well and you can continually monitor and advance his program each session as you work together. Unfortunately, that ideal scenario won't be the case for all your clients. For clients you're seeing intermittently, you need to provide precise direction on how and when to advance their program on their own, as well as set follow-up appointments that will enable you to reevaluate their fitness levels and make solid program changes.

When working with your clients whom you see less frequently, document everything when you're giving them a new program. You can even create a specific form just for program changes, with areas sectioned off to make notes so that your client will remember what to do when he's not with you.

Here are areas to cover when prescribing program changes for an intermittent client:

- **If/then scenarios:** Envision a few possible scenarios and tell your client what to do in each case. For example, you may say, "If this set is too easy, then next time increase your weight by 5 pounds."

- **Benchmarks for increasing intensity:** You want to make sure your client doesn't injure himself by being overeager. So you may say something like, "After your third week on this program, raise your repetitions to 15, keeping your weight the same."

- **Appointment for program change:** You need to tell your client how long he'll stick with this program before you implement another change. For example, you may say, "We'll need to reevaluate you for a new program in six weeks."

- **Recording his workouts himself:** It's important that your client record what he actually ends up doing for each workout so when you reassess him, you can see how well the program has been working for him.

- **Recording his intensity level during his workout:** As a trainer, you need your client to gauge how hard he's working when he's by himself. If he comes back to you with all his workouts at a perceived exertion rate of 4, you'll know that the program wasn't challenging enough for him.

Put it in writing! When you make program changes for an intermittent client, you end up giving him a lot of information in one session, which can be overwhelming. Most of the time, clients won't remember everything you've told them — but if you put it all in writing, they walk away with a solid program change that they can implement easily themselves.

Check out www.wiley.com/go/personaltrainer for sample workout log forms!

Strengthening Your Strength Techniques

You truly are only limited by your imagination when it comes to advancing your client. In the following sections, we provide some basic programming techniques to get you started. But remember, you're not limited to what you see here — be creative. Your clients will thank you for it!

Strength training routines

One strategy for taking your client to the next level is working out her body in smaller and smaller parts, starting with the full-body routine and ending with a five-day split where the client exercises a different body part each day. We outline these for you in the following sections.

Note: The full-body routine, two-day split, three-day split, four-day split, five-day split, and push-pull routine are all available at www.wiley.com/go/personaltrainer.

The full-body routine

The full-body routine assigns one exercise to each muscle group. This routine is an excellent format for beginning clients, because it provides a consistent format for creating a strong baseline conditioning level. When you're advancing the client within this routine, you can increase sets, weights, and intensity. This program can easily take your client from beginner to intermediate status.

Typically, beginning clients who are training two to three times per week will use this type of programming for their first three to four weeks of training. You can vary a client's exercises within the full-body-workout format, giving her the opportunity to keep the program fresh and interesting even though she's still training her full body each workout.

The two-day split

The two-day split is the next logical program progression after a client has mastered the full-body routine. When you're implementing the two-day split, you have your client devote one workout solely to upper-body exercises, then on the next workout, concentrate on lower-body movements.

By dividing the body into upper and lower regions, you enable your client to increase his *working volume* (how many sets he does per exercise) per session and per body part without risk of injury or overtraining. Alternating the body's regions each workout allows for adequate recovery time before you train the next region again.

The three-day split

The three-day split builds on the premise of the two-day split routine. After a client has adapted to the two-day split, her body will be ready to increase workload volume for more-specific body parts. Dividing the body further and adding an additional session to the program cycle allows the client to devote more training volume to each muscle group worked that session.

You can divide body parts in a three-day-split routine in a few different ways. ***Remember:*** How you choose your client's split depends on her individual training goals.

Here's one example:

- **Day 1:** Chest, shoulders, and triceps
- **Day 2:** Back, biceps, and abs
- **Day 3:** Legs

And here's another example:

- **Day 1:** Chest and back
- **Day 2:** Triceps and biceps
- **Day 3:** Shoulders and legs

The four-day split

Breaking down the body further for advancing clients, the four-day split is like the three-day split but divides the body into even smaller regions. Typically, when a client reaches this program level, she's considered to be advanced, and the intensity of this type of programming lends itself to more of a strength/power regime.

Here's a way to group body parts for the four-day split program:

- **Day 1:** Chest
- **Day 2:** Back
- **Day 3:** Shoulders and legs
- **Day 4:** Biceps, triceps, and abs

And here's another approach:

- ✔ **Day 1:** Chest and shoulders
- ✔ **Day 2:** Back and biceps
- ✔ **Day 3:** Legs
- ✔ **Day 4:** Triceps and abs

The five-day split

The five-day split is truly the pinnacle of programming for the serious trainer; the five-day split divides the body into even smaller regions to be worked out one day at a time.

By diving the body into even smaller regions, you can allocate more energy and intensity to training each muscle group. Although it may seem like you run out of weekdays for these sessions, the five-day split actually allows for more recovery per muscle group because you're only training each body part once a week.

Push-pull routines

A *push-pull routine* (in which you alternate a pushing movement with a pulling movement) can work well for any level client, because it allows for adequate muscle recovery. How you manipulate your client's rest and reps is what makes this program challenging.

Push-pull routines are a popular alternative for clients who have plateaued or who have been on a particular program style for an extended period of time. Push-pull training forces opposite muscle groups to work intensely back to back. This is great stimulus for the muscle fibers — it promotes confusion within the muscle, which can help "break through" any strength plateaus.

Advanced training techniques

In addition to giving your client new routine styles (see the preceding sections), you can try some advanced training techniques *within* the training routines. In the following sections, we provide a rundown of the most popular advanced training techniques.

Supersetting

Supersetting is when opposing muscle-group exercises are paired (such as a tricep push-down with a bicep curl) and performed back to back, without rest in between. After your client has performed the two back-to-back exercises, she rests. Then she performs the same set again.

This type of exercise pairing raises intensity without overloading the same muscle group. You extend the duration of the activity overall without over-stressing the active muscle group, because one muscle group rests while the other one works.

This method is great for advanced beginners, because it helps to raise their intensity level without overstressing their musculature.

Compound sets

Compound sets are based on the same principle as supersets (see the preced-ing section). The only exception is that same-muscle-group exercises are paired rather than opposing-muscle-group exercises. For example, you may pair a tricep pushdown with a tricep kickback if you're performing a com-pound set.

This method tends to be slightly more advanced, because the same muscle group is being worked for a longer duration, with no rest. We recommend this method for intermediate and advanced clients.

Strip sets

Strip sets are also known as *drop sets* or *breakdown sets.* When you strip a set, you have your client perform her regular set of a particular exercise. When she's reached the end of her set, you "strip" a certain amount of weight off her set (such as 5 or 10 pounds) and she continues to perform reps until she fails. When she fails, you "strip" some more weight off; she continues on until she can no longer perform another rep. Typically, this type of set is the last one of the workout, because she won't have anything left to do any more work otherwise!

This technique is advanced and should only be used with clients whom you know very well and who are very conditioned. If your client isn't that advanced, and you would like to try this technique with her, *don't* take her to failure. Instead, only perform two to three "strips."

Negatives

A *negative* is the eccentric phase (the lowering portion of a movement); typi-cally, it's the easiest part of a movement. A client is 130 percent stronger on the negative phase of a movement than she is on the positive phase (or lifting portion of a movement), which means she can *resist* 130 percent more force than she can *lift.*

Negative training occurs when you apply manual resistance during the lower-ing phase of a movement and the client resists the additional force, slowing the return to the start position, or when you assist the client in positively lifting

130 percent more weight in the eccentric phase, and she then resists all the way back to the start of the movement.

See Spot run: Spotting techniques

Spots on your uniform: bad. Spotting your client: good. Any trainer will tell you that a good spot goes a long way toward helping a client achieve fitness. You need to recognize *when* and, more important, *where* to spot.

A spot doesn't help your client if you aren't in a position where you can control her movement if she fails.

The most difficult movements to spot are free-weight and body-weight exercises. To spot free weights:

- ✔ Always spot from a position of strength.
- ✔ Place your hands by the joint closest to the weight (see Figure 15-1).
- ✔ Make sure you have stable body position.
- ✔ Make sure you can handle your client's weight yourself if she fails.

Figure 15-1:
When spotting free-weight movements, place your hands closest to the joints where the client is holding the weight.

To spot body-weight exercises:

- ✔ Spot from the client's nonmoving body part.
- ✔ Place yourself in a position to protect the client from falling (see Figure 15-2).
- ✔ Watch the client's posture.

Figure 15-2:
When spotting bodyweight movements, spot your client from your strongest position.

You can increase your client's intensity through your spotting technique. For example, you can apply additional light pressure to the arm of a machine to very gradually add extra resistance (as shown in Figure 15-3). Or, you can take the swing out of a client's movement by slowing her lift at the top of it. These are all good methods that can gently ease your client into more intense training methods in the future.

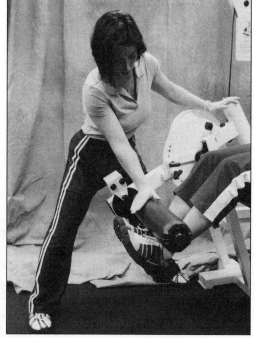

Figure 15-3:
Take the momentum out of a movement by placing your hand lightly on the arm of the equipment.

Let's Get Physical: Intensifying Your Client's Aerobic Workout

Strength programs aren't the only ones that need to be progressed. Your client's aerobic system will adapt just as easily as her musculature. Here, we cover two ways to intensify your client's aerobic program: interval training and mixing aerobic conditioning with strength training.

Introducing your client to interval training

Interval training uses moderately paced work interspersed with short, high-intensity work periods. Typically, the goal with interval training is to challenge your client's cardiorespiratory system enough that you can increase her aerobic capacity without overstressing her physiologically.

Whereas steady-state cardiovascular training is the common starting point for beginning clientele, interval training may be the next program type you want to incorporate into your intermediate client's programming repertoire. Two different types of interval training exist: aerobic interval training and anaerobic interval training. Aerobic interval training is when your client works to a level that is harder than what they are used to but not maximal during their interval phase (higher-intensity work). Anaerobic interval training is when your client pushes to his maximal work limit during his high-intensity bout.

Table 15-1 shows a sample interval program on the treadmill, for both an aerobic program and an anaerobic program. Notice that the anaerobic program's speeds are higher, meaning that the client is going to be working harder during those cycles.

Table 15-1	Sample Treadmill Interval Program	
Time	*Aerobic Program*	*Anaerobic Program*
Minutes 1:00 to 7:00	Warm-up (Speed 3.3)	Warm-up (Speed 4.0)
Minutes 7:00 to 8:00	Jog (Speed 5.0)	Run (Speed 8.0)
Minutes 8:00 to 10:00	Walk briskly (Speed 4.0)	Jog (Speed 6.0)
Minutes 10:00 to 11:00	Jog (Speed 6.0)	Sprint (Speed 10.0)
Minutes 11:00 to 13:00	Walk briskly (Speed 4.0)	Jog (Speed 6.0)
Minutes 13:00 to 14:00	Jog (Speed 6.0)	Sprint (Speed 10.0)
Minutes 14:00 to 20:00	Cool-down (Speed 3.5)	Cool-down (Speed 4.3)

Interval training is also great for:

- ✔ Breaking training plateaus
- ✔ Increasing VO_2 max (lung capacity)
- ✔ Increasing stamina
- ✔ Boosting metabolism

Mixing it up: Combining aerobic exercise with strength training

Another version of interval training — incorporating aerobic exercise in an interval manner into a strength program — can hike up the intensity of the session in a heartbeat. (No pun intended!) This style of programming is not for the fainthearted, as it puts together the best of both worlds — cardio and strength — and crunches them into one intense session.

For the intermediate client, after she has comfortably mastered performing her cardio and strength sessions separately on a regular basis, you want to incorporate this style of training gradually.

You still need to condition her body to the stress of this type of training, and the last thing you want to do is turn her off to it on the first session by working her too hard!

When beginning a client on this type of program, start her on pieces of cardiovascular equipment in between her exercises. This allows her to get the feel of performing cardio during her strength workout. Check out Table 15-2 for an example of this type of interval workout.

Table 15-2	A Cardio-Strength Interval Workout
Exercise	*Cardio Interval*
Lateral raise	Treadmill (2 to 5 minutes)
Chest press	Elliptical (2 to 5 minutes)
Lat pull-down	Stepper (2 to 5 minutes)
Tricep pushdown	Bike (2 to 5 minutes)
Bicep curl	Rower (2 to 5 minutes)
Leg press	Treadmill with incline (2 to 5 minutes)

As your client advances and comfortably masters the beginning stages of cardio-strength interval training, you can move her on to performing more intensive cardiovascular work in between exercises (such as jumping rope) and eventually between her sets. Bear in mind, however, that you still need to take it slow, because the higher the intensity of the session, the longer your client will need to recover and adapt.

For example, you may incorporate this type of session once a week, and during that one session, start out with your client only doing cardio intervals in between her exercises for a limited amount of time — say 20 to 30 seconds. As your client is able to comfortably perform the higher-intensity cardio intervals, increase her working interval time, up to two minutes. When your client is able to achieve that, you may want to consider switching her cardio intervals to in between her sets.

Some advanced examples of strength-cardio combinations are the following:

- ✔ Lateral raise with jumping jacks
- ✔ Chest press with jumping split squats
- ✔ Lat pull-down with jump rope
- ✔ Tricep pushdown with running in place (high-knee form)
- ✔ Bicep curl with box step-ups
- ✔ Leg press with jump squats

Watch your client carefully during these types of sessions — she can easily push too hard and potentially injure herself. Slow her down if her form is off — you won't sacrifice intensity if you can keep her form correct.

If your client needs a breather, give her the rest she needs. It will pay off in the long run, because she'll be able to perform more work if she's able to recover a bit during the session.

Part IV

Growing Your Personal Training Business

The 5th Wave   By Rich Tennant

Police SWAT Team
AEROBIC CLASS

SWAT

"Make sure everyone stretches before you begin, and this time don't frisk and pat them down while they're doing it."

In this part . . .

It's all about getting big. Your clients' muscles get bigger, your income gets bigger, and your business gets bigger. This part describes everything you need to expand your business.

First, we give basics on preparing for growth — how to document your systems and automate your processes so everything you need will be in place. Then, we describe all the ways you can expand your business, such as by adding massage services, nutritional services, and group classes; by giving seminars; and by selling fitness equipment.

When you start expanding, you'll likely need some help. That's why we also give you the scoop on hiring and — gulp! — firing employees, including information on placing want ads, conducting interviews, and staying on the right side of employment law.

Finally, we talk about how to build your business culture — that is, how to make the environment and atmosphere of your business conducive to great business, happy clients, and motivated employees.

Chapter 16

Preparing for Growth: Automating and Documenting Your Workflow

In This Chapter
- ▶ Getting ready to take on staff
- ▶ Creating an organizational chart
- ▶ Writing your employee manual

*T*he moment you realize, "Oh my gosh, I need more help!" is a defining moment in your career as a personal trainer. Needing help typically means that you've gotten where you want to go — you're at capacity and can't take any additional clients on yourself. Congratulations — this "problem" is a good one to have! But before you run out and post your help-wanted ad on Monster.com, take a few moments to consider this scenario:

> You hire your first employee. (Find more on *how* to hire your employees in Chapter 17.) You tell her, "Here's your staff shirt, your first client is Monday at 9 a.m. Don't be late."

How well do you think that employee will fare? Most likely, not too well. Studies have shown that the more energy and time you invest into on-the-job training, the more successful her career with you is going to be. Yes, taking on employees means that you're now responsible not only for your clients' success, but also for the success of your trainers as well.

In this chapter, we show you how to do the prep work that's necessary to make this important change a success.

Planning for Growth

So how do you ensure that you'll bring on successful hires? You plan for it! You developed your business plan to be a successful business owner, and now you need to develop your operating plan to be a successful employer.

Your *operating plan* outlines how your employees will carry out their responsibilities, defined by the steps needed to do so — the order of operations for your business, sometimes referred to as *workflow*.

Before you even think about hiring some help, you need to have an overall plan of how that employee is going to operate within your business, the role and responsibilities she will have, and how she'll contribute overall to the growth of your company. Sound like a lot? It is — but with a little work up front and the following information, you'll have your plan all mapped out in no time.

Thinking strategically

Strategic thinking sounds like a term you would hear thrown around in the Mergers and Acquisitions office of GiganticCo, Inc. Actually, strategic thinking is the process of developing your end vision for how your business will look when it's up and running successfully. It's a tool used by successful entrepreneurs — and no matter how large or small your company is, it's one that you should learn to use well.

Strategic thinking is a technique for framing and solving problems. Your first step is to assess your industry and your business — where you are currently — then identify where and how your efforts can be applied to reach your end goal.

Envisioning the end

If we were to ask you right now, "What is the end goal for you and your business?" would you be able to answer? When you plan for growth, you need to envision your ultimate goal as the end result, then work backward from there, planning what steps you need to take to reach your end goal successfully.

 Break out a pen and paper and write down your ultimate goal for your business. Don't be afraid to describe, in detail, what it will look like. This goal statement will be very useful to you later on as your business changes and evolves, to help keep you on track toward obtaining your goal.

Here are some things to keep in mind as you write:

- ✔ What will your business look like?
- ✔ What type of business structure do you need to create to support your vision?
- ✔ What type of employees do you need?
- ✔ How many employees will you need?
- ✔ What roles will they play in your company?

> ✔ What skill sets do your employees need to have?
>
> ✔ What types of problems will you need to be ready to handle?
>
> ✔ What types of obstacles will you need to overcome?

For some great resources on thinking strategically, check out the Small Business Association's Web site at `www.sbaonline.sba.gov/managing/growth/forecast.html`.

Working backward

Now that you've envisioned the goal for your business, write down the steps that you need to take to get your business there. (Does this sound familiar? This process is just like creating your business plan.) Working backward, think of everything you need to put in place to support your end vision. You may want to do some free-form brainstorming to help stimulate the old gray matter.

For example, say your goal is to own a personal training emporium with 20 employees. That means you'll eventually need to hire 20 people. To do that, you'll need to have enough revenues to justify bringing on more staff. To do *that,* you'll need to do more marketing to attract new clients. That's working backward.

This subject is one that a mentor, or someone who has grown her business before, can help you with. You may want to ask around for ideas and opinions as you go through this process.

Follow the Leader: Creating a System for Others to Follow

Now that you've defined your goal for your business, and you understand the type of staff it will take to get there, you're ready to create the how-to of your business — your business's rules and regulations, as well as the basics of how your company will run with others working in it.

Offering your clients consistent service

You have a special way of doing things — it's *your* way, the way that has worked so well that you now need to bring on other people to handle all the new clients clamoring for your stupendous services. And although you can't work with each client personally, you still want your clients to have the same exceptional experience with your new trainers as they would with you.

That exceptional experience comes from *consistency of service.* Consistency of service is what keeps your clients coming back. You want each trainer to have the same smiling mindset and upbeat, positive attitude for each client. You also want your trainers to dress the same way, spot your clients the same way, perform initial consultations and fitness assessments the same way, and so on.

To deliver consistent service, you need to:

- Document how you want clients to perceive your company and make sure your employees understand it.

- Document your business's steps of service — that is, the way and order in which employees carry out their duties with clients.

Developing your workflow

Without knowing it, you already have workflow systems in place. For example, when you perform an initial consultation or a fitness assessment, you follow specific steps unique to each of those sessions. Each step has a specific order that you execute it in; otherwise, you may not get the correct outcome. Each step and the order you execute it in are considered *workflow steps.*

When your staff performs those activities instead of you, outlining each step of a task, listing the details of how each step is performed, and identifying what happens after each step is important. How well your staff members perform those activities is reflected by how well you concisely detail each task's actions, and also by how well you train your staff to carry it out.

You want your business to run smoothly as much as you want your clients to receive excellent quality and consistency of service. You also want your employees to have a good working environment, where things are laid out well and they don't have to guess what to do if they don't know something.

Take some time to think about the recurring activities that you perform as a personal trainer. Then list the steps needed to complete each activity.

For example, let's say you want to outline for your employees how they should answer the phone and handle a call from a prospective client. Your workflow may look something like this:

> **Referred callers:** The bulk of our clientele is obtained through client and physician referral. Some of these people may want to speak to the referred trainer directly. If the trainer is not available, let the caller know that you have the trainer's schedule and would be more than happy to set up an initial consultation. If they still want to speak directly with the trainer, take their name, number, and ask who referred them. Tell them their call will be returned as soon as possible.

Phone book calls: When a prospect finds our ad in the phone book, she's generally calling for information about the services offered, pricing, and what we can do for her.

What to say: Generally, when a prospect calls to inquire about our services, price is the first question. Although we don't give prices over the phone, we can ask a few questions to help book the prospect. The following questions help to qualify the prospect:

> What's your name?

> How did you hear about us?

> What are you looking to accomplish?

Script: We're a personal training and nutrition company, offering one-on-one personal training and nutrition services to clients at our private facility, in your home, or the gym you belong to. The first step is to set up a free initial consultation. We will discuss your medical history and goals. Because we offer several different packages, from there we can decide the most efficient way for us to work together and packages and pricing will be discussed. The session lasts from 45 minutes to an hour. There will be no actual physical exercising during this session, just discussion. So what day would be good for you? (Slight variations of this are acceptable; this is the general idea of how we deal with new client calls.)

Who to book the consult with: After talking with the prospect, the next step is to have her come in for the initial consult. Schedule the prospect with the Client Care Specialist. Please be sure to appropriately code the appointment by obtaining the prospect's name, daytime phone, evening phone, referring source, and type of appointment. Allow one hour for the appointment.

Give directions over the phone or fax written directions to the prospect.

If the prospect doesn't schedule an initial consult, ask if she would like to be sent some information. Obtain her name, address, phone number, and referral source. Send articles and ad cards. Follow up a week later to see if she has any questions or if she is ready to schedule.

This is just one example of an everyday situation you may want to document for your employees. You can apply this approach to other scenarios as well, such as:

- Checking voicemail
- Answering phones
- Booking and rescheduling appointments
- Handling cancellations
- Performing the initial consult
- Selling a personal training package

> ✔ Collecting payment
>
> ✔ Performing a fitness assessment
>
> ✔ Performing a personal training session

When you've created steps for each activity that your employees will perform, the next step is to map out how all the activities and steps integrate with each other in the everyday flow of your business and assign who will handle each activity.

Mapping your workflow

Drawing a flowchart of the daily activities that occur in your business and how they integrate with one another is helpful. This chart will give you a bird's-eye view of your business and will let you spot conflicts and problems before you have people and systems actually performing these steps on a day-to-day basis. Figure 16-1 provides an example flowchart.

Administrative	Trainer
Opening	
Reception AM	**Trainer AM**
1. Check voice mail.	1. Disarm alarm.
—Return all calls and distribute messages.	2. Turn on lights, fans, radio.
2. Complete items on to-do report.	3. Check AND save messages.
3. Confirm next day's new appointments.	—Respond to urgent ones.
Mid-day	
Reception AM—End of Shift	**Trainer AM—End of Shift**
1. Validate sessions in schedule.	1. Pick up cups and towels.
2. List to-do's.	2. Wipe down showers.
3. Face front.	3. Wipe down equipment.
4. Stock bathrooms.	4. Stock bathrooms.
5. Bag towels.	5. Bag towels.
6. Check trash.	6. Check trash.
Administrative Manager	**Head Trainer—End of Team Trainer Shift**
1. Count bank.	1. Approve team trainer leave.
2. Approve reception AM leave.	
Reception PM—Beginning of Shift	**Trainer PM—Beginning of Shift**
1. Review and complete to-do's.	
2. Validate sessions in schedule.	
Closing	
Reception PM	**Trainer PM**
1. Enter next day's appointments on daylog.	1. Pick up cups and towels.
2. Print out trainer schedules.	2. Wipe down showers.
3. List to-do's.	3. Wipe down equipment.
4. Face front.	4. Stock bathrooms.
5. Stock bathrooms.	5. Bag towels.
6. Bag towels.	6. Check trash.
7. Take out trash.	7. Turn off lights, fans, radio.
	8. Arm alarm.

Figure 16-1: A flowchart can help you and your employees manage the day-to-day operations of your business.

You can create flowcharts for any system in your business, such as selling, training, hiring, and so on. All you need to do is list out the steps and actions involved, who performs them and when — and you have the meat and potatoes of your operations manual!

Writing Job Descriptions

Now that you have all your systems mapped out, and you know which employee is going to do which activities, you need to write job descriptions for each position you're planning to hire for (see Figure 16-2).

A job description is important, because it defines what your employee will be doing within your company. Making the job description functional and current is crucial — a poor job description can prevent your employees from doing a good job. A well-written job description will avert the oh-so-familiar "but it isn't in my job description!"

A well-written job description contains a concise summary of everything important about the job, such as:

- ✔ **The job title**
- ✔ **Individual tasks involved**
- ✔ **Methods used to complete the tasks**
- ✔ **The job objective:** This statement is generally a summary designed to orient the reader to the general nature, level, purpose, and objective of the job. The summary should describe the broad function and scope of the position and be no longer than three to four sentences.
- ✔ **The purpose and responsibilities of the job**
- ✔ **The relationship of the job to other jobs**
- ✔ **Qualifications needed for the job**
- ✔ **The relationships and roles relevant to the employee's position within the company, including any supervisory positions, subordinating roles, and other working relationships.**
- ✔ **The job location (that is, where the work will be performed)**
- ✔ **The equipment to be used in the performance of the job:** For example, does your company's computers run in a Mac or Windows environment?
- ✔ **The range of pay for the position**

Keep in mind that the job description you're creating now will serve as a base for future employees' job development and training.

Job Description
Team Trainer Position

1. Description

The UltraFit Team Trainer (TT) position is a part-time, salaried training position. The TT reports to the Manager.

2. Qualifications

The TT is required to have current personal training certification from one or more of the following certifying bodies: ACSM, NSCA, or ACE. The TT must also maintain current CPR certification from the American Red Cross or the American Heart Association. The TT must have two years of practical experience prior to employment.

3.Duties

The duties of the TT include, but are not limited to:

3A.1 Personal Training/Nutrition—General Duties

Maintaining and promoting client relationships

The TT will provide all clients with an exceptional, five-star training experience. To do this, the TT will:

  i.   Be ready 5 minutes prior to all training sessions.
 ii.   Train clients no fewer than 45 minutes, or no more than 75 minutes (unless otherwise agreed upon by management).
iii.   Train each client uniquely and specifically for his individual goals.
 iv.   Be a positive source of encouragement, education and feedback for each client.

3A.2 Personal Training/Nutrition — Specific Duties

  i.   Become completely knowledgeable about the exercise and nutrition methodologies practiced by the company.
 ii.   Become completely knowledgeable about each new client's needs, goals, location of training, package purchased, and assessment parameters prior to assessment.
iii.   Provide fitness and nutrition assessment, evaluation, prescription, education, and follow-up to clientele of the company, utilizing company-set protocols.
 iv.   Accurately record each workout in client's workbook, providing date of session, session number, exercises performed during session, and weights and repetitions performed per set per exercise per session.
  v.   Provide accurate, detailed notes of client progress in client files.

3B. Administrative

Maintain all paperwork critical to the operations of the company

The TT is responsible for all paperwork pertinent to the daily functions and overall health of the company and the company's clientele.

3C. Maintenance

Maintain equipment and fixtures of facility

The TT is responsible for the maintenance of the company's equipment and facilities on a daily basis.

4. Compensation

Compensation for this position is $32,400.00 annually.

I acknowledge and agree to the above statements and terms:

Signed:

Employee: _____   Date: _____

Manager: _____   Date: _____

Figure 16-2:
Have your new hire sign a job description and keep a copy on file in case you ever need to gently remind your employee what you expect.

When writing your job description, keep each statement short and clear. Be sure to structure your sentences in classic verb/object and explanatory phrases.

Charting Your Progress: Creating Your Organizational Chart

An organizational chart shows who's in what position and their relationships to one another. The *org chart* (as it's sometimes called by those who are super-busy) shows employees who their superiors are, as well as what positions they may be able to advance to within the company.

When you build your own org chart, you want to make the level of each position clear to your employees. Too often, org charts can become confusing, so keep it as simple as possible.

Here's how to build your own org chart:

1. **Start with yourself — create a box and enter your name and your title.**

2. **Create a row of boxes below yours for all the positions that will report to you; enter the title and position for each one.**

3. **Create connecting lines between your box and those of the people who report to you.**

4. **Create smaller boxes below the row of boxes directly beneath you to demonstrate the positions that report to your subordinates.**

Figure 16-3 shows an example of an organizational chart for a personal training company.

Here are some tips for creating organizational charts that will help — and not confuse — your employees.

✔ Draw your org chart on paper or use charting software like Visio.

✔ Make the box sizes correspond to the ranking in the company. Boxes are usually larger for higher-ups, the same size for peers, and smaller for subordinates.

✔ Draw all positions, even if you don't have an employee in place for that position yet. Show the position as TBH (to be hired) or TBD (to be determined).

✔ For positions that report to you for direction but report to another position primarily, use a dashed line rather than a solid line to connect their boxes to yours.

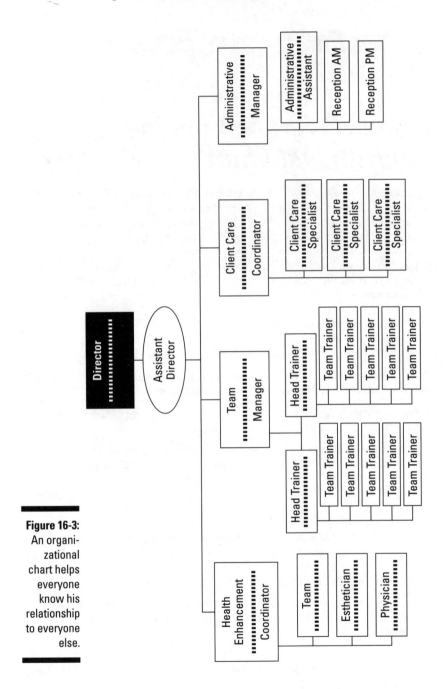

Figure 16-3:
An organizational chart helps everyone know his relationship to everyone else.

Creating Your Employee Manual

An employee manual will save you energy and effort in the long run. It will also help to protect your business against employees who can potentially be dangerous to the health of your company by their conduct.

An employee manual clearly communicates your business's policies, benefits, and expectations for your new hire. It also will lay out conduct policies and other hard-to-address issues.

Having a well written employee manual will:

✔ **Save you time.** Most times, new employees will ask you the same questions over and over again. By having all the answers consolidated in the form of a manual, you'll eliminate the need for employees to always come to you with questions about office procedures, and so on.

✔ **Improve your on-the-job training.** Your employee manual will serves as a roadmap for your employee to do his job correctly. The more procedures that employees are officially trained in, the more confidence they'll have in performing their jobs well.

✔ **Improve your consistency of service.** If you don't spell out exactly how you want an employee to perform his job, he probably won't do things the way you want them done. Your clients want consistent, reliable service — and they want to know what they're receiving every time they work with one of your employees.

✔ **Show your new hire that you're serious about your business.** After all, as they say, "There it is in black and white"!

✔ **Reduce employee misconduct by laying out your discipline policies.** This information can also come in handy if an employee ever disputes your rules or policies.

See Chapter 18 for details on how to create an employee manual.

Many resources are available to help you create an employee manual. You can even find employee-manual software and entire books devoted to the topic. Check out Employee Manual Maker by Jian Software (www.jian.com) to get started on the right path.

Chapter 17

Hiring Additional Staff

. . . .

In This Chapter

▶ Outsourcing to other professionals

▶ Hiring trainers

▶ Keeping your employees happy

▶ Laying off employees

. . . .

For years, you were probably someone else's employee — working hours you didn't want to for a paycheck that you didn't set. Now it's payback time — time for you to hire employees of your own!

But you'll find that there's more to hiring trainers than sticking a want ad in the local paper. You have to figure out the employment laws, understand how to find the best trainers, and know how to keep employees whistling while they work. That's what this chapter is all about.

Even if you aren't hiring other trainers, you probably *are* hiring such professionals as PR people, attorneys, and even designers and printers. In this chapter, we tell you how to find the best professionals for your business.

Outsourcing Is In: Hiring Professionals

Even if you don't need employees, you need employees. Does that make sense? Well, let's put it another way: Even if you don't plan on hiring other personal trainers in your business, you need to outsource certain tasks to professionals.

You can take the time to master the skills needed to handle these tasks yourself, but your clients probably aren't looking to hire a personal trainer/lawyer/painter/tailor. They want a personal trainer who knows her stuff inside and out, so focus on these needs and leave nontraining tasks to the professionals.

You probably need to consider hiring the professionals listed in the following sections. For more information on hiring an attorney, accountant, and insurance agent, check out Chapter 6.

Graphic designer

As we discuss in Chapter 8, you can create your own business cards and letterhead at home with paper from a supplier such as Paper Direct (www.paperdirect.com). But if you want to look truly professional — and not like someone who runs his business cards out of his inkjet printer — you need to hire a designer to create your logo and other designs.

To find a designer who will create graphics that will have clients flocking to your doors, try these suggestions:

- ✔ Check out the local Yellow Pages.

- ✔ Search online in graphic-designer directories such as the one at Open Directory (http://dmoz.org/arts/graphic_design). With the Internet, you can hire a designer who lives across the country!

- ✔ Ask other small-business owners and personal trainers who they use.

Can't afford a designer? Try these tips:

- ✔ **Barter your services for the services you need.** In Chapter 8, we give tips for bartering with other professionals. Perhaps you can trade personal training sessions for professional design services.

- ✔ **Contact a design school to find designers-in-training, who may be willing to charge less than full-time professionals in order to gain experience and credentials.**

Printer

A printer is the person who will make your letterhead, brochures, and business cards so beautiful that clients will weep with delight.

Getting your marketing materials professionally printed sounds like an expensive endeavor, but a printer can give you tips on how to save money, for example by using cheaper paper or by sticking to stock colors.

As with a designer, you can find a printer by browsing the Yellow Pages or asking other business owners who they use. Or try an online service such as iPrint (www.iprint.com).

An electrician

If you have your own facility, you may need to hire an electrician to make sure you have enough juice for all your equipment, to install lights, and so on. Whether you find an electrician through the phone book or through other business owners, ask to speak to some references.

Fix-it person

If you own your own facility, what happens when the air conditioning breaks or the ceiling starts leaking? You probably won't need to have a professional waiting in the wings, but you do need to know who you can contact to fix various parts of your facility, from the plumber to the air-conditioning repairperson.

Deciding on these individuals and building a relationship with them before you actually need them should lead to faster fixes when trouble does arise.

Internet service provider

If you plan to have a Web site, send out an e-mail newsletter, or answer inquiries via e-mail, you need an Internet service provider (ISP). Your ISP keeps you connected to the Web, hosts your Web site, and gives you an e-mail address. You can find good deals in ISPs at Freedomlist (`www.freedomlist.com`).

PR person

So you don't have the time or the ability to publicize your business. That's where a PR person comes in. She'll seek out PR opportunities, write press releases, contact editors and journalists on your behalf, and more. You can find independent professionals who may charge less than those who work at bigger PR firms, by searching on the Internet with a search engine like Google (`www.google.com`) or browsing through the business-to-business directory on Yahoo! (`http://dir.yahoo.com/business_and_economy/business_to_business/`).

A PR person can be pricey, but you can always try to barter. Melyssa netted free services from a hospital's PR person when she offered to hold free classes at the hospital.

Payroll company

A payroll company cuts checks for your employees' pay and handles tax withholdings as well. You can find a payroll company in the phone book or through an online search.

Pumping Up Your Ranks: Hiring Other Trainers

So you're ready to expand your business and take on more trainers. Congratulations! This is what many trainers dream of. You can't add more hours to the day, after all, so hiring help who will let you serve more people (and make more money) than would otherwise be possible is almost always a boon.

Don't write that want ad just yet, though. First, we want to give you the scoop on hiring, dealing with, and (gulp!) firing employees.

Uncovering where trainers hide out

Unfortunately, walking into the local gym and shouting, "Who wants to quit this dump and come work for me?" is bad form. But we have the scoop on how you can find trainers who would be happy to become your disciple and pave the way toward your goal of world domina— um, your goal of a healthy world for all:

- ✔ **Place an ad in the newspaper.** Be sure to outline exactly what you expect so you'll face no surprises. For example, if you want someone with a four-year degree and CPR certification who can work a 40-hour workweek, say so in the ad.

- ✔ **Use word of mouth.** Your clients know you well and can suggest trainers who fit in with your work environment and training style.

Melyssa had a client who came to her because she was dissatisfied with her current gym. The client said, "Y'know, the girl who took me through my orientation session at the other gym would be great over here." So Melyssa contacted the other trainer — who was so unhappy with her current work situation that she was ready to leave the profession. Melyssa hired her, and she ended up working with Melyssa for three years.

✔ **Contact the association you're certified through.** Associations' Web sites often have job-search boards or online forums where you can post an ad.

✔ **Use online job boards such as Monster.com.** Just as with a newspaper ad, make sure your ad at an online job board states exactly what you're looking for.

Evaluating a trainer's potential

If it were a perfect world, you'd be able to pull random trainers off the street and they'd be model employees. But alas, the world is not perfect — so if you want good employees, you have to do some research on the people who are applying to work with you.

Melyssa had a three-step process that helped her understand everything she needed to know about a potential trainer before hiring him.

Step 1: The written assessment

Before she even interviewed a trainer, Melyssa would hand him a written exam that she made up using information from training certification textbooks. The test included basic questions on anatomy, physiology, kinesiology, and exercise science. The assessment sure helped separate the wheat from the chaff — the test had a 75 percent *failure* rate.

Some applicants may be offended when you hand them a test, but don't let it faze you. Melyssa had one applicant who whined that she clearly didn't believe he knew what he was talking about. Guess what? He didn't — he failed the test. The lesson here: Those who can't will try to stop you from proving it; those who can will prove it and move on.

If the applicant failed, Melyssa sent him a letter saying that they couldn't continue the interview process, but that he could contact her when he was ready to try again. If the applicant passed, she would go on to Step 2.

Step 2: The interview

During the interview, Melyssa would ask the typical questions (more on that later), but she would also give a verbal test. For example, she asked the trainer to explain which muscle group would move the leg on the saggital plane, or to demonstrate adduction from the hip and from the shoulder, or what type of movement a dumbbell press is.

Melyssa would also give scenarios such as the following:

> You have a client who's been training with you for four years. She recently injured her back picking up a heavy box. Her doctor gave her moderate workout parameters. What exercises would you do and not do?

In addition to testing an applicant's knowledge, you discover how well she can present the information and where she may need polishing.

Step 3: The practical assessment

If the applicant passed the verbal test and Melyssa felt comfortable with him during the interview, the final step was a practical assessment — kind of like role-playing but without the blonde wig. One of her trainers would pose as a client and act out a scenario; for example, she might be a 55-year-old woman who has a rotator-cuff injury and likes to play sports on the weekend. The applicant would then help the "client" go through five exercises while Melyssa judged him on his communication skills, knowledge, spotting technique, and comfort level working with others.

If the applicant passed this final test, she would hire him for a 30-day trial period, in which he would trail Melyssa's trainers and their clients. Melyssa let the trainer go after 30 days if she found he wasn't suited for her business.

Being your own human-resources officer

Major companies have human-resources officers who hire employees and make sure that everything regarding the hiring and firing of employees is on the up-and-up. You don't have this luxury, so it's up to you to hire and fire employees, do interviews, and understand employment law. In the following sections, we show you how.

Doing background checks

If you've ever tried renting an apartment, you know that the landlord does a background check to make sure you're not some sort of psychopath (and that you can afford the rent). In the same way, you may want to do some sleuthing into your applicants' criminal backgrounds before you hire them.

You generally have the right to access arrest and conviction records that are public information,

but whether you can use such information for hiring decisions varies from state to state. Some states allow employers to discriminate based on criminal convictions but not on arrests. Other states apply varying rules depending on the position or industry the candidate is applying for. Check with your lawyer for the scoop.

Understanding labor or employment law

Labor law and *employment law* are the same thing — statutes found at all levels of government, from county to federal, that determine the rights and obligations that arise out of an employment contract. Labor law regulates everything from the initial hiring process and benefits to job duties and termination of employees, and protects employees from discrimination and unfair labor practices.

Your lawyer (see Chapter 6 for tips on finding one) can help you understand labor law as well as write up employment contracts and other contracts and forms you need in your business relationship with an employee.

Knowing the costs of hiring others

Think that wages are your only employee-related cost? Think again. You also have to pay for workers' compensation insurance, unemployment tax, and Social Security tax:

- ✔ **Workers' compensation insurance:** Workers' compensation insurance (or as the cool kids say, *workers' comp*) covers your employees if they get sick, injured, or even killed on the job. The benefits they receive include medical expenses, lost wages, vocational rehabilitation, and death benefits. Workers' comp doesn't protect just the employee — it also protects the employer (that's you). Before workers' comp existed, a serious injury to an employee could put you out of business. Now, all the lost wages, rehab, and so on are paid by the insurance, no matter who's at fault.

   Workers' comp requirements vary from state to state, so call your state's insurance commissioner's office for more info (you can find the phone number in the government pages of the phone book). Your insurance agent can also help you with the details.

- ✔ **Social Security and Medicare taxes:** Social Security (also known as FICA) taxes provide for benefits for retired workers and the disabled and their dependents. Medicare taxes provide medical benefits for certain people when they reach age 65. Not only are you required to withhold Social Security and Medicare taxes from your employees' paychecks, you also have to match their contributions. So if the employee owes $7,000 in Social Security and Medicare taxes, you deduct half of that from the employee's paycheck and pay the other half yourself as the employer. (You may have noticed that if you were self-employed, you would have to pay the whole $7,000 yourself.)

- ✔ **Federal unemployment tax:** Most employers have to pay federal unemployment tax, though if you're a sole proprietorship or partnership, you don't have to pay the tax on your own compensation.

Before you start putting out want ads, you should know that all these taxes and benefits can cost you an additional 20 to 35 percent over and above an employee's gross wages.

We could write another book just to explain all the taxes and other costs associated with hiring employees! Contact your accountant for more-detailed information.

Identifying when an independent contractor is really an employee

You may find hiring independent contractors (sometimes called *freelance trainers*) more convenient. But the government sets strict rules on who is an employee and who is an independent contractor, and the distinction is important because it determines how you handle taxes and what laws govern your relationship with the person you hire. For example, if the person you hire is an independent contractor, you don't have to match his Social Security and Medicare contributions.

How do you know if what you have is an employee or an independent contractor? An independent contractor:

- Is in business for herself
- Makes quarterly federal and state income-tax deposits
- Pays the entire contribution for Social Security and Medicare taxes
- Provides her own insurance and benefits
- Is not subject to wage and hour regulations
- Has no employer-employee relationship with you
- Controls the means by which work is performed

If you're confused about whether someone you've hired counts as an employee or an independent contractor for tax purposes, consult your lawyer or accountant.

Interviewing Potential Employees

So many times you've been interviewed for jobs, and now it's your turn to put someone in the hot seat. But it can be just as nerve-wracking to be the person on the other side of the desk. Here we tell you everything you need to know about planning for and conducting interviews.

Arranging and setting up interviews

Set up the interview in a place you're comfortable in. You can interview applicants:

- ✔ In your home (make sure you have a desk and chairs set up)
- ✔ At your gym
- ✔ At a café — as long as you pick up the tab!

As for what time to conduct the interview, try to be accommodating; many people have full-time jobs and find it hard to get away during the 9-to-5 work-day. Melyssa has interviewed applicants at both 6 a.m. and 6 p.m., in addition to more-typical business hours.

Conducting the interview

When you're interviewing a potential employee, don't be nervous! Here are tips that will help you conduct a great interview and make the right hiring decisions for your business:

- ✔ **Dress for success.** Melyssa wore her training uniform for interviews.

- ✔ **Write out your questions.** You won't be reading from them like a robot, but having them in front of you will help you remember what to ask and will ensure that you ask all applicants the same questions so you can compare apples with apples. Avoid questions that can be answered with a simple "yes" or "no." (More on what questions to ask — and not ask — is later in this chapter.)

- ✔ **Make a mental note of your first impression.** How is the applicant dressed? She should be wearing a pantsuit or other casual business attire (no three-piece suit needed!). How is her handshake? Does she smile and look enthusiastic about the job?

- ✔ **Put her at ease.** Try some friendly small talk to break the ice. A good way to do this is to explain your company and the job the candidate is applying for.

- ✔ **Ask your questions, and give the applicant time to formulate answers.** Ask follow-up questions such as "Why did you do that?" and "How did that happen?"

- ✔ **Take notes during the interview.** After the dust clears, remembering whether it was Applicant A or Applicant B who said such-and-such can be difficult. But be unobtrusive — you don't want the applicant to feel like you're grading her on everything she says!

✔ **Near the end of the interview, ask the applicant if she has any questions for you.** This not only gives the applicant a chance to clarify the job in her mind, but also shows you whether she's done her research. Does she ask questions about things she should already know (such as what client population you service), or does she ask intelligent questions about your training process? There's a big difference between the applicant who asks, "I noticed that your main competitor has a new Web site. Do you plan to build one?" and the one who asks, "How many vacation days do I get?"

✔ **Let the applicant know what to expect.** Will you call her with the results, and if so, when? Will you want her to take a test or demonstrate her skills?

What you should ask

They're what make an interview an interview — the questions. But how do you know what to ask? Here are some suggestions:

✔ What made you choose this field as a career path?

✔ What experience have you had training people?

✔ Tell me about your *worst* personal training experience and why it was bad.

✔ Tell me about your *best* personal training experience and why it was good.

✔ What was the most recent mistake you made with a client?

✔ Have you ever injured a client?

✔ What interests you most about this company?

✔ What are your greatest strengths and weaknesses?

✔ If you could design the perfect job for yourself, what would you do? Why?

✔ How would you describe your current supervisor?

✔ What are three things you like about your current job?

✔ What were your three biggest accomplishments in your last job?

✔ What do you like best and least about personal training?

✔ What do you do for your own workout and why?

✔ What are your career goals?

Why are you asking these questions? Do you really care what the applicant's career goals are (unless they're to take over your job) or how much he works out? If you listen carefully, you can glean valuable information from your candidate's answers.

For example, Melyssa asked applicants about bad experiences working with clients. If the applicant replied that he was upset because a client wouldn't stop talking, Melyssa would know that he had communication issues and didn't like to hear about others — after all, it's only natural that clients will want to talk. When the applicant gives his answer, listen for potential red flags. When Melyssa asked, "How would you describe your current supervisor?" one applicant replied, "She's a real witch!" See how easy it can be to narrow down your field with these open-ended questions?

What you should never ask

In a nutshell, you can only ask about the applicant's skills and experience as they relate to the job. Other questions can be considered discriminatory — as you probably know, strict laws prohibit discriminating against job applicants based on sex, race, disability, religion, marital status, and so on. Here are some questions that are taboo:

- ✔ **Do you have any disabilities?** Ask this question, and you can run afoul of the Americans with Disabilities Act.

- ✔ **Do you plan to have children?** Although it's true that parents sometimes have to take time off to care for their kids, basing a hiring decision on this fact is considered discrimination.

- ✔ **Are you married?** If you ask this question, it can be interpreted that you discriminate against married or unmarried employees.

- ✔ **How old are you/what is your date of birth?** Age discrimination is another no-no. However, if you're interviewing a teenager, you can ask if he is at least 16 years old.

- ✔ **Have you ever filed a workers' compensation claim or been injured on the job?** This question is considered a disability-related one.

- ✔ **What is your sex/race/creed/color/religion/national origin?**

- ✔ **When were you discharged from the military?** Discriminating based on military duty is illegal.

- ✔ **What is your maiden name (for female applicants)?** This is just another way of asking whether the applicant is married and is just as illegal.

- ✔ **Are you a U.S. citizen?** However, you *can* ask if he has the legal right to work in the United States.

- ✔ **Have you ever been arrested?** You may, however, ask if the person has been convicted, as long as the question is accompanied by a statement saying that a conviction will not necessarily disqualify an applicant for employment.

Payday!: Dealing with Compensation

The best things in life may indeed be free, but those people you hired will expect something from you besides a hearty "Good morning!" and the occasional pat on the back. It's called money. Here, we tell you how to develop a payment plan that will tickle your employees pink without putting your business in the red.

Developing a pay/commission schedule

Determining what to pay your employees can be difficult. You want them to be able to make a living — but at the same time, you don't want to go broke yourself.

Your business plan (see Chapter 5) should help you make a decision. According to the plan, what are your overhead costs? What are your taxes and other expenses? Melyssa's overhead costs were 40 percent (that's pretty high, but she had a very nice facility), and after factoring in taxes and other expenses (like money for emergencies and her own income), she was able to pay her employees 40 percent of the take.

Find out how much other personal trainers are charging clients and paying employees. You should have a range of numbers. Where do you want to land on that scale?

Did you ever notice how you can walk into certain stores and the sales clerks are all over you like ants on a donut crumb? And the sales clerks make sure you know their names when they help you? These employees are on commission — they get a percentage of every sale they make. The good news is that commissions motivate your employees to work harder, and you pay only for results. The bad news is that working on commission can be stressful for employees. Also, determining how to pay commissions can be difficult. If a trainer sells a $2,000 package and collects only $1,000 before the client quits, do you pay commission on the $2,000 or the $1,000?

Your accountant and mentor (see Chapter 6) can help you decide whether to pay commissions, and if so, how to do it.

Motivating employees

A client walks in, and the trainer, after finishing his conversation with another trainer about the latest *New York Times* bestseller, saunters over and greets the client with a grunt. That's one unmotivated employee.

Unmotivated employees — employees who don't feel valued, appreciated, or challenged — are unhappy employees, and unhappy employees equal unhappy clients.

Believe it or not, motivation isn't about money. Even if you pay your employees sky-high rates, if they're working in a poor environment or you let clients treat them badly or you don't praise them for a job well done, they'll be unmotivated. Read on to find out how to keep your employees engaged and productive.

Rewarding employees with perks and benefits

Which employer would you work harder for: the one who offers a paycheck and that's it, or the one who rewards you above and beyond the expected paycheck for doing a good job? If you're like most people, you'd prefer the job with the rewards.

Here are ways to motivate your employees through perks and benefits.

- ✔ **Offer extra time off, such as an extra 30 minutes for lunch or a day off.**

- ✔ **Offer benefits like a 401(k) plan and health insurance.** Talk to your accountant and insurance agent for more information.

- ✔ **Give praise.** Employees love to hear they're doing a good job. A nice thank-you note or even a simple "Good job!" can go a long way toward keeping an employee motivated.

- ✔ **Give employee discounts on products you carry.**

- ✔ **Give gift cards for local businesses.**

Creating sales incentives

Many businesses, both personal training and otherwise, motivate employees with sales incentives. For example, the employee who sells the most personal training packages may get a cash bonus or other prize.

Melyssa doesn't recommend using sales incentives. In her opinion, the personal training industry is sales-driven enough as it is, and sales incentives can turn your employees from caring trainers into hard-sell machines whose goal is not to train clients, but to sell packages and products. In addition, the hard sell can burn out clients and trainers alike.

If you don't want to go the sales-incentive route, you can use the motivating techniques from earlier in this chapter to reinforce behavior you want to see in your trainers. Motivated employees are happy employees, and happy employees equal happy clients.

Offering flexible and part-time schedules

If you can swing it, offer part-time and flexible schedules to trainers who love working with you but don't love the hours. For example, if one of your trainers is a single parent or has a second job, she may appreciate the ability to work odd hours.

Melyssa had a trainer who had a government job and who wanted to train only part-time. She gave him the okay, and he was one of the best trainers she had. If she could have had ten of this guy working only part-time rather than five other people working 40-hour weeks, she would have been a very happy camper.

Providing a happy place to work

A poor working environment can lead to unhappy employees. Would *you* be motivated to go to work in a dank, smelly gym? If you have your own work-space, follow these tips to keep it pleasant for your employees (and your clients).

- ✔ **Keep it clean!** Make sure the equipment and other surfaces are dust-free, that the bathrooms are clean and sanitized, and that the air is fresh. Yes, your employees are likely the ones doing this grunt work, but a little work from each of them will provide a fantastic work environment for all of them.

- ✔ **Make sure the equipment is in good shape.** After all, what trainer wants to train clients on equipment that's rusty or falling apart?

- ✔ **Keep a small fridge stocked with water and sports beverages.**

- ✔ **Make sure employees have a place they can go to eat lunch and take breaks in private.**

- ✔ **Set the tone for the environment that you work in.** Melyssa's environment was fun and upbeat, with music that kept everyone moving.

- ✔ **Play games and have parties.** Who doesn't like games and parties? Try healthy potlucks on Fridays, or birthday parties with games like Pin the Tail on the Muscle Group. Melyssa's business had pizza (with grilled chicken and soy cheese) and Chinese food (steamed, not fried) on Friday nights.

Parting Is Such Sweet Sorrow: Firing and Laying Off Employees

Downsize, lay off, pink slip — no matter how you say it, it's an unpleasant task. But the sad fact is, you may need to fire an employee. Maybe she's had disciplinary problems, like showing up late for sessions, or maybe she's proven to be less competent than you would like (though if you read the earlier section on hiring the best employees, you may improve your chances). Here, we show you how to make the process as painless as possible.

Understanding the law

Before you take on an employee, you explain the job requirements and make a deal: "You do X for me and I'll pay you Y dollars per month." If the person is not able to do X, you're not obligated to keep that person on the payroll; you're entitled to find someone else who can do the job.

Under the *at-will* employment doctrine, either the employee or the employer can terminate employment at any time, for any reason, except for reasons involving illegal discriminatory action. Talk to your lawyer for more information.

If you implied or expressed job security for a certain amount of time (that is, you gave the employee reason to believe that he would have a job for a certain length of time — for example, you said the job would last one year), you need proper justification to fire the employee. Examples of proper justification are neglect of duty, dishonesty or unfaithfulness, misuse of trade secrets, and theft.

As always, consult your lawyer, who can help you draw up employment contracts and make sure you're always on the right side of the law.

Documenting disciplinary actions

Remember when you were in high school and your teacher threatened to put a negative note in your permanent file? Well, she'd make a great personal-training-business owner because she understood that you have to create a paper trail when it comes to disciplinary actions. If you don't record your employees' violations and the actions you took as a result, you can be sued for wrongful termination.

Make sure you have a plan for handling employee violations. For example, Melyssa had a three-strikes policy:

- **Strike 1:** The employee got a verbal warning, which lasted for 30 days.

- **Strike 2:** The employee got a written warning, which went into his permanent file.

- **Strike 3:** The employee got paid time off — what Melyssa called *decision-making leave*. The employee was to use this time off to either choose to change his behavior or to leave the company. If the employee left, it was voluntary. If he decided to stay on, he had 30 days to prove he had reformed, or she would let him go.

Melyssa hired someone as a receptionist who planned to become a trainer after she got her certification. But this employee was bad news — she would disappear for days at a time. Melyssa finally had to fire the employee. But because Melyssa didn't thoroughly document the employee's slip-ups and the disciplinary actions she had taken, the state magistrate ruled that Melyssa had fired the employee unjustly. The former employee was allowed to collect unemployment insurance, and Melyssa's unemployment tax rate went up as a result. Don't let this happen to you. Always keep detailed records!

Making the break

It's time to do the deed — you just can't keep that employee on any longer, and you need to let her go. Here's how to do it with a minimum of emotional (and legal!) trauma:

- ✔ **Think hard before you do it.** Remember that even a very weak job performance can be brought up to snuff with enough effort. Remember also that firing someone can have a traumatic impact on your staff and exposes you to potential lawsuits. Do you really need to fire this person?

- ✔ **Give the person a chance to change.** Don't fire someone out of the blue — make sure you give her every chance to improve her job performance. If you do and she doesn't, you're less likely to be faced with legal action. If you document all employee violations and disciplinary actions, you won't take her by surprise when you hand her a pink slip. In addition, your other employees will feel less threatened if they know that the employee blew every chance you gave her.

- ✔ **Talk to your lawyer.** If you have any doubts or questions about firing someone, talk to your lawyer. It may seem like a hassle, but compare that to the hassle of a lawsuit!

- ✔ **Plan what you're going to say, and stick to it.** Believe it or not, if you offer kind words about the employee's performance to soften the blow, you open yourself up to potential lawsuits. After all, if you liked the employee's performance enough to compliment it, why are you firing her? Plan what you're going to say — and don't even hint at anything positive regarding the employee's performance. Focus on why you're firing her.

- ✔ **Stay cool.** Soon this person will be gone from your company forever, so don't let her get to you if she lashes out, irritates you, or becomes verbally abusive.

- ✔ **Be nice.** Although you shouldn't say anything positive about the employee's job performance, that doesn't mean you have to be cruel. Being fired is a traumatic experience for most people. Be kind.

Chapter 18

Building Your Business Culture

*B*usiness culture — it sounds like your personal training company is traipsing around European museums *oohing* and *aahing* over Picassos and Matisses. But really, your business culture is everything that makes your business what it is — your leadership skills, your mission, your attitude, your employees. It's your beliefs and values, the unwritten rules in your company, the "way we do things here."

In this chapter, we tell you how to build a business culture that keeps clients and employees — and yourself! — happy and motivated.

Lead, Follow, or Get Out of the Way

Guess who your employees are looking to for leadership? Don't look around like that — we mean you. Now that you have a business and employees, you're a leader. You've got the power!

No one can really define what leadership is, but they know it when they see it and they miss it when it's not there. In the following sections, we help you become a leader employees will want to follow.

The buck stops here

Realizing that the health and well-being of your entire business — including your clients, your employees, and yourself — rests directly on your well-conditioned shoulders can be scary. Your business will succeed or fail based on your own behavior.

Your employees may love you, they may adore your business — but if your company were to go belly up, they'd simply find different jobs. They don't have as much invested in the business as you do. That's why you need to take responsibility for your business — because nobody else is going to do it for you. For example:

✔ **If an employee continuously makes mistakes, fails to follow up with clients, or comes in late, you need to take quick action to put a stop to the bad behavior and to reinforce the behavior you want.** You can't just let it slide, hoping the problems will go away. They won't. And when other employees see what one staff member is getting away with, they may decide to try it for themselves.

✔ **If sexual harassment occurs in your workplace, you may be held liable if you knew about it and didn't take steps to stop it.**

✔ **If clients continue to make the same complaints — for example, that your training space is too hot or that they don't like one of your policies — it's up to you to fix the problem if you want your clients to keep coming back.**

✔ **If an employee is out sick, you need to make sure that the tasks he usually does are taken care of by someone else (even yourself if it comes to that).** Yes, this means you may have to take out the trash sometimes.

This doesn't mean that you have to do everything yourself, from cleaning the toilets to plotting your business growth. Later in this chapter, we give advice on delegating tasks to your employees.

Envisioning your vision and philosophizing on your philosophy

Most people say they'll follow a leader who stands for something, who has good values and a good business philosophy. Think about why you're in business, where you want to go, and how you hope to help people. You may even want to break out some paper and write this down.

The vision of Melyssa's business was "to educate clients through hand-tailored exercise and nutrition prescriptions while improving their lives through successful lifestyle-modification formulas." Who wouldn't stand behind that? Melyssa's philosophy was, "True success comes from hard work, integrity, and knowledge. We believe in completely educating our patrons so that they can make well-informed, positive lifestyle decisions."

The key is to write a vision statement and philosophy that works for you and your business.

Leading by example

If your employees see you doing something, they'll do it, too. If they see you snapping at clients, forgetting to follow up, and cutting corners, guess what? They'll probably do the same. If, on the other hand, they see you providing service with a smile, acting like a professional, and putting all your energy into doing a good job, they'll be inspired to do likewise.

Here are some ways you can lead by example:

- ✔ **Dress the way you want your employees to dress.** Your employees will hate wearing that yellow company polo shirt if you show up every day in jeans and a T-shirt that reads, "Born to fish."

- ✔ **Eat right.** No snacking on candy bars while on the job!

- ✔ **Don't call in sick if you aren't actually sick.** Yes, they *will* find out.

- ✔ **Show up on time.** Why should employees bust their rear ends getting to work on time if you always saunter in at 9:30?

- ✔ **Treat people well.** Put on your best smile and show your employees, by example, how you want them to treat clients and each other.

Communicating effectively

Leaders (that's you, remember?) need to be able to communicate clearly. They need to be able to say what they want done and know that it will be done.

Most people think of communicating as a one-way process. One person talks, and then when there's a pause, the other person talks. Where's the listening? When someone talks, you should listen. Don't think about what you're going to say next or wait impatiently for a pause so you can jump in. Actually listen to what the other person is saying and try to understand what he wants.

Your body language says a lot about you. For example, if you're tapping your finger on the desk, chances are you're feeling impatient or combative. If you're leaning forward, you're seen as open and engaged. That's why it's important to make sure your body is giving the message you want to give. For example:

✔ **When talking with someone, make sure you look directly into the other person's eyes.** (But don't stare — that's just creepy.) Wandering eyes signal wandering attention.

✔ **Mirror the other person's body language, which keeps the two of you in harmony.**

✔ **Don't cross your arms or lean away from the other person.** Either of these behaviors indicates hostility or that you're rejecting what he's saying.

✔ **Keep your hands open with your palms showing to signal openness and warmth.**

You can also decipher other people's body language as a way of figuring out how they're really feeling. See Chapter 9 for a table of body signals and what they mean.

If you don't know the answer to something, say so; people will respect your honesty. On the other hand, if you fake it, people will think you're, well, a fake.

To make sure you're understanding what the other person is saying, say it back to him in your own words — for example, "So, what's concerning you is that we don't have a candy machine in the lobby. Is that right?"

Try to understand and address how the other person is feeling. For example, "It must be frustrating for you that you need the day off on Thursday but no one can stand in for you. I appreciate the fact that you're missing the log-toss competition to be here today."

Asking questions shows that you're listening and heads off problems before they begin. Questions also offer great learning opportunities — after all, if you don't ask, you'll never know! Here are some tips on asking (and receiving!):

✔ **Try to ask questions before stating your point.** You may discover something that changes what you planned to say.

✔ **Don't just stick question marks on the ends of statements.** Think about what you can find out from someone or from a situation and formulate questions accordingly.

✔ **Question, don't interrogate.** Make sure you're asking because you want to find out more, not because you want to attack or cast doubt on someone's idea.

For more information on improving your communication skills, check out *Communicating Effectively For Dummies* by Marty Brounstein (published by Wiley).

Considering what other people want

Some really hard-core trainers just don't know — or care — where their employees and clients are coming from. They think, "If I can bench-press 200 pounds, why can't my clients?" (Maybe because they've been injured?) Or, "If I can arrive at 6 a.m. and work until 10 p.m., why can't the other trainers?" (Perhaps because the other trainers have lives?)

Bulldozing your way to what you want isn't the way to build a positive business culture — or to be a good leader. To get the most from your employees and clients, you need to find out what they want and figure out how you can reconcile that with what *you* want.

For example, if a client wants to look great at his 20-year class reunion without straining his already-injured back, you can come up with appropriate exercises and explain how they'll help the client reach his goal of looking buff by June 20.

Or say an employee wants the evening off to watch the season finale of *Survivor* and you're short-staffed. You can ask the employee to find a replacement, let the employee take his dinner break while the show is on, or let the employee borrow your VCR to tape the show because you just can't give him the evening off.

Now, isn't that better than telling a client, "Just lift the weight, you wimp!" or saying to your employee, "Look, we're short-staffed. You'll be here and you'll like it"? That's called being empathetic, and it's an important part of building and improving your business culture. It's also what a true leader does, instead of bullying people to get what he wants.

Managing micromanagement

If you haven't had time to think about where you want your business to go because you're too busy trying to get the copy machine to work, if you view excessive employee supervision as "mentoring," if you check up on your employees on an hourly basis, you may be the dreaded micromanager. A *micromanager* is a business owner who has to manage every aspect of the business, from bringing in the mail to writing the business plan, even though she has employees who can take on some of the work.

You may have several reasons for micromanaging your employees:

- ✔ **You didn't hire right.** If your employees can't do the job, then you'll have to do it for them.
- ✔ **You don't trust your employees.**

✔ **You feel you can do a better job yourself.** After all, it *is* your business.

✔ **You're used to doing everything yourself, because you didn't used to have employees.**

✔ **You're afraid that something will go wrong if you're not there to fix it.**

These reasons are compelling ones to keep an eye on everything and everyone in your business at all times, but micromanagement brings several risks:

✔ **You can stunt your business's growth.** After all, you can't do strategic planning if you're busy taking out the trash and tracking your employees' every moves.

✔ **You may burn out.** Running a business all by yourself is tough!

✔ **Your employees will feel unmotivated.** How would *you* feel if your employer didn't trust you to do your job?

Follow these tips to figure out how to delegate and let your employees do their own thing — so you have the time and energy to attend to growing your business:

✔ **Admit to your employees that you need their help.** After you've tested your employees (and yourself) and know where everyone's strengths lie, you need come clean with your employees and admit to them that you need their expertise to make the business succeed. Your employees will be more eager, committed, and loyal when they know that you need them.

✔ **Create a vision.** Determining goals for the future, making plans for new products or services, and setting sales targets will help you see where your talents are needed the most — so you can stop mismanaging your time and skills. As you delegate more and more, you can start looking at the company's future needs rather than running around putting out fires.

✔ **Hire the right people and pay them well.** Every cell in your cost-conscious brain is telling you to hire cheap — but don't do it. Remember that you get what you pay for. Don't consider it spending money on an employee — instead, consider it investing in your business. Because skilled employees free you up to do the things that generate more income for your business, they will be worth every dollar you've spent. (You can find more on hiring employees in Chapter 17.)

✔ **Make a list of every task you no longer want to do, and then write out the steps an employee needs to take to accomplish each task.** The resulting policies-and-procedures manual will help you let go, because it's a guide for employees on how to handle the small things — so you don't have to.

✔ **Trust your employees.** After you've trained your employees, trust them to do what needs to be done. Take comfort in knowing that the business won't fall down around your ears if employees do things their own way — or even if they make mistakes.

Higher Education: Encouraging Your Employees to Grow

What would happen if your employees stopped learning about the personal training industry? Chances are, they'd miss out on all sorts of important developments and would also be way behind on their skills and knowledge. That's why personal training business owners need to foster a learning environment in the workplace.

Staying certified

As we mention in Chapter 2, most certifying organizations require trainers to keep their credentials up-to-date by earning continuing education credits (CECs). For example, to renew and maintain ACE personal training certification, trainers must earn 1.5 CECs every two years through ACE-approved courses or professional activities.

Be sure that your trainers have what they need to stay certified. For example, you can:

✔ **Find out about the certification standards for each of the certifications you accept in your business and include this information in your employee manual.** This way, your employees will be kept up-to-date on what they need to do to maintain their certifications.

✔ **Encourage your employees to attend professional activities that will count toward their CECs.** Give them time off to do so, if necessary.

✔ **Keep a list of upcoming professional activities, such as seminars, and post it somewhere where employees will see it.**

✔ **Make sure your employees keep their CPR and Advanced First Aid certifications current.**

Creating a learning atmosphere

If you want your employees to continue to grow, you can foster a learning atmosphere right in the workspace. For example:

- ✔ Subscribe to fitness-industry magazines (for example, *Club Industry, Fitness Management,* and *Health Products Business*) and loan them out to employees.

- ✔ Keep health books, fitness books, and business-management books on a shelf that employees can access.

- ✔ Keep health and fitness magazines available for employees to read. These can be a great way for your employees to glean useful bits of information. Such magazines include *Health, Fitness, Men's Fitness, Body & Soul, American Health & Fitness, Muscle & Fitness,* and *Muscle & Fitness Hers.*

- ✔ During staff meetings, encourage your employees to share things they've learned since the last meeting. Other trainers (and their clients) may benefit from knowing this information.

Continuing your own education

Not only do you need to keep your own certification up to date, but you should also continue learning about business management. Here are some ways to keep the learning going:

- ✔ Subscribe to small-business magazines like *Inc., Entrepreneur, Entrepreneur's Business Start-Ups,* and *MyBusiness.*

- ✔ Check out small-business-management books like the following:

  - *Small Business For Dummies,* 2nd Edition, by Eric Tyson and Jim Schell (published by Wiley)

  - *Essentials of Entrepreneurship and Small Business Management,* 3rd Edition, by Thomas W. Zimmerer and Norman M. Scarborough (published by Prentice Hall)

  - *Beating the Odds in Small Business* by Tom Culley (published by Simon & Schuster)

  - *The Ultimate Small Business Guide: A Resource for Startups and Growing Businesses* (published by Basic Books)

- ✔ Take continuing education classes in business management and entrepreneurship at your local college.

- ✔ Take continuing education classes online. World Wide Learn (www. worldwidelearn.com) offers business-skills training courses over the Internet.

Be sure to tell your employees about all the continuing education you do yourself. You'll set a good example and may inspire them to do the same.

Training Your Employees

Training your employees is the best business investment you'll ever make. Employees are happier when they know what's expected of them and how to do their jobs — and clients are happier when they're looked after by well-trained, competent employees.

Creating a training manual

Imagine taking a six-hour course on how to run a dentist's office. At the end of the six hours, how much do you think you'd remember about filing, reception, answering the phone, handling patients, filling out insurance forms, cleaning, and handling receipts? Not much, we'd wager.

That's why having an employee training manual that spells out your business procedures is so important. Whenever an employee has a question about how to maintain a piece of equipment or fill out an assessment form, he can just flip open the training manual and find the answer.

Writing out all the procedures in your business will show you where you they may be lacking. For example, maybe you don't have any procedures in place for handling bounced checks, or maybe you'll discover that you need some sort of chart that shows who's responsible for cleaning what.

Here are some of the procedures you'll want to include in your training manual:

- ✔ **Instructions on filling out forms:** Personal training requires a lot of forms, and remembering who fills out what when, as well as what you do with the forms after they're filled out, can be difficult. Along with the instructions, you can even include copies of each form.

- ✔ **Client retention information:** This is information about how to keep clients happy. For example:

  - How to handle an unsatisfied customer: Do you give her a free session? Call in the supervisor?

  - When and how to follow up on clients: This includes check-in phone calls as well as thank-you notes, special offers, and so on.

  - How to keep clients motivated.

  - How to change up the client's training program.

✔ **Client-service details:** This is information on how to interact with clients, and includes the following:

- How to answer the phone: Do you want your employees to answer with "Good day, Perfect Personal Training. This is Janet speaking. How may I help you?" No matter how you want people to answer the phone, write it down.

- How to take money: Do you accept cash, checks, credit cards? How many sessions do clients pay for at a time? What happens if a check bounces or a credit card is declined?

- How to write a receipt.

- How to answer potential clients' questions about free trial sessions, prices, packages, and so on.

✔ **Equipment maintenance:** This is information on how and how often to "tune up" equipment. It includes answers to the following questions:

- Who is responsible for maintaining equipment?

- How often does it need to be maintained?

- How are different pieces of equipment maintained, and where are the tools kept?

✔ **Cleaning procedures:** This gives details on how to clean everything that needs to be cleaned, from floors to equipment, and includes the following:

- Who is responsible for cleaning? Do trainers take turns?

- How often does cleaning need to be done?

- What gets cleaned — equipment, floors, the bathroom? What are the procedures for cleaning?

- Where are the cleaning tools located?

Creating an employee manual

An employee manual? What do we think you are — a Fortune 500 company with 10,000 employees? Nope. We think you're a small business with just a few employees — but we think that every business with employees, no matter what the size of the business, needs an employee manual. The employee manual documents your rules, policies, and standards so that every employee is working in the same way toward the same goal.

The employee manual is also a safeguard — if a reprimanded employee complains that he didn't know the rules, you can point out that the rules are listed in the manual that he was given when he started working for you. The manual ensures that everyone is treated fairly and consistently, because everyone is given fair notice of the rules.

Your employee manual should contain these elements:

- ✔ **Information on vacation time, sick days, family and maternity leave, medical benefits, and pay periods.**

- ✔ **Policies on drugs and weapons in the workplace, sexual harassment, and safety matters.**

- ✔ **Details about lines of authority:** Whom do the employees report to? An organizational chart will help employees understand who their supervisors are.

- ✔ **Rules regarding lateness and attendance.**

- ✔ **Information about disciplinary actions:** What will happen if an employee needs to be reprimanded? Will you have a three-strikes-and-you're-out rule? See Chapter 17 for more on reprimanding employees.

- ✔ **Expectations for your employees:** When and how often will the employees be reviewed for job performance? What will you be looking at? What will happen if the review is positive or negative?

- ✔ **Information on regulatory compliance:** Have policies in place to make sure you comply with regulations such as the Americans with Disabilities Act. Have your lawyer check the employee manual to make sure it contains everything necessary regarding these laws.

- ✔ **Information about trade secrets and confidential information:** What do you want kept confidential? For example, employees should not share information about clients with outside people, or information about your business with competitors.

- ✔ **Employee acknowledgement:** Include a form that acknowledges receipt of the manual. Have the employee sign it when he gets the manual, then keep the receipt in the employee's personnel file. This way, the employee can't claim that he didn't know about a rule or policy.

Getting your employees up to speed

Training your employees involves more than showing them what you want and then throwing them out onto the gym floor. In the following sections, we provide suggestions that will help you get your employees up to speed.

Throw the book(s) at them

We cover the operations manual in Chapter 16. Make sure each new employee gets — and reads — a copy of the manual. It's not exactly a *New York Times* bestseller, but it will help your employees get a grasp on your business and what's expected of them. Each employee should also get a copy of the training manual and the employee manual.

Employee manual templates: A place to start

Don't have the time to pound out an employee manual? Try these template software packages that can help you create a manual on the double:

- **Instant HR Policies,** Web site: www.instanthrpolicies.com, phone: 800-437-3735

- **Employee Handbook Plus,** Web site: www.hrnonline.com, phone: 800-940-7522

- **Sample Employee Handbook,** Web site: www.sampleemployeehandbook.com, e-mail: support@sampleemployee-handbook.com

- **Office Employee Manual,** Web site: www.writeexpress.com/or/employee-manual/employee-manual.html, phone: 800-974-8339

- **Employee Handbook Template,** Web site: www.employeehandbookstore.com, e-mail: CustomerService@the-guru-group.com

- **HRIT Employee Handbook Template Package,** Web site: www.hrit.com, phone: 800-774-4870

The employee should sign a receipt for each of the three manuals. Place those signed receipts in the employee's personnel file so she can't later claim that she wasn't aware of the rules.

Identify their skills

An important step in working with new employees is identifying the skills they're lacking so you don't waste time telling them what they already know.

You should already know your new employee's strengths and weakness from observing the trainer during the hiring process — the written assessment, interview, and practical assessment that we cover in Chapter 17.

Role-play

By *role-play* we don't mean to don a wig and hit the singles bar. We mean that you and the employee being trained will act out different situations that are likely to arise in a personal training business. For example, you can pretend to be:

- **A disgruntled client:** How can the trainer soothe your sore feelings?

- **A potential client who has just walked in the door:** How can the trainer make you feel welcome and explain your options — *without* the hard sell?

- **A client who doesn't comply with the trainer's exercise prescription:** What does the trainer do when he's bombarded with excuses from a client who's not improving?

> ✔ **A client with an injury, such as a pulled shoulder:** What exercises should the trainer avoid, and which should he prescribe?
>
> ✔ **A client with a health issue, such as high blood pressure:** Again, what exercises should the trainer avoid, and which should he prescribe?

Acting out various situations helps the new trainer experience different customer-service scenarios and work out the solutions. It also lets you evaluate the trainer's strengths and weaknesses — and take action to work on those weaknesses.

Monkey see, monkey do

Let the new trainer *shadow* (follow around and observe) a more experienced trainer (even you) to see how things are done. Let him ask questions afterward to make sure everything is clear.

Assign a more experienced trainer to be the new employee's best buddy until he can work on his own. The trainer should be prepared to answer questions, explain procedures, and encourage the new hire through tough times.

It's showtime: Starting new employees in their jobs

Now it's time to let the trainer fly on his own — but you need to make sure he starts with supervision. Explain to the client that the new trainer wants to take her through a session, and that you're there if any questions or concerns arise.

Frequently, observe the new employee to make sure everything's going smoothly. If you see the employee taking shortcuts or making mistakes, this is your chance to reinforce the right way to do the task.

Continuing the training long-term

The training process should continue throughout the employee's career with your company. Help your employees continue to learn about the business, and they'll acquire skills and knowledge that will keep your business competitive.

These tips apply to training clients but also to other tasks, such as taking payments, maintaining equipment, cleaning the workspace, answering phones, and so on.

Part V
The Part of Tens

The 5th Wave   By Rich Tennant

"I'm with my personal trainer right now. Yes, the one who works with the seals at Aqua Land."

In this part . . .

Every *For Dummies* book has a Part of Tens, and this one is no different. In this part, we give you ten ways to add more services and products to your business, ten pieces of equipment every personal training business needs (they're not all what you think!), and ten ways to wow your clients by being the best personal trainer this side of the Mississippi. We also include an appendix of resources you can turn to.

With this section, we draw the curtain on *Becoming a Personal Trainer For Dummies*. We wish you (and your clients) much health, wealth, and happiness!

Chapter 19

Ten Great Ways to Expand Your Services

*1*t's inevitable — when the entrepreneurial bug has bitten you, you see things in a whole new light as a business owner. The day will come when you've mastered the art of the personal training session — and that will no longer be challenging enough for you. You'll ask yourself, "What else can I do to offer my clients more — and increase my revenue?" Or maybe you'll be talking with a client and realize she has a need outside of personal training that you can fulfill. However it happens, here are a few suggestions to help quench your entrepreneurial thirst — and, oh yeah — expand your services to grow your bottom line.

Adding Nutrition Services

Clients will naturally ask you not only "How should I exercise?" but also "What should I eat?" Correct diet and exercise practices go hand in hand to help clients achieve their wellness goals, so this seems like an easy add-on to your existing menu of services. But before you hang out your diet banner, you need to know what you can (and can't!) do legally, in terms of providing nutritional advice for your clients.

Forty-six states have enacted legislation regulating the practice of dietetics. And if you plan to provide specific nutrition services, you'll fall under your state's dietetic laws. If you decide to add nutritional counseling to your repertoire of services, consult your lawyer and contact your state regulatory agency first; in many states, practicing dietetics without a license is a violation of state law.

Selling Supplements

Meal-replacement bars, protein powders, vitamins, and other nutritional supplements accompany personal training and nutrition services well.

Check out www.europasports.com for information on how to obtain a wholesaler's account. They have a great selection of products and an awesome customer-service staff that will help you get started in choosing the right products to carry for your business.

Depending on your state's laws, these types of items may be considered taxable goods, and you may have to apply for a resale tax certificate to sell them legally.

For more info on how to obtain a resale permit, consult your accountant or go to www.irs.gov.

Adding Group Sessions

If you do it for one person, why can't you do it for a whole group of people? If you have the space, providing group classes can be a great way to extend your services to those who may not necessarily be able to afford you one-on-one.

For example, you can provide "buddy" sessions where you train two people at once; while one person rests, the other one works with you. This type of training scenario may work well for clients who like to have someone to work out with.

Or you can offer personal training circuit classes, where you take five to eight people through a preset circuit course. Screen your participants before they start (to make sure they're familiar with the equipment you're using), and during the session correct their form, provide verbal encouragement, and generally keep them moving. Once again, this allows you to fit more clients into less time.

Giving Workshops and Seminars

In the same vein, giving workshops and seminars is a great way to add extra income while not placing too much strain on your available working hours.

If you're working in a gym, speak with the management about using their aerobics room for an hour or two to hold the seminar or workshop. If you don't have an aerobics room available to you, try your local hospital — hospitals typically have a room available for lectures and presentations. Or try your local community college.

Contact local high schools and ask about giving seminars there if you're interested in sport-specific training. Parents are always willing to shell out a little coin to get a sports scholarship for their kid or just to help them improve. And working with kids can segue into training the parents.

In planning the topics for your lecture or workshop, think through the most common issues with clients. Here are some ideas for lectures and workshops:

- ✔ Making Fitness Achievable
- ✔ Living a Healthy Lifestyle
- ✔ Fitness Myths Debunked
- ✔ Making Fitness Work for You
- ✔ Healthy Back
- ✔ All Abs
- ✔ Working Out 101

In preparing for your lecture/workshop, you'll want to outline your speech or presentation and prepare written materials to hand out afterward. Be sure to include your name and contact information so if anyone in your audience wants to work with you, they know how to do so. See Chapter 8 for more information on giving seminars.

Adding Massage Services

Another very synergistic service is to be able to offer your fatigued client an invigorating sports massage postworkout. But before you order your portable massage table, check into your state's laws regarding massage therapy.

Currently, 33 states regulate the practice of massage, with stringent requirements regarding schooling, hours of specialized training, and a national or state certified exam. Unlike personal training, which has no state regulatory board, massage has crossed over into the realm of being regulated, which means you'll have to go to school and pass your boards to legally practice it. So if you plan to offer massage, get ready to go back to school again, or hire a Certified Massage Therapist (CMT). A CMT has passed her state boards and can legally practice massage therapy.

Selling Fitness Equipment

A great and easy way to make extra money is to sell fitness equipment to your clients. You'll find that most of the time, after a client has discovered the joy of exercise, sooner or later she'll want some type of fitness equipment at home so she can exercise at her leisure.

You can go about selling fitness equipment in a few ways. One way is to sell the equipment directly, where you become a vendor for a manufacturer and sell their products to your clients. This way definitely requires that you have a resale license and requires a little more work come tax time; for example, you have to pay quarterly taxes on the equipment that you sell, and you need to charge your clients sales tax as well.

Another way to sell fitness equipment is to team up with a local fitness-equipment store and help them sell their products to your clients. Work out a deal where you receive a commission on whatever equipment you help to sell to your clients. This way is a little cleaner, because you don't need to worry about inventory or sales tax.

Providing Corporate Wellness Services

Corporate wellness, also known as *worksite wellness,* is providing health and fitness programs for employees of companies. With healthcare costs rising, companies are turning to fitness to help reduce their costs. A solid worksite wellness program can

- ✔ Lower healthcare costs
- ✔ Reduce employee absenteeism
- ✔ Increase employee productivity
- ✔ Reduce employees' use of healthcare benefits

✔ Reduce workers' compensation/disability claims

✔ Reduce employee injuries

✔ Increase employee morale and loyalty

Here are some ideas for different services you can provide to a company for corporate wellness:

✔ Sell fitness equipment to businesses and corporations to set up their worksite fitness facilities.

✔ Train employees how to safely use the fitness equipment.

✔ Provide weekly workout classes.

✔ Hold proper lifting seminars.

✔ Hold back-strengthening workshops.

For more information on worksite wellness, visit the Wellness Council of America's Web site at www.welcoa.org.

Offering Specialty Training Sessions

Specialty training sessions can open up a whole new world of clientele. Although it may require you to obtain another certification, it's worth your time and investment. Having different areas of expertise allows you to expand your client base, keeping the referrals coming in so you have continuous client flow — and your work as a trainer won't get stale.

Here are some ideas for specialty session types:

✔ Golf-specific training

✔ Flexibility training

✔ Sport-specific training

✔ Endurance training

✔ Bodybuilding competition training

✔ Fitness competition training

✔ Pre/postpregnancy training

✔ Kid workouts

✔ Pilates training

Check out your certifying association's Web site to see if they offer any specialty certifications that you can get at a discount (as a member).

Selling Fitness Apparel

Like selling fitness equipment, selling fitness apparel is another way to make money that fits right in with your work. Typically, to become a reseller for fitness apparel, you need to provide the clothing company with proof of:

- ✔ A valid federal tax ID number
- ✔ A valid tax reseller's certificate
- ✔ A bank account with your company name on it

You may also need to place a minimum order of up to $1,000 to open your account with them.

Anytime you resell anything, you need to check with your state to see if it's considered taxable goods. If it *is* considered taxable goods, you need to charge and collect sales tax, as well as pay that sales tax back to the state quarterly. Consult with your accountant on your state's specific guidelines and how to go about obtaining a resale certificate.

Offering Other Services

Y'know, this is *your* business — and you can offer any type of service you feel would benefit your clients! If you have your own place, you can even offer a shoeshine service or car detailing. Services that save clients time while they're training with you are called *value-added services,* and it's those little things that keep your clients sticking around. Or you may want to consider selling things like motivational tapes, books, or workout music.

The moral of the story here is that no one can say what's right or wrong for you to offer with your personal training services. Only *you* will know what works best for your business!

Chapter 20

Ten Essential Pieces of Equipment

In This Chapter

▶ Identifying equipment that isn't equipment

▶ Knowing which equipment really *is* equipment

▶ Keeping the right attitude

As we stress throughout this book, you wear many hats in your role as a personal trainer. You're a salesperson, scientist, friend, coach, motivator, teacher, employer, bookkeeper, and business owner, to name just a few. To be successful wearing any of these hats, you need to be equipped properly — and that means you need to have the right tools to use at the right time.

As you've discovered by now, your "equipment" as a trainer won't always be big, heavy pieces of workout equipment! Read on for the ten pieces of essential equipment *every* personal trainer needs.

Your Mindset

The equipment available to help you be a successful trainer is limitless: cellphones, computers, software programs, weight-training equipment, cardiovascular equipment. . . . The list goes on.

But trust us, no matter what types of toys you have (or how expensive or cutting edge they are), it won't matter if you don't have the most important one: the right mindset.

Important factors for having the right mindset are:

✔ **Honesty:** You need to be honest with yourself about what you realistically can and cannot do; this flows through to your clientele as well.

✔ **Determination:** Not every day is easy; you won't always have a full book, and sometimes those slow days end up being weeks. Pushing ahead and staying on track when the going gets tough takes determination and focus.

✔ **Willingness:** You need to be willing to change if your original course of action isn't producing the results that you want. You also need to be willing to keep an open mind when your client is complaining that she's not happy with your services. Willingness is more about what you should do as opposed to what you want to do — after all, sometimes you'll have to do things that you don't *want* to do.

Your Certification

As we discuss in Chapter 2, certification is your badge of honor — it tells everyone who works with you, from employers to clients, that not only do you *say* you know what you're doing, but you can also prove it. You have your sheet of paper that states, "I studied, I tested, and I passed — I know what I'm talking about here!"

Certification gives you the edge over your competition. If you and your competition are equally matched, service for service, price point for price point, but you're certified and they're not, whom do you think your prospective client will choose to work with? Nine times out of ten it will be you — because you're certified. Certification assures your client that you're a true fitness professional; you've undergone stringent studies and testing protocols to figure out what to do and what not to do as a personal training professional. It ensures your client that you know what they don't — which is how to help her reach her fitness goals, safely and efficiently.

Certification is also a means of qualifying your credibility. Have you ever seen a trainer quoted in a newspaper or on television who was introduced with "an *uncertified* personal trainer, John Q. Smith, states that exercise is . . ."? Most likely not! Being certified gives you the credibility you need for other professionals and clients to take you seriously. Certification helps you to build a solid rapport with the people you will be doing business with, such as:

✔ Employers

✔ Clients

✔ Mentors

✔ Media contacts

✔ Doctors with whom you have a referral relationship

In other words: If you're not certified yet, don't wait any longer!

Your Business Card

You get a lot of bang for your buck with a little 2½-x-3-inch piece of card stock! Your business card helps to create a lasting impression with a potential client. No matter how impressed she is with you when she meets you, she'll be even more impressed when you hand her your business card — which says to her, "I'm serious about what I do, which means I'm serious about helping *you.*"

You never know when you're going to meet someone who will become a client, business associate, mentor, or referring physician, so always carry your business cards with you in an easily accessible place. When you easily pull your business card out of your cardholder rather than fumble around searching for it in your purse or gym bag, it says to the person you're giving your card to, "I'm organized and professional."

Here are some tips for making a long-lasting impression with your business card:

- ✔ In the case of a chance meeting, when someone asks you, "What is it that you do?" have a brief summary (called an *elevator pitch*) prepared that makes you memorable as you hand her your business card. For example, you can say, "I help people look great naked" or "I build muscles."

- ✔ Make sure the information on your card is correct and up to date. If your area has just recently implemented ten-digit dialing, if your area code has changed, or if you've just gotten an e-mail address, make sure you invest in a new set of business cards to reflect your new contact information.

The impression you leave with a potential client is the one that will bring her back to you for business. Make sure that your business card reflects everything you want your potential client to remember about you — professionalism, integrity, quality, and trustworthiness.

Tape Measure

The tape measure can be used for many different things. You can record your client's *anthropometric measurements* (body circumference) with it to show change and make sure she's on track to achieving her personal goals. You can also measure degrees of flexibility as well as how far your client can reach past her toes in the sit-and-reach flexibility test (see Chapter 11). Other uses for the tape measure are:

✔ Measuring vertical jump height

✔ Measuring *plyometric* (explosive) movement distances

✔ Measuring length of stride

✔ Measuring stance distances

Body-Fat Calipers

If we surveyed all the personal trainers in the world and asked them for the number-one reason clients come to them, the unanimous answer would most likely be "to lose weight." You know, however, that if a client loses the wrong type of weight — that is, muscle rather than fat — it's counterproductive to the client's long-term goals.

So how do you make sure your client is losing the right type of weight? Body-fat calipers! That's right — these handy-dandy little pinchers are light, portable, and the personal trainer's best friend when it comes to body-composition assessment. We cover where to get body-fat calipers and how to use them in Chapter 11.

Body-Weight Scale

Going hand in hand with recording baseline *biometrics* (body measurements), a scale is useful and important in determining gross bodyweight. After you've recorded your client's gross body weight, you can assess body-fat percentage, BMI, and one-rep-max percentages to determine how heavy your client needs to be to train for her workouts.

Heart-Rate Monitor

Having a heart-rate monitor for your client to use while you train her has multiple benefits:

✔ It allows you to see where her heart rate is without stopping her exercise.

✔ A heart-rate monitor is a lot more accurate than the palpation method.

✔ Your client will get instant feedback from it — it is an invaluable tool when it comes to teaching clients about perceived rate of exertion and working intensity.

✔ You can use it to teach your client stress management, breathing, and biofeedback techniques.

Check out Chapter 11 to find out where to get a heart-rate monitor.

Blood-Pressure Cuff

Recording blood pressure prior to performing the fitness assessment is very important. Knowing your client's systolic and diastolic readings will help you to determine if she's ready to start working with you or if she needs to see her doctor to get clearance before doing so.

Check out www.quickmedical.com for a wide selection of manual and automatic blood-pressure cuffs.

Jump Rope

A jump rope is a light, inexpensive, very portable, and excellent tool for challenging your client's cardiovascular system. Anyone at any fitness level can use it — and as exercises go, your client will burn more calories per minute jumping rope than doing any other activity! Skipping rope is a challenging workout that burns about 360 calories per half-hour (by comparison, moderate running or jogging burns about 330 calories per half-hour).

Experts suggest rubber, leather, or *beaded ropes* (ropes with small plastic tubes on a cord). The grip should be foam-based to absorb sweat and give your client a firm grasp. The client should be able to stand on the rope and hold the handles slightly above waist height. Jump ropes generally come in 6- and 9-foot lengths, and many have detachable handles so you can trim the rope yourself.

Resistance Tubing

A solid alternative to dumbbells for the beginning client, resistance tubes are very easy to travel with because they weigh practically nothing. Resistance tubing typically come as a set in its own bag, with different tubes providing different levels of resistance — light, medium, and heavy.

Tubes are great for clients who may have problems with their wrists, hands, or fingers and may not be able to grasp a dumbbell. Another bonus is that almost all free-weight movements can be duplicated with them.

Chapter 21

Ten Ways to Be the Best Personal Trainer You Can Be

*P*ersonal training is a competitive field. Big George's Deep Discount Personal Training down the street would love to take your clients away from you — and if you don't give your clients what they're looking for, they just might give George a try.

Your clients want more than just a good workout. They want a personal trainer who motivates them, cares about them, and sets a good example.

That's why we give you this chapter. When all else is equal, your professionalism, your attitude, and your knowledge of business etiquette are what will put you ahead of the pack. These ten tips will help you be the best personal trainer you can be.

Don't Be a Know-It-All

You're having a conversation with a new acquaintance at a dinner party and he starts talking about the works of Umberto Eco. Instead of saying, "Who in the ever lovin' world is Umberto Eco?" you nod along, pretending that you're deeply familiar with *The Name of the Rose* and the other works of whatshisname.

C'mon, you know you've done this before. We all have.

Although you may get away with this tactic at a dinner party, you won't get away with it as a personal trainer. If you give false information because you don't want to look stupid in front of your client, you can do more than get found out — you can injure the client.

Melyssa had a trainer on her staff who told a client that he knew how to rehabilitate a rotator-cuff injury — even though he had no clue. He had the client doing exercises that were contraindicated by the client's surgeon, and the client later complained to Melyssa that the exercises hurt her instead of helping her. Needless to say, that trainer didn't last long with Melyssa's company.

Admit When You're Wrong

Everyone makes mistakes. The difference between a good trainer and a bad trainer is that the good trainer owns up to her mistakes, and the bad trainer tries to sweep the evidence under the proverbial rug.

Like most personal trainers, Melyssa has unintentionally hurt clients by working them too hard. Every once in a while, a client has complained that he couldn't walk all week without being reminded of his training session! Instead of trying to pin the blame on the client — "You should have told me" or "You shouldn't have worked out so hard" — Melyssa apologized. It's simple, easy, and appreciated.

Be There for Your Client

Being there for your client doesn't mean you have to trail her, handing her warmed towels when she gets out of the shower and feeding her chicken soup when she has a cold. We mean that you have to put your own ego and wants aside and focus completely on the client.

Don't ever take your eyes off your client during a session; many's the time Melyssa has seen a trainer staring off into space rather than watching the client as she hoists a heavy weight. That trainer is thinking about himself — how bored he is, what he'll be having for lunch that day, how much he likes that hot trainer across the room — rather than about the client.

Your job is to be the most motivating, inspiring trainer you can be, and to set a good example for your client. That requires you to put yourself aside and be there for your client.

Stay within the Boundaries

You have your personal self, and your professional self. Your professional self does not offer relationship advice, does not eat candy bars in front of the client, and does not make comments about the client's home or its contents.

Personal training is just that — personal. Your client may come to think of you as her friend. That's a good thing, but it also invites unprofessional behavior. If a client starts, say, complaining that her husband doesn't pay attention to her, you need to draw that boundary line. Say, "I hear you, I understand" — but don't offer advice or tell her what a jerk her husband is. If a client asks you to train her for an extra half-hour free of charge, or to drive 15 miles outside your regular area to train her daughter, tell her you can't do it. If you do, the client may come to expect this from you all the time — and it can hurt your business.

Do What You Say, Say What You Do

When you tell the client to do something, you should do it. Sounds simple, right? Well, you'd be surprised at how many personal trainers forget this simple concept.

The best way to keep your word is to be prepared, to always be on time, and to follow the tips in this chapter about getting your bag and files ready ahead of time. To make sure you always have a program ready for the client, have the client's file with you when you need it, and have a place where you can work — a place with a desk, adequate lighting, and all the tools you'll need to stay on top of things. And be sure to have access to all the health information you need so that if you tell a client you'll bring her a recipe or a new exercise or information about heart disease, you can have it ready the next time you see her.

When it comes to being a person of your word — that is, doing what you say and saying what you do — the Boy Scouts were right: Be prepared.

Showing Clients You Care

Care is more than just a four-letter word. It also stands for "Clients Are Really Everything." You may know everything there is to know about personal training, but you wouldn't be much of a personal trainer without your clients. Clients can make or break your business. That's why you have to care about them.

Here are some tips for showing clients that you care:

- Return phone calls promptly.
- Return e-mails promptly.
- Follow up with your clients to make sure the sessions are working for them.
- Send your clients thank-you cards for doing business with you.
- Send clients holiday cards or small gifts.
- Always be sympathetic to your clients' complaints.
- Keep individual files on each client so you can track them and create the most personalized programs for them.
- Follow the rest of the suggestions in this chapter!

Always Be on Time

Imagine having a weekly appointment with someone at 4 p.m. What if the other person always showed up at 4:15, or even 4:05? It may not seem like much, but over time, the other person's tardiness would likely irritate you.

Being late shows a lack of respect for the person who is waiting. Not only that, but if you have a personal training session and you show up late, what are your choices? You can either cheat the client out of a few minutes of training so she can be done at 5 p.m., or you can run late — which is annoying for a busy person (and who *isn't* busy?).

If you're always late, ask yourself why and come up with a solution. Do you get stuck in traffic? If so, find alternate routes or leave earlier. Do you have trouble getting yourself out the door? Have your bag, your client folder, and everything else you need ready by the door early in the day so you can grab it and leave when the time comes. You can even buy a shelf or hook to keep your stuff on — it may motivate you to use it.

Do you just dread working with the client? Then you need to think seriously about whether this client is right for your business, or whether you're the right personal trainer for this client. See Chapter 9 for information on how to "fire" a client.

Carry a cellphone so that if you're late despite these tips, you can call the client and let her know.

Dress Professionally

Which trainer inspires more confidence — a personal trainer dressed in an embroidered polo short, sweatpants, and workout shoes, or one dressed in skintight neon spandex? The spandex may make you look hot, but your job is not to look hot. Your job is to look professional and set a good example for your clients.

Here are some dress-for-success tips:

- We'll say it again — no skintight spandex!
- Don't wear jeans and a T-shirt, no matter how comfy they are.
- Make sure your clothes aren't too baggy. If you demonstrate a machine, your clothes may get caught.
- Women, don't slather on the makeup. (Guys, this goes double for you!)
- Keep jewelry to a minimum. Long, dangly jewelry can get caught in the machines.
- The same goes for long, loose hair. If you have long hair, you may want to pull it back.
- The best uniform may be a collared polo shirt, well-fitting sweatpants, and good-quality exercise shoes.

Stay Educated

One of our favorite mottos is "When you're green, you grow; when you're ripe, you rot"? This means that in order to keep growing as a personal trainer, you need to keep learning. Become complacent, and you'll be, well, a rotten personal trainer.

Personal trainers need to stay up-to-date in medicine, fitness, business, and even psychology and nutrition. These fields are constantly changing, and researchers are uncovering new information every day.

Here are some ways to keep learning:

- Attend continuing education courses.
- Talk to other personal trainers.
- Go to conferences and workshops.

- ✔ Read industry magazines.
- ✔ Read medical journals.
- ✔ Read health, fitness, and business magazines (many are available at the local library).
- ✔ Talk with doctors.

Do What You Love, Love What You Do

When you love what you do, it shows. You have an enthusiasm that's contagious, and your positive attitude motivates your clients.

Unfortunately, though, personal trainers do burn out. And if you burn out, you'll do yourself — and your clients — a favor by either altering what you do or doing something else altogether. Make a change while you still have a good reputation.

Here are some ideas for changing up your career to get rid of or avoid burnout:

- ✔ Move into corporate wellness.
- ✔ Write a fitness book.
- ✔ Write magazine articles on fitness.
- ✔ Conduct group sessions.
- ✔ Change your client population.
- ✔ Consult.
- ✔ Sell fitness equipment.
- ✔ Go on sabbatical to refresh yourself and learn something new.
- ✔ Take classes in nutrition or another field related to fitness.
- ✔ Go back to school full-time.

Melyssa had the same problem — after 13 years of personal training, the day-in and day-out demands of running her business lost its appeal. She closed her business in order to expand her professional horizons — such as work in corporate wellness and write a book (the book you're holding in your hands, in fact). Melyssa does still have personal training clients — just not as many — and her schedule is varied with many different projects that keep her interested and fresh. Her schedule is no longer jam-packed with sessions like it used to be.

Appendix

Resources

*W*e'd like to say that this book has every single thing you need to become a successful personal trainer — but if it did, it would be bigger than *War and Peace* and the 20-volume *Oxford English Dictionary* combined! That's why we're suggesting that you find out more by joining one or more of these professional organizations, reading these books, or checking out these Web sites.

Professional organizations often offer educational conferences, journals, networking opportunities, and career boards, so check out the ones we list here. Some of them don't require you to be credentialed through them to be a member and get the benefits.

In addition, you need a library of books you can flip through whenever you have a question or need inspiration. You can start with the books we list here.

Finally, the Web offers a wealth of neat tools like calorie calculators, message boards for fitness professionals, career centers, and nutrition databases. We've given you a few of our favorites.

Professional Organizations

American Council on Exercise (ACE)
4851 Paramount Drive
San Diego, CA 92123
Phone: 800-835-3636 (toll-free) 858-279-8227
Web site: www.acefitness.org

The American Council on Exercise (ACE) is the largest nonprofit fitness certification and education provider in the world. This organization's Web site (www.acefitness.org) is brimming with useful information for the personal trainer, and a public bulletin board lets fitness consumers and fitness experts ask and answer questions and exchange ideas. The site also has a section that's off-limits to those who are not ACE-certified, and that includes a calendar of events, communication center, recommended reading list, and more.

The most useful part of the site may be the Career Center, which includes articles on topics like salary survey results; how to write an effective résumé; the secrets of an effective business letter; how to dress for success; and keys to a successful interview. ACE also runs GymJobs.com, a site for employment opportunities in the health, fitness, recreation, and sports industries.

ACE-certified professionals receive:

- *ACE FitnessMatters,* a bimonthly publication featuring fitness news and information and the latest product studies

- *ACE Certified News,* a newsletter with in-depth information about the fitness industry

- Resource Center access for answers and advice on complicated fitness-related questions

- Professional Referral System, a tool for job placement

International Health, Racquet & Sportsclub Association (IHRSA)
263 Summer Street
Boston, MA 02210
Phone: 800-228-4772 (toll-free) or 617-951-0055
Web site: www.ihrsa.org

As the name implies, the International Health, Racquet & Sportsclub Association (IHRSA) is for owners of and executives at fitness clubs. However, personal trainers can find a wealth of information at the organization's Web site. The site includes stats — such as lists of health clubs by type, health-club members by age, and attendance at health clubs — that can come in handy for market research, writing your business plan, or applying for a loan.

Free IHRSA Trend Reports (available as downloadable PDF files) include such topics as "Health Clubs and Public Policy: Three Predictions for 2004," "Taking Charge of the Baby Boomer Market," and Understanding and Motivating Your Gen X Employees."

The IHRSA Job page (accessible through the Site Map) is where job seekers can connect with employment opportunities in the health and fitness industry; however, these are mostly club-management positions.

American College of Sports Medicine (ACSM)
P.O. Box 1440
Indianapolis, IN 46206-1440A
Phone: 317-637-9200
Web site: www.acsm.org

Besides credentialing, the American College of Sports Medicine (ASCM) offers its members professional and educational meetings such as the *ACSM Health & Fitness Summit,* specialty conferences, and scientific roundtables.

Three ACSM journals *Medicine & Science in Sports & Exercise, Exercise and Sport Sciences Reviews,* and *ACSM's Health & Fitness Journal* are included as member benefits or are available by subscription for nonmembers.

The site is also affiliated with the LWW Classifieds, a job board for fitness professionals.

Membership fees range from $50 to $190 per year, depending on your status (student, graduate, professional, and so on) and the type of membership.

National Strength and Conditioning Association (NSCA)
3333 Landmark Circle
Lincoln NE 68504
Phone: 888-746-2378 (toll-free) or 402-476-6669
Web site: www.nsca-cc.org

The National Strength and Conditioning Association (NSCA) puts on an annual NSCA National Conference that features a preconference symposium with speakers on strength training and conditioning, a career center, NSCA certification exams, a trade show full of fitness companies, and three days of sessions with professionals in the industry.

As for networking, NSCA Special Interest Groups provide members who share a common interest the opportunity to share ideas and address issues relating to their area of interest.

The NSCA also offers a career center that contains hundreds of job postings in the strength and conditioning field.

Membership costs range from $70 to $195 per year depending on your status (student or professional) and other factors.

Web Sites

Personal Training on the Net (www.ptonthenet.com)

This personal training site is heavy on interesting research and helpful articles. Personal Training on the Net offers several different "libraries"; for example, the Flexibility Library has nearly 300 stretches and variations, detailed descriptions, pictures and videos, while the Program Library offers premade program templates including sport-specific programs and programs for stability, strength, and power.

The site also offers 800 articles in the fields of Advanced Workout, Sports Specific, Programming, Functional Anatomy, Nutrition, Special Populations, Aquatic Fitness, Workout, Post Rehabilitation, Research Reviews, Business Development, Holistic Health, and Safety, Standards and Ethics.

Other online tools include Create-A-Program, which allows members access to the Exercise and Flexibility libraries in order to build, store, print, e-mail and monitor multidimensional programs online, and Client Profiles, which gives trainers online access to a handful of leading-edge profile and assessment tools. From general profiles to complex postural and movement assessments, site members can create, edit, and store profiles online, print and e-mail them to clients, and chart progress between original and subsequent assessments over time.

All these goodies don't come for free; membership costs $9.95 per month or $95 per year.

The USDA Nutrient Data Laboratory (www.nal.usda.gov/fnic/foodcomp/search/)

If you offer nutritional services — or even if you don't — this site is indispensable. Created by the U.S. Department of Agriculture, the site is a search engine that lets you search for nutritional data on any type of food you can imagine, from apples to zucchini. You then choose a serving size, and the site gives a readout of the calories, fat grams, sodium, amounts of vitamins and minerals, and other information. So if you need to suggest some snacks for a client who's on, say, a low-sodium diet, you can zip over to this site and enter different kinds of foods — even brand names — to come up with a list of healthy choices.

National Institutes of Health American Body Mass Calculator (http://nhlbisupport.com/bmi/bmicalc.htm)

Just enter your client's height and weight, and this calculator will tell you the client's body mass index.

SportsInjuryClinic.Net (`www.sportsinjuryclinic.net`)

This virtual sports injury clinic offers a wealth of tools for diagnosing and treating sports injuries. For example, the Virtual Therapist lets you "click where it hurts" and helps you determine what the problem is and how to treat it. The site also includes step-by-step sports massage instructions.

CalorieKing.com Food Database (`www.calorieking.com`)

Need to find nutritional information on restaurant foods? Visit the CalorieKing.com Food Database. The database holds nutritional information for over 30,000 American generic and brand-name foods, including over 150 fast-food chains.

C.H.E.K Institute (`www.paulchekseminars.com`)

The C.H.E.K. Institute offers many resources, from videos to correspondence courses to specialty equipment.

Personal Training University (`www.personaltraineru.com`)

This site includes articles, interviews with "faculty members," ideas for expanding your business, a business start-up guide, a discussion group, and more. A three-month subscription costs $24.95.

Books

Fitness For Dummies, 2nd Edition, by Suzanne Schlosberg and Liz Neporent, M.A. (published by Wiley)

Fitness For Dummies, 2nd Edition, is full of jargon-free information on exercise, from stretching to buying cardio equipment. You can use this book to get a solid understanding of fitness basics, or recommend it to your clients.

Nutrition For Dummies, 2nd Edition, by Carol Ann Rinzler (published by Wiley)

Chances are, your clients will ask you for nutrition advice — and this book is for you. The book gives in-depth information on vitamins, minerals, fat, carbs, as well as shows readers how to build a healthy diet.

Small Business Marketing For Dummies by Barbara Findlay Schenck with Linda English (published by Wiley)

Although you probably love reading up on the body, exercise, nutrition, and fitness equipment (if you don't, you may be in the wrong field!), this book is essential if you own your own personal training business and want to get the word out about your services and what you have to offer. Geared specifically toward small-business owners, the authors don't assume you have a massive marketing budget to work with — which, if you're like most people, is true (especially when you're just starting out).

Program Design for Personal Trainers: Bridging Theory into Application by Douglas Brooks (published by Human Kinetics)

Program Design for Professional Trainers: Bridging Theory into Application is dense — much like a high-school algebra textbook — but it *is* thorough. It includes information on the science behind exercise programs and how to bridge that science into program design.

Client-Centered Exercise Prescription by John C. Griffin (published by Human Kinetics)

Client-Centered Exercise Prescription is another of Melyssa's faves. This book tells trainers how to delve into the minds (and physiques) of their clients and use this information to create exercise programs that work. For example, one chapter goes into how to determine clients' motivators and commitment levels, and another tells how to match exercise equipment with clients.

The E-Myth Revisited: Why Most Small Businesses Don't Work and What to Do About It by Michael Gerber (published by HarperBusiness)

E-Myth is short for *Entrepreneurial Myth,* and this book explains why most businesses (and business owners) fail to achieve their true potential. The book's main premise is that, as a business owner, you need to work *on* your business, instead of always working *in* your business, doing the day-to-day tasks that at some point can be delegated to someone else.

The E-Myth Web site (www.emyth.com) offers multiple programs designed to show you how to run a successful and efficient operation, without relying solely on your daily presence.

Grassroots Marketing: Getting Noticed in a Noisy World by Shel Horowitz (published by Chelsea Green Publishing)

This is one of Linda's favorite marketing books. The book is full of information and ideas for small-business owners (like you!), from bumper stickers to direct mail. It offers great basics for the newbie marketer.

Index

common mistakes, 150
definition, 8
employee evaluation, 279–280
function, 8
good versus bad, 7–8
love of job, 7, 324
required skills, 8–13
shadowing, 35
personal training business. *See also*
    business; job
  accounting methods, 107–109
  advisory board, 83–85
  business name, 87–89
  consistency, 20
  growth, 19–20
  independent spirit, 44–46
  legal forms, 93–97
  licenses and IDs, 86–87
  lifestyle needs, 43–44
  logo, 89–92
  networking, 83
  policies, 99–104, 151
  pros and cons, 46–49
  quality, 17, 20
  record-keeping, 104–109
  structures, 85–86
  support system, 46, 75–84
  tips for getting started, 14–16, 17
Personal Training on the Net
    (Web site), 328
Personal Training University
    (Web site), 329
personality
  classification systems, 138–139
  population selection, 116
  trainer characteristics, 10, 45
Peterson, Steven *(Business Plans Kit
    For Dummies)*, 65
Petersons Guides *(Internships 2004)*, 37
petty-cash fund, 108
philosophy, 292–293

phone call
  follow-up, 145
  marketing, 157–164, 267
  positive reinforcement, 144
  workflow steps, 267
physical feedback, 228
physical therapy, 56, 125
physician, 124–126, 173–174
plan, business
  components, 64–65
  content, 63–64
  definition, 63
  employee compensation, 286
  financial plan, 71–73
  location selection, 68–69
  marketing plan, 71–72
  marketing research, 67–68
  mission statement, 65–67
  rate-setting guidelines, 69–70
  resources, 64
plan, program
  baseline program, 200
  cardio exercise selection, 200–207
  change, 143–144, 248–249
  client's lifestyle, 141
  client's needs, 195–200
  equipment, 197–198
  introduction to client, 172–173
  medical history, 199–200
  overview, 18
  progression through sessions, 199
  rationale, 141
  strength program selection, 207–211
plastic folder, 168
plastic surgeon, 125
PNF (proprioceptive neuromuscular
    facilitation), 223
Polar (equipment company), 177
policies, 99–104, 151. *See also
    specific types*
polo shirt, 166

• U •

Notes

Notes

Notes

Notes

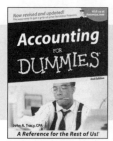

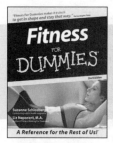
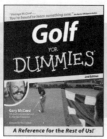

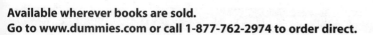

FOR DUMMIES®

A world of resources to help you grow

HOME, GARDEN & HOBBIES

0-7645-5295-3

0-7645-5130-2

0-7645-5106-X

Also available:

Auto Repair For Dummies
(0-7645-5089-6)

Chess For Dummies
(0-7645-5003-9)

Home Maintenance For
Dummies
(0-7645-5215-5)

Organizing For Dummies
(0-7645-5300-3)

Piano For Dummies
(0-7645-5105-1)

Poker For Dummies
(0-7645-5232-5)

Quilting For Dummies
(0-7645-5118-3)

Rock Guitar For Dummies
(0-7645-5356-9)

Roses For Dummies
(0-7645-5202-3)

Sewing For Dummies
(0-7645-5137-X)

FOOD & WINE

0-7645-5250-3

0-7645-5390-9

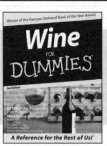

0-7645-5114-0

Also available:

Bartending For Dummies
(0-7645-5051-9)

Chinese Cooking For
Dummies
(0-7645-5247-3)

Christmas Cooking For
Dummies
(0-7645-5407-7)

Diabetes Cookbook For
Dummies
(0-7645-5230-9)

Grilling For Dummies
(0-7645-5076-4)

Low-Fat Cooking For
Dummies
(0-7645-5035-7)

Slow Cookers For Dummies
(0-7645-5240-6)

TRAVEL

0-7645-5453-0

0-7645-5438-7

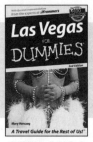

0-7645-5448-4

Also available:

America's National Parks For
Dummies
(0-7645-6204-5)

Caribbean For Dummies
(0-7645-5445-X)

Cruise Vacations For
Dummies 2003
(0-7645-5459-X)

Europe For Dummies
(0-7645-5456-5)

Ireland For Dummies
(0-7645-6199-5)

France For Dummies
(0-7645-6292-4)

London For Dummies
(0-7645-5416-6)

Mexico's Beach Resorts For
Dummies
(0-7645-6262-2)

Paris For Dummies
(0-7645-5494-8)

RV Vacations For Dummies
(0-7645-5443-3)

Walt Disney World & Orlando
For Dummies
(0-7645-5444-1)

Available wherever books are sold. Go to www.dummies.com or call 1-877-762-2974 to order direct.

FOR DUMMIES®

Plain-English solutions for everyday challenges

COMPUTER BASICS

0-7645-0838-5

0-7645-1663-9

0-7645-1548-9

Also available:

PCs All-in-One Desk Reference For Dummies (0-7645-0791-5)

Pocket PC For Dummies (0-7645-1640-X)

Treo and Visor For Dummies (0-7645-1673-6)

Troubleshooting Your PC For Dummies (0-7645-1669-8)

Upgrading & Fixing PCs For Dummies (0-7645-1665-5)

Windows XP For Dummies (0-7645-0893-8)

Windows XP For Dummies Quick Reference (0-7645-0897-0)

BUSINESS SOFTWARE

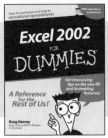

0-7645-0822-9

0-7645-0839-3

0-7645-0819-9

Also available:

Excel Data Analysis For Dummies (0-7645-1661-2)

Excel 2002 All-in-One Desk Reference For Dummies (0-7645-1794-5)

Excel 2002 For Dummies Quick Reference (0-7645-0829-6)

GoldMine "X" For Dummies (0-7645-0845-8)

Microsoft CRM For Dummies (0-7645-1698-1)

Microsoft Project 2002 For Dummies (0-7645-1628-0)

Office XP For Dummies (0-7645-0830-X)

Outlook 2002 For Dummies (0-7645-0828-8)

Get smart! Visit www.dummies.com

- **Find listings of even more *For Dummies* titles**
- **Browse online articles**
- **Sign up for Dummies eTips™**
- **Check out *For Dummies* fitness videos and other products**
- **Order from our online bookstore**

Available wherever books are sold. Go to www.dummies.com or call 1-877-762-2974 to order direct.

FOR DUMMIES®

Helping you expand your horizons and realize your potential

INTERNET

0-7645-0894-6

0-7645-1659-0

0-7645-1642-6

DIGITAL MEDIA

0-7645-1664-7

0-7645-1675-2

0-7645-0806-7

GRAPHICS

0-7645-0817-2

0-7645-1651-5

0-7645-0895-4

FOR DUMMIES®

The advice and explanations you need to succeed

SELF-HELP, SPIRITUALITY & RELIGION

0-7645-5302-X

0-7645-5418-2

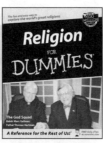

0-7645-5264-3

Also available:

The Bible For Dummies
(0-7645-5296-1)

Buddhism For Dummies
(0-7645-5359-3)

Christian Prayer For Dummies
(0-7645-5500-6)

Dating For Dummies
(0-7645-5072-1)

Judaism For Dummies
(0-7645-5299-6)

Potty Training For Dummies
(0-7645-5417-4)

Pregnancy For Dummies
(0-7645-5074-8)

Rekindling Romance For Dummies
(0-7645-5303-8)

Spirituality For Dummies
(0-7645-5298-8)

Weddings For Dummies
(0-7645-5055-1)

PETS

0-7645-5255-4

0-7645-5286-4

0-7645-5275-9

Also available:

Labrador Retrievers For Dummies
(0-7645-5281-3)

Aquariums For Dummies
(0-7645-5156-6)

Birds For Dummies
(0-7645-5139-6)

Dogs For Dummies
(0-7645-5274-0)

Ferrets For Dummies
(0-7645-5259-7)

German Shepherds For Dummies
(0-7645-5280-5)

Golden Retrievers For Dummies
(0-7645-5267-8)

Horses For Dummies
(0-7645-5138-8)

Jack Russell Terriers For Dummies
(0-7645-5268-6)

Puppies Raising & Training Diary For Dummies
(0-7645-0876-8)

EDUCATION & TEST PREPARATION

0-7645-5194-9

0-7645-5325-9

0-7645-5210-4

Also available:

Chemistry For Dummies
(0-7645-5430-1)

English Grammar For Dummies
(0-7645-5322-4)

French For Dummies
(0-7645-5193-0)

The GMAT For Dummies
(0-7645-5251-1)

Inglés Para Dummies
(0-7645-5427-1)

Italian For Dummies
(0-7645-5196-5)

Research Papers For Dummies
(0-7645-5426-3)

The SAT I For Dummies
(0-7645-5472-7)

U.S. History For Dummies
(0-7645-5249-X)

World History For Dummies
(0-7645-5242-2)

Available wherever books are sold. Go to www.dummies.com or call 1-877-762-2974 to order direct.